CW00683877

BETWEEN WAR AND POLITICS

The Changing Character of War Programme is an inter-disciplinary research centre located in the University of Oxford, and funded by the Leverhulme Trust.

Between War and Politics

*International Relations and the Thought
of Hannah Arendt*

PATRICIA OWENS

OXFORD

UNIVERSITY PRESS

OXFORD
UNIVERSITY PRESS

Great Clarendon Street, Oxford OX2 6DP
United Kingdom

Oxford University Press is a department of the University of Oxford.
It furthers the University's objective of excellence in research, scholarship,
and education by publishing worldwide. Oxford is a registered trade mark of
Oxford University Press in the UK and in certain other countries

First published 2007
Reprinted 2013

Published in the United States of America by Oxford University Press
198 Madison Avenue, New York, NY 10016, United States of America

British Library Cataloguing in Publication Data
Data available

Library of Congress Cataloging in Publication Data
Data available

ISBN 978-0-19-929936-2

Cover illustrations: courtesy of the Hannah Arendt Archive/iStockphoto.
Cover design: Grounded

For Francis, Ella, and Tashi

Acknowledgements

It gives me enormous pleasure to recognize those who have supported the writing of this book. I am especially grateful to George Welton and Michael Jago who gave extensive comments on the entire manuscript. Lyn Boyd Judson, Tony Lang, Keith Stanski, and Nina Silove commented on many, if not all, of the chapters. Ken Booth and Nick Wheeler were excellent advisers of the dissertation where some of these ideas were first worked out. Bhikhu Parekh and Tim Dunne were first-rate examiners. For comments on the book proposal, chapters and conference or workshop papers I warmly thank two anonymous reviewers, Hayward Alker, Tarak Barkawi, Molly Cochran, Martin Coward, Lisa Disch, Jean-Francois Drolet, Pauline Ewan, Alexandra Gheciu, Patrick Hayden, T. X. Hammes, Lene Hansen, Helen Kinsella, Jerome Kohn, Richard Little, Bryan Mabee, Jennifer Mitzen, Norma Claire Moruzzi, Mark Philp, Richard Price, Henry Shue, Steve Smith, Hew Strachan, Ann Tickner, Dan Twining, John Williams, and Michael C. Williams.

The Department of Politics and International Relations at the University of Oxford and Oriel College have provided a first-rate home for the past three years. The Oxford–Leverhulme programme on the Changing Character of War provided financial support. I am very grateful to my editor, Dominic Byatt, who has been supportive, encouraging, and patient. Keith Stanski has been a diligent and good-humoured assistant in the final weeks double-checking quotes and doing last minute library runs. I am also grateful to Jerome Kohn and Jessica Reifer of the Hannah Arendt Blucher Literary Trust.

A few paragraphs of the material are reprinted from: 'Accidents Don't Just Happen: The Liberal Politics of High-Tech Humanitarian War', *Millennium: Journal of International Studies*, Vol. 32, no. 3 (2003), pp. 595–616 and 'Hannah Arendt, Violence, and the Inescapable Fact of Humanity', in John Williams and Anthony F. Lang, Jr. (eds.), *Hannah Arendt and International Relations: Reading Across the Lines* (London: Palgrave Press, 2005), pp. 41–65. Chapter 7 originally appeared in *Review of International Studies*, Vol. 33, no. 3 (2007). I am grateful to Viking/Penguin, Harcourt, Chicago University Press, and Random House for permission to use scattered quotes from Hannah Arendt's works.

Patricia Owens
Oriel College, Oxford

Contents

Abbreviations of Books by Hannah Arendt

1

Introduction

> Events, past and present,—not social forces and historical trends, nor
> questionnaires and motivation research, nor any other gadgets in the
> arsenal of the social sciences—are the true, the only reliable teachers of
> political scientists, as they are the most trustworthy source of information
> for those engaged in politics.
>
> —Arendt, *Origins of Totalitarianism*, p. 482

Hannah Arendt (1906–75) is often considered to be one of the leading writers
on political non-violence. She was the theorist of political speech as action and
claimed on numerous occasions that violence was mute and brought the death
of politics. Yet we also find in Arendt's work praise for the experience of war
as the quintessential moment for humans to be most fully alive and political.
In an introductory essay she wrote to J. Glenn Gray's *The Warriors: Reflections
on Men in Battle*, Arendt approvingly cited the story of a French woman who
lived through the Second World War. 'Anything is better than having nothing
at all happen day after day', said the woman. 'You know that I do not love
war or want it to return. But at least it made me feel alive, as I have not felt
alive before or since' (1970*a*: xii). This cannot merely be an interesting though
random observation given the nature of the book Arendt was introducing. We
are left with the same message in the opening of *Between Past and Future* and
the concluding passages of *On Revolution*, the book in which Arendt set out
to capture the 'lost treasure' of revolutionary politics, the basis of her general
theory of political action.

While finishing *On Revolution*, Arendt recalled the poet René Char, leading
member of the French Resistance during the Second World War, and his
'frankly apprehensive anticipation of liberation' (OR, 284). 'If I survive', she
quotes him, 'I know that I shall have to break with the aroma of these essential
years, silently reject (not repress) my treasure'. Like the words of the French
woman, these remarks hold significance to Arendt because 'they testify to the
involuntary self-disclosure' to others, 'to the joys of appearing in word and
deed without equivocation and without self-reflection that are inherent in
action' (OR, 285). Arendt is suggesting that both the famous poet and the

ordinary woman revealed who they were, they 'self-disclosed', through violent action or action in support of violent resistance. Her singular example of the 'age-old treasure' of public freedom is the individuals who 'found themselves' in the midst of the struggle against the Nazis. She suggested this form of political action was more interesting than 'the old empty strife of conflicting ideologies which after the defeat of the common enemy...split the former comrades-in-arms into innumerable cliques...and to engage them in the endless polemics and intrigues of a paper war' (BPF, 4). 'Could boredom', she asked in the *Warriors* essay, 'be more terrifying than all of war's terrors?' (1970*a*: xii). We assume and hope that Arendt's answer is no. But the question is revealing.

Arendt was one of the most important and original political thinkers of the twentieth-century. Her theory of politics was constructed in response to what she saw as the causes and consequences of totalitarian violence in Europe. The Second World War and the Holocaust were shattering events she would try to understand for the rest of her life. 'At the outbreak of the war', she noted, 'Germany was not yet completely totalitarianized' (OT, 409). Arendt's political theory, a response to totalitarianism, is also therefore importantly a response to war. Everything she subsequently wrote was shaped by her conviction that the disasters of the twentieth-century had led to a monumental rupture in human history. What had led up to and occurred during the war had altered the political and moral landscape so profoundly that the traditional categories of Western political and moral thought were revealed as wholly inadequate. 'We can no longer afford to take that which was good in the past and simply call it our heritage, to discard the bad and simply think of it as a dead load which by itself time will bury in oblivion' (OT, ix). Arendt's response was to construct a new (partly through recovering an old) vocabulary for political thought and action. This was necessary not only to understand the recent past, but to search for a new political guarantee for human dignity in the future.

The narrative just presented is the standard account of the dominant influences on Arendt's work (Canovan 1992; Isaac 1992; Villa 2000). And yet the relationship of her thought to war, and even violence, has hardly been explored. A small number of short studies exist on her essay 'On Violence' (Elshtain 1986: ch. 8; McGowan 1998; Bar On 2002: ch. 7; Young 2002).[1] It is noted that violence is a constant theme in Arendt's work; in her account of the violence of necessity (in the activities of labour and work) and of totalitarian terror. Most commentators observe that Arendt sought to exclude violence and war from being 'properly political', which she understood to be the freedom to speak and act in concert with plural equals. The exemplary moments of political action highlighted by the secondary literature are overwhelmingly non-violent. Arendt's formal definition of politics did indeed exclude violence.

But time and again she found in wartime evidence of the best kind of politics. Was Arendt's effort to exclude war from the 'properly political' in vain?

This book argues that Arendt's political theory is fundamentally rooted in her understanding of war and its political significance. War was more than the mere occasion for Arendt's reflections on political action and brute violence. Her writings on war and violence are more subtle and important. The vast secondary literature on Arendt is sophisticated and broad. But it has underestimated this engagement with war by equating war with brute violence and focusing on those passages in which she does indeed exclude violence from being properly political. This book assesses the full range of Arendt's writing on war, a subject that has been largely neglected in political theory, and critically engages with this material to shed light on an important area of contemporary world politics. Re-reading Arendt's disparate and dispersed ideas on war reveals a more serious engagement than her earlier readers have recognized. Pulling together the threads of violence and war in Arendt's writing suggests that her treatment of the subjects is as illuminating as the classical sociology tradition and more compelling than some of the more recent work in the political theory of war.

Arendt's writing on the war question has not only been neglected in the political theory scholarship on her work. It has been overlooked in the relevant branches of international thought, which has only recently and belatedly turned to her work (Saurette 1996; Lang 2001; Lang and Williams 2005). Given the high volume of scholarship on Arendt in recent years, it has been suggested that it is becoming difficult to say much that is original about her (Reinhardt 2003). If true, this says more about the limitations of political theory than the quantity and quality of recent Arendt scholarship, which has been exceptionally high (see Honig 1995; Villa 1996, 1999, 2000). Just as international thought has become more open to the insights of social and political theory, these fields have not systematically engaged with the subject matter Arendt once described as the 'the foremost political issue' of her time: 'what role force should have in international affairs' (PP, 147). The fields of international history and theory have a great deal to learn from Arendt. As she wrote, 'in one form or another world politics has been an adjunct to politics' (OR, 47).

Under the impact of the legacy of the First World War and the more direct encounter with the Second World War and the attempted annihilation of the Jews, Arendt developed a political theory that places her in the rank of one of *the* key thinkers of the twentieth-century. She can be read as a resistance intellectual, a political writer as much as a political theorist (Isaac 1992). Like many others of her generation, she had been 'sucked into politics as though with the force of vacuum' (BPF, 3). She belonged to a generation of intellectuals whose ideas about war and politics were forged through first-hand experience of occupation and struggles for liberation, political founding, and resistance in time of war (JW, Part II).

From the 1930s, as it became ever more evident that the tide of anti-Semitism was about to overwhelm life in Germany, a young Arendt became directly involved in politics. She was arrested by the Gestapo in 1933 when found gathering material to research anti-Semitic propaganda in the Prussian State Library. Released eight days later, she fled the country without documents, leaving Germany for Paris. Arendt had become a stateless Jew. But she was perhaps more actively political during this period than at any other time during her life. She went to work for Youth Aliyah, an organization that rescued Jewish children and prepared them for the exodus to Palestine. But as an 'enemy alien' in Nazi-occupied France she was detained at a camp in Gurs. After escaping in 1941, she fled to the United States. Arendt continued as a writer and editor in New York arguing passionately for the need for a Jewish army to fight against Hitler. The taking up of arms as Jews to fight fascism, the creation of a Jewish army, she believed, would be the beginning of Jewish politics. But she also wrote unflinchingly about the consequences for Palestinians of the war to found Israel arguing against Zionism and for the establishment of a dual-state for both Arabs and Jews (JW, 199–263).

Arendt's direct engagements with these questions of war are clear. But in her later writing she seems more reluctant, awkward, she says 'haunted', when writing about modern war (1962: 15). Perhaps she felt that to pursue fully the war question would indeed have undermined her effort to theorize authentic politics. From a first glance at her major works in political theory, *The Origins of Totalitarianism*, *The Human Condition*, *Between Past and Future*, *On Revolution*, and *The Life of the Mind*, it might appear that Arendt rarely addressed humans as 'homo furens', as warriors (1970a: xi), or the 'military world of war' (PP, 171; Canovan 1992: 186). Her engagement with what she called 'the war question' was irregular and, at first glance, uninspired (see the treatment by Cocks 2002: ch. 2; Keane 2004: 6). Why did Arendt appear to pay so little direct and sustained attention to what she saw as the most important political issue of her day? This harshest critic of modern political philosophy also seemed to commit one of its gravest errors in leaving war to the government strategists. One could respond by noting that Arendt's apparent lack of sustained engagement with war was in line with her more familiar views on violence; she did not believe violence was truly political; 'coercion and brute force are always means for protecting or establishing or expanding political space, but in and of themselves are definitely not political' (PP, 130). From this reading it would follow that Arendt's idealized image of political action is—or should be—non-violent.

Wars, like revolutions, are not 'wholly determined' by brute force. Yet unlike revolution, within which Arendt's paradigm of political action most often occurred, war, she believed, was less amenable to sustained political thought because the brute violence of war was 'mute'. 'Where violence rules absolutely, as for instance in the concentration camps ... everything and everybody must turn silent. It is because of this silence that violence is a marginal phenomenon in the political realm', properly understood (OR, 9). Somewhat frustratingly, Arendt offered as supporting evidence for the speechlessness of violence the defining characteristic of what violence is not. Violence is not in essence 'political' because this is the realm of speech and 'for man, to the extent that he is a political being, is endowed with the power of speech' (OR, 9). Political theory, inasmuch as it can only deal with what 'appears' as speech or action in the political realm, 'has little to say about the phenomenon of violence and must leave its discussion to the technicians' (OR, 9). We appear to be back with the strategists.

But there is an important distinction between the phenomenon of violence and the social practices of war. And as Arendt also remarked in her argument for a Jewish army to resist the Nazis directly and violently, 'war is too serious a matter to leave to the generals' (2000: 48). Brute violence and war are not the same. There is much more room to think politically about war with Arendt than the conventional reading of her work appears to suggest. Politics is precisely what distinguishes war from sheer violence, although Arendt sometimes elides the distinction. War is part of human affairs, 'what politics is about' (PP, 154), and she understood revolution and war as the two phenomena that have most determined the 'physiognomy of the twentieth century' (1962: 10). We might say that to place war outside any theory of politics, to borrow Arendt's words from a different context, 'is tantamount to not living in the world in which in fact we live' (PP, 191).

It will be argued throughout this book that Arendt offered her readers the beginnings of a sophisticated and original political theory of war. However, to the extent that such an account can be derived from Arendt's thought it must meet at least two criteria. First, it depends on the existence of a meaningful distinction between politics and war. Second, it must 'only deal with the justification of violence because this justification constitutes its political limitation' (OR, 10). Arendt argued that politics truly begins when actors start to justify, rationalize and give reasons for their actions. 'Men in the plural', she wrote, 'that is, men in so far as they live and move and act in the world, can experience meaningfulness only because they can talk with and make sense to each other and to themselves' (HC, 4). Strictly speaking, a political theory of war, as distinct from a social theory or a military history, deals with the elements most closely associated with the political, that is, the justificatory (or condemnatory) language surrounding warfare. At the same time, political theory becomes 'antipolitical' 'if, instead, it arrives at a glorification or justification of violence as such' (OR, 10). Any such glorification of violence was a denial of speech, the essence of authentic politics and the 'most human form of intercourse'.

There is some space for a political theory of war after all. But, again, why did Arendt not explicitly pursue it? Another possibility is that the political–military issues of her day were undergoing such revolutionary changes that the kind of war most often discussed could no longer be justified. In the nuclear age, Arendt believed that 'the whole war question has undergone another decisive change' (OT, 442n). Carl von Clausewitz's idea of war as the continuation of politics by other means was simply beside the point. 'What is now at stake' with weapons that could annihilate human life 'is something that could…never be a matter for [political] negotiation: the sheer existence of a nation and its people. It is at this point…that war first truly ceases to be a means of politics and, as a war of annihilation, begins to overstep the bounds set by politics and to annihilate politics itself' (PP, 159). In such circumstances it appeared to Arendt that sustained engagement with the most profound and difficult dilemmas of war seemed 'idle'. In Arendt's words, 'there is little we can do about the whole business one way or another' (1962: 15). A political theory of war recedes further from view. In the nuclear age at least, its only purpose was to salvage some self-respect for humanity.[2] Fortunately, Arendt did not leave it at that.

In recognizing Arendt's contribution to thinking about politics and war we need not accept every idea she expressed.[3] For example, she appeared to take sides with the military profession against the evidence of social science on the core issue of combat motivation, the question of why soldiers fight. She believed that, 'no ism, not nationalism and not even patriotism, no emotion in which men can be indoctrinated and then manipulated, but only comradeship, the "loyalty to the group is the essence of fighting morale"' (1970a: ix). This is the standard view within military circles and Western popular culture. The emotional bond between soldiers is the basis of effectiveness in combat. The classic studies supporting and challenging this view concern the brutality of war on the Eastern Front during the Second World War and the resilience of German soldiers who continued to fight as Berlin fell.[4] Arendt did not address combat motivation at length. And she rightly rejected the idea that soldiers were mere killers. Indeed, 'killers—those with "personal aggressiveness"—are probably not even good soldiers' (CR, 159f).[5] She is better known for her study of the functionaries of mass killing, men such as Nazi war criminal Adolf Eichmann. She faced head-on the realization of what ordinary humans were capable of doing and believed that this must be 'the precondition of any modern political thinking' (EU, 132).[6]

Arendt matters because the issues that she dealt with throughout her life and work continue to shape the political world and her approach to political thinking remains a source for those in search of guidance not in what to think but how to think about politics and war today (BPF, 14). And yet Arendt was not concerned with offering any straightforward theory that might be applied by those who read her work or those whom she taught. Rather than offering any such 'application' this book follows a number of theoretical 'thought-trains' inspired by Arendt (LM, 160). The intention is to assemble and critically analyse her political writing on war and to introduce international theory and students of war to the distinct language she used to talk about war and the political world. It builds on her rethinking of old concepts such as power, violence, greatness, world, imperialism, evil, hypocrisy, and humanity and introduces some that are new to international thought like plurality, action, agonism, natality, political immortality, and making.

An historian, as well as a theorist, Arendt's writing was inspired by facts and events and not intellectual history or the history of ideas (Krieger 1976). Her historical method mirrored her thinking about politics; the approach to history was attentive to what she took to be the 'rules of the political realm' (BPF, 248), anti-authoritarianism, based on persuasion, attentive to the necessary perspectival character of all politics. The basic fact of human plurality, that there are unique beings, that there are many and not one of us, is unassailable. The different human perspectives that plurality implies Arendt considered an objective fact itself. We find that her approach to political thought and history merged into one another, each shaping the other. The best method of persuasion in the political realm, Arendt believed, was through examples of past incidents or individual characters. This was a form of persuasion 'by inspiration' (BPF, 248). Ideas and theories only mattered if they directly illuminated politics. Karl Marx, 'for decades...' she wrote, 'was highly esteemed, or deeply resented, as the "inventor of the class struggle", of which he was not the "inventor" (facts are not invented) but not even the discoverer' (2002: 275).

Arendt's writing is best described as philosophically informed 'large-scale historical social science', with science broadly understood as rigorous and systematic enquiry (Katznelson 2003: 93). Her thinking did not roll 'along...accustomed paths', which she found to be more 'in keeping' with the nature of political events themselves (AJ, 176). Asked by Hans J. Morgenthau whether her position was 'liberal' or 'conservative', she responded as though the question itself were truly silly; she 'couldn't care less' because 'the real questions of this century will [not] get any kind of illumination by this sort of thing' (1979: 334). Arendt constantly read the politics of her day against the grain and, of course, she sometimes made mistakes. She did not shy away from controversy in her life-time and some of her most controversial and important ideas continue to shape political discourse. The staleness and the polemics that pass for debate in the aftermath of the 9/11 attacks and the response of the US government only makes her mode of thinking more attractive.

Consider Arendt's relation to 'realism', often considered the dominant approach to international theory. She enjoyed numerous affinities with classical realism. She praised the practical philosophies of Thucydides and Machiavelli, the former for his understanding of theory as both historical and political and the latter for his appreciation of the 'splendor of the public realm' (OR, 29). Her understanding of the causes of war derived from what she called 'well-known realities of power politics—such as conquest and expansion, defence of vested interests and preservation of power or conservation of a power equilibrium' (1962: 13). But Arendt's thought could scarcely be confused with neo-realism (Waltz 1959, 1979) for she railed against the effort of behaviourist social science to predict and control political action. Arendt was unimpressed by the methodological quarrels afflicting social and political science, which tended to overshadow 'more fundamental issues' (BPF, 53). She considered social science vocabulary as it was emerging in her day as 'repulsive' and its effort to ' "manage" human affairs ... frightening' (BPF, 59). She also rejected the tradition of political realism associated with Max Weber and her criticism of Hobbes overlaps with elements of other international theories. But her thinking cannot be contained in any of its schools. No one 'owns' Arendt's legacy despite the constant effort of various schools to claim her.

Chapter 2 introduces Arendt's understanding of the basic meanings of politics and war, violence, and power. Her definition of power, a collective capacity that emerges between people as they act together, is supported through a number of historical examples including partisan resistance during the Second World War and the Hungarian Revolution of 1956. Her position on partisan warfare and the uses and limitations of revolutionary violence are contrasted with the important writing on these subjects by Carl Schmitt and Franz Fanon. The distinction between power and violence forms the basis of Arendt's understanding of the different meanings of politics and war. Arendt shared with Clausewitz, the leading theorist on the subject, a view of war as an act of force, a violent contest whose essence is violence and compulsion. However, political action, though sometimes occurring during wartime, is fundamentally different from the act of waging war. Politics is full of conflict and disagreement. But it is also limited by the condition of plurality, that there are many and not one of us, the very condition for speech and political action among equals. In contrast to a recent trend in the philosophy of war, Arendt maintained that a distinction between politics and war was indeed possible and necessary for there to be politics at all.

Chapter 3 addresses Arendt's method of thinking about politics and war. It was a fundamental conviction of her work that the most significant changes in social and political life, including wars, could not be understood through the projection of continuous historical laws. It was the nature of both politics and war to bring about the unexpected and unpredictable. She found war to be perfect for her kind of 'historical narrative' because like history itself it is the product of events brought into being by the actions of men and women; here 'accident and infinite improbability occurs' all the time (BPF, 170). Inspired, in part, by the tradition of historiography that emerged out of the writing of Homer and Thucydides, Arendt argued that it was essential to divorce the meaning of events from our ethical judgement of them. We should and do make ethical judgements. The difference is that we must also pay attention to the distinctly political criteria for judging action, which Arendt believed to be greatness. This understanding of the history of war and forms of agency in wartime is illustrated with the contemporary and controversial practice of suicide bombing. 'Who', if anyone, is revealed in such acts? The men and women who believe that they are dying for their political community may not conceive politics as Arendt did. But we can nonetheless see them in her terms.

After establishing Arendt's understanding of the basic meanings of politics, violence, and war, as well as her methodology, Chapter 4 looks at her historical analysis of a form of war that still shapes the contemporary world. In particular, we assess her far-sighted and prescient claim that late-nineteenth-century wars of imperial conquest helped sow the seeds of twentieth-century total war in Europe. The implications of Arendt's insight are potentially great for how we might think through the social and political processes unwittingly unleashed by various forms of violence, including so-called 'small wars'. Arendt's historical writing not only illuminated her conceptual claim that there was an almost overwhelming logic for violent means to over-run the ends. Her writing on imperialism and European total war reveals some of the flaws in conventional military history and strategic studies which have understood these practices as unrelated. Both Arendt and Clausewitz were concerned with war not simply as a rational act of state policy. Arendt points us towards relationships that are much closer to Clausewitz's more fundamental insight about war as a social process that transcends the nation-state. Moreover, Arendt may have been the first to articulate what today we call 'blowback' and she termed the 'boomerang effect', the negative and unintended consequences of aggressive foreign policy.

Chapter 5 explores the implications of Arendt's historical and conceptual account of the relationship between war, law, and territorial expansion. Arendt understood the importance of law and territorial boundaries as the principle limitations on the otherwise unpredictability and boundlessness of political action. But she condemned the ancient Greeks for building their polis around the ideals of agonistic contest while simultaneously excluding all legal and political recognition of the 'barbarians' outside. This non-recognition was directly linked to the Greek propensity for total war, the annihilation of their enemies, rather than coming to political terms with the defeated. The Romans, in contrast, endowed the 'other' with a legally recognized status. Indeed, Arendt argued that such recognition was essential to the construction of the Roman Empire and was the beginning of the Western tradition of foreign policy. This legalism was productive rather than just constraining of bureaucratic and political domination, which, as both Arendt and Weber showed, made it both faceless and unforgiving. What does this relationship reveal about forms of subjectivity produced through the laws of war in our present context? How are subjects of violence produced such as the 'accidental' civilian casualties of our own wars? What relationships of hierarchy and subordination, responsibility and punishment, are created?

Imperialism and the Holocaust demonstrated to Arendt that 'human dignity' needed 'a new guarantee' (OT, ix). But she was wholly ambivalent about the liberal discourse of human rights and by extension, it will be argued in Chapter 6, wars justified in their name. Arendt can be read as far less sanguine about the apparent progressiveness of human rights ideologies than other of her readers have suggested. This argument is made through an analysis of her writing on violence and hypocrisy. Some liberals have argued that hypocrisy is less bad than cruelty. We may therefore support wars justified as a response to cruel and systematic abuses even when the human rights discourse of powerful states is hypocritical. Arendt's work is filled with examples of violent rage against hypocrisy, but also how hypocrisy can enable cruelty. She argued that efforts to 'unmask' hypocrisy are problematic. But this is not because the exposure increases the prospects for cruelty (because we become cynical about human rights). Above all, Arendt was a defender of the created, public world where it is only possible to judge words and actions, not motives. To hunt for and expose inner-motives is to misconstrue the fundamentally constructed, artificial nature of the public realm. And yet Arendt does not leave us without grounds to act against genocide, the greatest of all political sins. But these grounds are not based on the large numbers of dead, on levels of cruelty as such. Wars of annihilation cannot be tolerated because they attack the fundamental basis of all politics which is human plurality—different peoples living and acting in our common world. It destroys the world that is created by action and which cannot be rebuilt.

Each of the previous chapters engages Arendt's writing in dialogue with various schools of political and international theory, including political realism, liberalism, and constructivism, post-structuralism, and post-colonial thought. The final two chapters offer more sustained engagements with two very different, but increasingly important, approaches to politics and war in political and international theory. Neoconservatism and Habermas-inspired critical theory each claim Arendt's influence. To illustrate Arendt's fundamental divergence from these schools, Chapter 7 contrasts her writing with the philosophical roots of neoconservatism as articulated in the writings of Leo Strauss. We pay particular attention to their different evaluation of the antagonistic relationship between philosophy and politics. This, in turn, sheds light on contemporary neoconservative claims about the power of ideas to change the world, for example through the invasion and occupation of Iraq, and widespread, but misguided, claims about their propensity to condone political lies. There is always a temptation to lie in politics because the lie is itself an intervention into the common world. Arendt argued that there is an inherent clash between politics and truth of all kinds, philosophical and factual. The denial of political reality is only made worse by ideological thinking. Ideologies possess a hubristic 'contempt for reality' and assume that political action and conflict can be mastered (OT, 458). For Arendt, in contrast, 'the freedom of plurality entails an inescapable contingency: action's futility, boundlessness, and uncertainty of outcome' (HC, 175).

Chapter 8 contrasts Arendt's political writing with that of a leading figure in critical and normative international theory on the relationship between war and cosmopolitan democracy, now often heralded as the best alternative to US global hegemony. Jürgen Habermas has argued that humanitarian intervention is justified, in part, because it places international relations on the path towards cosmopolitan society, a global public realm. There are a number of problems with Habermas's historical and conceptual understanding of the relationship between publics and violence. This chapter suggests that Habermas has unwittingly—and perhaps surprisingly—endorsed a model of global political founding that has something in common with Machiavelli's notion of politics and violence being two sides of the same coin. Habermas envisages a political end, a global public; 'humanitarian' war is endorsed as a means to make it. Arendt's judgement is more sobering. Her account of founding and political freedom foregoes the temptation to reduce politics to a relationship between ends and means. She held a deeply ambivalent view of the concept of and justifications for political action based on 'humanity'. Her thought was rarely couched in what she took to be the rather abstract and even dangerous language of humanitarianism. We seem no more ready in contemporary times than in Arendt's to acknowledge in full the awesome responsibility implied in taking seriously the idea of humanity and certainly humanity in wartime.

In the scholarship on Hannah Arendt it is a commonplace to note that she sought to observe and describe types of political action, past and present, which might counter the re-emergence of totalitarian political forms, and that these forms of political action were non-violent. Arendt did indeed wish to exclude war from political action. She rejected the view that politics and war were on a mere continuum of degrees of violence, that there was no meaningful distinction that could be drawn between them. But Arendt never banished war from her vision of the political. War is the context in which she developed her ideas about political thought and action. She believed that the central question concerning the meaning of politics had become 'the appropriateness or inappropriateness of the public means of force' (PP, 146). War was the backdrop for her reflections on politics in the ancient and the modern world. Digging a little deeper we see that Arendt's apparent exclusion of war from politics, her definitionally enforced distinction, linked politics and war together in a historically and conceptually rich relationship. She criticized the dominant Western traditions of social and political thought for borrowing their models of politics from the realm of organized violence, of command and obedience. But it is her political thought that is deeply influenced by the enduring significance of war. Hannah Arendt's most important insights about history and theory, political agency and identity, imperial and totalitarian crimes show that her engagement with war runs deep.

2

Violence and Power, Politics and War

> Since in foreign relations as well as domestic affairs violence appears
> as a last resort to keep the power structure intact against individual
> challengers—the foreign enemy, the native criminal—it looks indeed as
> though violence were the prerequisite of power and power nothing but a
> façade, the velvet glove which either conceals the iron hand or will turn
> out to belong to a paper tiger.
>
> —Arendt, *Crises of the Republic*, p. 146

Revolutionary uprisings and violent resistance to oppressive authority have
been two of the defining features of the twentieth-century. Hannah Arendt's
writing is filled with examples of popular violence and of the non-violent
action and resistance by the materially less powerful but the numerically
superior. She never referred to methods of non-violent protest in the language of 'passive resistance', which may be taken to imply *in*activity. What can
emerge, she wrote, is 'an almost irresistible power' and 'one of the most active
and efficient ways of action ever devised, because it cannot be countered by
fighting' (HC, 200, 201). Arendt believed that under certain conditions acts of
non-violence could be more effective and potentially more revolutionary than
even small-scale violent demonstrations. She gave the example of the resistance to the deportation of the Jews of German-occupied Denmark during
the Second World War (EJ, 171–5).

Hitler's order to send ships for the deportation of the Danish Jews was
leaked to the leader of the Jewish Community in Denmark in September
1943. Days before the transportation was due to begin the entire community
went into hiding assisted by large numbers of Danish citizens. Jewish men,
women, and children were secretly taken to the coast where local fishermen
transported them the two-miles across the water to Sweden who had remained
neutral during the war (Werner 2002). Over a number of days, more than
7,000 were rescued from imminent deportation to the death camps. It was
extremely significant to Arendt that prior to the war the Danish had not
treated their Jews especially well. Like other European states, Jews were not
naturalized or given visas to work. Nonetheless, their right to asylum 'was

considered sacrosanct'.[1] Although Denmark was not the only country 'by hook or by crook' to save the majority of its Jews, it was only the Danes who spoke openly about what they were doing. 'And the result', in Arendt's words, 'was that under the pressure of public opinion, and threatened neither by armed resistance nor by guerrilla tactics, the German officials...were overpowered by what they most disdained, mere words, spoken freely and publicly'.[2]

The facts of this case, Arendt believed, 'should be required reading in all political science courses which deal with the relations between power and violence'. They challenged the dominant tendency to treat power and violence as synonymous and to assume that violence is simply the ultimate expression of power. Arendt had identified a troubling agreement across the political spectrum and in the major traditions of social and political theory 'to the effect that violence is nothing more than the most flagrant manifestation of power' (CR, 134). Power has been seen as a possession, an instrument of rule that produces a hierarchical, indeed coercive, relationship between rulers and ruled. This relationship has been considered the essence of politics in virtually all traditions and is closely related to the idea that domination and ruling are the most basic categories of politics and violence is the essence of power. Those who have power command and those who do not obey; even in a democracy, the rotation of rulers is still a system of rule. It has seemed like common sense to equate the essence of political power with violence, to argue that the central political events in human history 'stand under the sign of brute force' (PP, 192). This view was most forcefully expressed in the words of Karl Marx and Mao Zedong. 'Violence is the midwife of history'. 'Political power grows out of the barrel of a gun' (quoted in CR, 113).

Arendt's comprehensive goal was to end the modern fascination with reducing politics to violent domination and to uncover an alternative 'vocabulary no less old and time-honored' so 'that the original data' of the political realm might be revealed (CR, 139, 143). At the heart of Arendt's argument was a deconstruction of the relationship between power and violence that emerged in the modern period and became the basis of modern social and political thought about politics and war. However, in order to retrieve a deeper understanding of politics and war from Arendt's political theory, we must be clear about and be attentive to her unique lexicon. This is all the more important given the lack of agreement in wider social and political thought concerning the meaning of the key terms under consideration. Arendt always carefully structured her political thought around a number of important distinctions. And as we can see, her terminology tended to depart from the traditional understandings in social and political thought (Parekh 1981).

Steven Lukes, in his own theory of power, suggests that the whole purpose of Arendt's definitions was intended 'to reinforce certain theoretical positions'

(2005: 34). This is partly right. But we should not take this to mean that Arendt's definitions and distinctions between power and violence, politics and war were arbitrary, mere utopian theoretical constructs. Her argument about the flaws of the tradition of political philosophy is not based on some alternative normative vision of what ought to be. It is a claim based on what is real, but has been concealed in both the political philosophy tradition and the historical development of the West. Modern historical and intellectual trends may move in the direction of obliterating the distinctions between power and violence, politics and war altogether. Yet to ignore the evidence and fail to properly distinguish between them, Arendt argued, resulted 'in a kind of blindness to the realities' to which 'they correspond' (CR, 142).

The concepts of power and violence, and politics and war, refer to basically different things. The purpose of this chapter is to introduce and analyse Arendt's understanding of them. *Power* springs up between people as they act together; it belongs to the group, and disappears when the group disperses. It is a collective capacity. Until this coming together, it is only a potential. *Violence* is an instrument. It is the use of implements to multiply strength and command others to obey. Power can be channelled by the state apparatus. Indeed, this is the necessary precondition for the accumulation of the means of violence by the administrative state. When power and violence are combined, Arendt wrote, 'the result is a monstrous increase in potential force'. It is for this reason that under modern conditions power and force appear to be the same and why violence and power, which is 'derived from the power of an organized space', are combined in modern states (PP, 147). This combination is historically contingent rather than intrinsic and necessary.

To illustrate the non-identity of power and violence the chapter takes a number of examples from Arendt's own writing: the Vietnam War; the Hungarian Revolution of 1956; the argument for a Jewish army to face down Hitler; and the French Resistance. Her analysis of partisan activity and unconventional warfare is distinguished from the ideas of the authoritarian German jurist Carl Schmitt and the revolutionary anti-colonial writing of Franz Fanon. Arendt had more in common with Fanon, but she occupies no liberal 'middle ground'. This is clear when we come to the distinction between politics and war. What is politics, and can it be distinguished from war? Arendt argued that if Marx was right, and 'we are essentially moving across a field of violent experience' then the consequences are 'fatal' (PP, 192). There can be no politics and indeed no distinction between politics and war necessary for a political theory of war. Arendt's goal was to salvage politics from brute violence, to show that it is not as meaningless as it might seem. The meaning of *politics* is the freedom to act in concert with plural equals. The meaning of *war* is coercion and being coerced, the force of compulsion. Its end is security or conquest. Arendt criticized the two dominant ways of distinguishing politics from war in the West, the ancient Greek and the liberal. But in contrast to a recent trend in the philosophy of war, she maintained that there was indeed a valid distinction between them.

DISTINGUISHING POWER FROM VIOLENCE: UPRISINGS AND PARTISANS

The histories of invasion and occupation, of insurgency and counter-insurgency, suggested to Arendt that the likelihood of violence increases when those we usually understand as 'holding' power 'feel it slipping from their hands' (CR, 184). In such cases, the expression of violence is not the man-ifestation of superior power but of weakness. It is a sign that power is in jeopardy. Arendt pointed to the inability of the United States to terminate its involvement in the Vietnam War as evidence of the 'impotence of power', that there is no necessary correlation between technological sophistication and power or between military capability and victory (Hammes 2004).[3] The Viet-cong famously utilized only the most modest of instruments and gained crit-ical political support—power—in the countryside. North Vietnamese forces emerged victorious because they understood the political dimensions of the conflict in a way the United States could not. In a futile effort to reverse a decline, militarily strong states often resort to force to compel others to obey. In such circumstances, the more extreme the violence used the weaker the 'superior power' appears, 'bogged down under the monstrous weight of their own bigness' (CR, 181).

Perhaps Arendt's most singular example of the difference between power and violence was the Hungarian uprising of 1956. At the root of this event was the same desire to speak openly and freely in public made manifest in Denmark in 1943. Arendt described this anti-Soviet, pro-democracy revolt in Budapest 'as the best thing that has happened for a long time ... regardless of how it ends' (AJ, 306). It did end in the death of 2,500 Hungarian dissenters and it lasted for just 12 days. But for a time, millions participated in a revolt that led to the people temporarily wresting control of institutions and terri-tory from the pro-Soviet regime. The spontaneous emergence of voluntaristic councils during the revolt seemed to Arendt strong evidence against the con-servative view 'of the ... lawless "natural" inclinations of a people left without the constraint of its government' (OR, 275).[4] These councils, the political organs established to determine the new political organization, were Arendt's quintessential examples of the power of people acting in concert and creating a new public realm.

Arendt wrote something of a eulogy to those individuals who had been killed or silenced by the Soviet army and their Hungarian co-conspirators.[5] In her words,

This was a true event whose stature will not depend on victory or defeat; its greatness is secure in the tragedy it enacted. For who can forget the silent procession of black-clad women in the streets of Russian-occupied Budapest, mourning their dead in public, the last political gesture of the revolution? And who can doubt the solidity of this remembrance when one year after the revolution the defeated and terrorized people have still enough strength of action left to commemorate once more in public the death of their freedom...What happened in Hungary happened nowhere else, and the twelve days of the revolution contained more history than the twelve years since the Red Army had 'liberated' the country from Nazi domination (1958b: 5).

The unexpected, spontaneous character of the uprising once the revolutionary spirit had taken grip was significant for Arendt. There were no leaders, she argued, and 'the few instances of public hanging...were conducted with remarkable restraint and discrimination' (1958b: 28). There was no civil war, no chaos; there was the emergence of small councils born out of the demands of the people to institutionalize their new found freedom. This is not freedom in the sense of choice or free will. It is a freedom that only exists, Arendt believed, through acting with equals in the public realm. The political promise of freedom is quite literally found in the ability to initiate new beginnings and found new political spaces.

We should not confuse Arendt's praise for these examples of non-violence, and her distinction between power and violence, with a form of pacifism. Pacifism, she wrote, is 'devoid of reality' (OT, 442). She argued for the creation of a Jewish army to fight 'against Hitler as Jews, in Jewish units, under the Jewish flag' (2000: 46). Indeed, the creation of such an army she maintained would constitute the very *beginning* of Jewish politics. Writing in 1941, she continued,

A Jewish army need not be a utopia if Jews from every country demand it and are prepared to join it as volunteers. It is, however, utopian to believe that we could profit in any way from the defeat of Hitler if this defeat is not in part our doing. Only a real war of the Jewish people against Hitler will put an end—a well-deserved end—to the fantastic talk of the Jewish war. 'Freedom is not a gift' as the old and yet very relevant Zionist saying has it. *Neither is freedom a reward for suffering endured* (2000: 47).

But freedom may be—in fact it too often is—a reward for suffering inflicted. Twenty-two thousand survivors of the 'Final Solution' took part in Israel's 1948 War of Independence, or Catastrophe for the Palestinians. Two thousand of the six thousand Israeli dead were survivors from the Nazi camps (Yablonka 1999). Anything up to 15,000 Arabs died and 700,000 Palestinians, half of the population, were forcibly removed or fled (Moran 2001). Arendt did not believe that freedom had to be achieved at such a price. She felt enormous ambivalence towards Zionism, in part, for this reason and she did not flinch in her descriptions of the violence of 1948.[6] In a letter to Karl Jaspers she wrote, that 'in order to set an example' an Arab village, Deir Jassim, was 'wiped out', leading to a 'mass exodus' of Palestinians. The 'massacre', she observed, 'was widely characterized then as a second Lidice', the Czechoslovak town destroyed by the German SS in June 1942 in revenge for the assassination of the governor who was helping to organize the genocide of the Jews (AJ, 358; JW 397). Arendt was realistic and prescient about the problems and consequences associated with the founding of Israel.[7]

Political freedom need not always be achieved through violence. But when it was we find that Arendt's political sensibilities were much more in tune with the side of the partisans, or the guerrillas and resisters, than with the 'regular' side in military encounters. Arendt wrote from the perspective of the irregulars and accordingly distinguished between civilians who took up arms and the professional soldier; 'the moment the "partisan" is backed by the machinery of state power, he changes' (JP, 239; JW, 145). The partisans or 'challengers' are distinct from the regulars because 'without knowing or even noticing it', she argued, they 'had begun to create that public space between themselves where freedom could appear' (BPF, 4). Partisan activity is evidence of common conviction, where the power generated by the many counters the military force mobilized by the state. In a struggle for national liberation, for example, it is the creation of new political space 'where—without the paraphernalia of officialdom ... —all relevant business in the affairs of the country [is] transacted in deed and word' (BPF, 3).

Arendt attached immense value to the stories of the men and women who turned to guerrilla warfare to resist Nazi occupation in the Second World War. The principle and most effective military acts in France were the disruption of German reinforcements, supplies, and communications. Partisans gathered and disseminated military intelligence, and also engaged in relatively minor acts of violence and sabotage (Laqueur 1976). Given the speed of the collapse of several national armies in the face of the German advance, a number of national resistance movements sprang up throughout Europe. As is often the case with such activities the real significance of armed resistance is the polit-ical component, the defiance against invasion or occupation. That such acts often have greater political than military consequence may explain Arendt's attraction to the form. In France, where Arendt was interned for part of the war, men and women came together and created such political space even if only briefly and 'without premonition and probably against their conscious inclinations, they had come to constitute willy-nilly a public realm' (BPF, 3).

Hanna Fenichel Pitkin believes it is 'startling' that Arendt could describe the Resistance as forming a public realm. 'What could be less public than a clandestine resistance organization...? Even the members may not know each other as such, lest they betray others if captured and tortured'. Arendt must have been prompted to describe their activities as 'public', Pitkin suggests because she shared 'the goals or principles that motivated the members, their serious commitment to the cause of France, of justice, freedom, of self-government' (1998: 108–9). But Arendt explicitly stated that the experience of public freedom did *not* depend on the justice of their fight 'against... things worse than tyranny—this was true for every soldier in the Allied armies' (BPF, 4). Arendt's politics meant that she viewed the central cause of the Partisans, the removal of German occupation and eventual defeat of Nazism, to be just. For the Resistance too, foreign enemy occupation provided an element of simplicity. There was conflict between Gaullists and Communists. Yet these did not amount to 'armed clashes' (Laqueur 1976: 206). They were *resisting* and this enemy acted as a uniting force. But the different motivations of the actors were not Arendt's principal concern.

To illustrate, we can compare Arendt's writing on the Partisans to Carl Schmitt's *Theory of the Partisan*. We know that the activity in France was more or less contained in the classical international legal norms and conventions that regulated and responded to the European experiences of the Second World War. France, after all, was on the side of the victors. Many of those who resisted believed themselves to be fighting for more than just the removal of an occupation. But Arendt's partisans, in the language developed by Schmitt, were nonetheless 'the defensive-autochthonous defender of home' (2006: 20). The French case was a 'barricade war'. The power, the public freedom that emerged among the resisters—and this was central to Arendt's lament—largely ceased with the end of the war. They did indeed 'return to the old empty strife of conflicting ideologies..., the endless polemics and intrigues of a paper war ... They had lost their treasure' (BPF, 4). But Schmitt's partisan allegedly reveals a deeper source of enmity.[8] If the power that emerges between partisans *cannot* be channelled into the conventional nation-state, if the resumption of 'peace' is not possible after a limited victory, then we are describing a fundamentally different form of warfare and participant in war.

In one sense, both Schmitt and Arendt believed that the theory of the partisan, as he put it, 'proves to be the key to recognizing political reality' (2004: 43). But their conception of that reality—and the meaning of political action—is very different. Truly revolutionary partisans not only create new spaces for politics and war, Schmitt argued. They adopt new methods and means of combat that totally disrupt the existing military and political order. Conventional warfare between states is understood to be contained by more or less limited goals and the political–legal distinctions within which conduct in such war is understood: between war and peace, combatant and civilian, between the legitimate enemy and the unlawful criminal. The revolutionary partisan—Schmitt cites Lenin, we might cite bin Laden—is declared to be beyond the pale. They are outside the 'conventional game' of inter-state law and war (2004: 35). But Schmitt's partisan makes a similar move declaring 'the enemy a criminal and all concepts of law, statute, and honor an ideological fraud' (2006: 20). The classical state and inter-state model is rejected.

Schmitt's theory of the partisan is a theory of enmity. For Arendt, it is a theory of agency. She expressed little sympathy for grandiose and ideologically motivated agendas of violent political change. Such agendas revealed no deeper political meaning. They were, in fact, anti-political, representing a 'conspicuous distain of the whole texture of reality' (OT, viii). On the other hand, as we will further discuss in Chapter 3, Arendt distinguished the meaning of political action from the justice of the cause and whether it was a failure or success. Here we pause to note that although the European resistance as described by Arendt was historically specific, it was not necessarily unique. The Second World War initiated and fuelled a number of revolutionary anti-colonial struggles both inside Europe and without. Many of the doctrines and tactics of the anti-colonial struggles were inspired by the Allied special warfare units and guerrillas (Shy and Collier 1986). Arendt's writing on the public character of partisan activity centred on activities in Europe. But is it right to suggest that 'what she recognises in the European she fails to see in the non-European'? (Serequeberhan 1994: 77) Did she condemn the very same acts by non-Europeans in the colonies? She did not. But we explore the suggestion for it reveals Arendt's ideas on what violence can and cannot achieve.

RESISTANCE AND INSTRUMENTAL VIOLENCE

The suggestion of a Eurocentric double standard in Arendt's writing on partisans is based on her essay 'On Violence', which was written in the context of the turn to armed violence across US society in the 1960s. This violence emerged out of the clashes over the Vietnam War, the struggle for free speech on the college campuses and for African–American civil rights. Some of this activity was inspired, in part, by the writings of both Franz Fanon and Arendt (Young-Bruehl 1982: 404). The assertion of a Eurocentric double standard derives from Arendt's assessment of Fanon's influential book *The Wretched of the Earth* (1963) and the preface to this volume by Jean-Paul Sartre. This is Arendt's most direct engagement with Fanon and she does indeed criticize him. But this was not a wholesale attack and had little to do with anti-colonialism as such. Arendt supported the move to decolonization and had sympathy with Fanon's idea that 'decolonization is always a violent phenomenon' (1963: 35). She was not oblivious to the political and strategic reality central to his work: the anti-colonial violence signalled an end to the imperial state's monopoly on the means of violence with global reach. Arendt's analysis of imperialism and its devastating results suggests that *The Origins of Totalitarianism* anticipated *The Wretched of the Earth* (Cocks 2002: 47). It was the nature of Fanon's specific justification of violence to which she took exception.

Arendt criticized the treatment of violence in a number of traditions of social and political thought. In 'On Violence', however, she singled out Marxism for two particular failings. First, Arendt objected to the teleological assumption that anti-colonial violence might contribute to a new more humanistic order of global freedom led by the Third World, of the formerly oppressed 'starting a new history of Man' (Fanon 1963: 315).[9] This was not based on any belief that domination was natural and inevitable; that if Africans had been the first to explore overseas and industrialize, white Europeans would be the subject races, not them. Rather, she rejected all efforts to assimilate violence into any broader theory of historical movement, human creativity, and new beginnings; the idea of violent resistance as the embodiment of historical progress. Fanon understood that hatred and the craving for revenge could not 'sustain a war of liberation' (1963: 139). Arendt made it clear that Fanon was far closer to reality in his understanding of the limitations of violence than some of his followers. But Fanon nonetheless revived an older and problematic tradition of thinking of violence as an expression of life and creativity, the idea that there is some 'creative madness' to violence (1963: 95).

The association between violence, life, and creativity, is the basis of Arendt's second criticism of Fanon. She acknowledged that the idea was indeed plausible. 'Is not violent action a prerogative of the young', she wrote, '—those who presumably are fully alive? Therefore are not praise of life and praise of violence the same?' (CR, 166). As Fanon put it,

for the colonized people this violence . . . invests their characters with positive and creative qualities. The practice of violence binds them together as a whole, since each individual forms a link in the great chain, a part of the great organism of violence which has surged upward in reaction to the settler's violence in the beginning (1963: 93).

This is not purely an argument for the strategic necessity of violence to rid the colonized of their oppressors. It is an argument for its physiological necessity.

Violence is understood as a 'cleansing force' for the body and the bringer of 'new meanings'. Practices of violent struggle are understood as creating new knowledge; the colonized can now 'understand social truths' (Fanon 1963: 147). Arendt too had written of the physiology of violent action which, she wrote, could be 'the most elemental experience of human strength' and 'elation...of a strength with which man measures himself' (HC, 140). But she was speaking of the element of violence in fabrication, the work involved in making the human artifice, the durable man-made world (see Chapter 8). This violence does not reveal any new truth; violence as such is 'mute'. For Arendt, only words, not violence, have the power to reveal and bring out new meanings and new knowledge.[10]

Fanon had good reason to be suspicious of bourgeois colonial discourse. In contrast to this hypocritical talk it seemed obvious that violence could teach or reveal the truth of oppression. Marx had shown bourgeois discourse to be 'mere...pretexts for, or justifications of, violent deeds', past and present (Arendt 2002: 290). From here it was but a small step to suggest that it was only in periods of war and violent revolution that history showed its true undistorted face; only violence 'dispel[s] the fog of mere ideological, hypocritical talk' (BPF, 22). Marx, Arendt, and Fanon shared a distrust of the bourgeoisie and their political categories (see Chapter 6). But the *general* 'mistrust of speech', Arendt could not share; 'for man, to the extent that he is a political being, is endowed with the power of speech' (OR, 9). As we will discuss momentarily, Arendt understood violence principally in terms of its instrumentality. The only meaning that could be revealed through the brute force of violence was compulsion.

There is no double standard in Arendt's treatment of anti-colonial resistance. Margaret Canovan notes that Arendt went 'so far as to declare that a people that does not defend itself is no more than an animated corpse' (1992: 186; also see Cocks 2002).[11] Like Fanon, who with brilliant cogency showed how colonialism shaped the subjectivity of the colonized, Arendt's own identity as a Jew and her understanding of the principles of political struggle were shaped by a violence that was colonial in nature. From the 1930s, Arendt had to deal with the inescapable fact of Jewish identity increasingly imposed by the German regime and she asked herself, 'What can I specifically do as a Jew?' (EU, 12). The question was purely conditional on being attacked in these terms and the belief that it was the only appropriate, realistic basis from which to fight back (1979: 333); 'you cannot say, "Excuse me, I am not a Jew; I am a human being". That is silly'. In such circumstances, to defend oneself as anything else (such as a world citizen) would have been 'nothing but a grotesque and dangerous evasion of reality' (MDT, 18; JW, 465–71; also see Chapter 8).

Arendt argued for the necessity of Jewish men and women to take up arms to resist *as Jews*. This was a justification of violence for an immediate and concrete goal of self-defence and self-definition. Nazi aggressors tried to define and then destroy the Jews. Resistance in Arendt's terms enabled the Jews to define themselves (JW, 222). However, Arendt's most compelling claims about violence concerned its practical limitations and dangers. Violence could be a rational and justifiable response to aggression. But it is important to understand what violence cannot achieve and why. Here it may be helpful to return to the conceptual language Arendt used to distinguish power from violence. In an important sense they are opposites; 'where one rules absolutely, the other is absent' (CR, 155). Power needs people. But in theory and actuality violence does not; it can manage with only one.[12] In an extreme situation the violence of one may destroy the power of many in the political form of tyranny or in pressing the nuclear button. But what kind of victory is that? Arendt noted that even the so-called 'victor is defeated, cheated of his prize, since nobody can rule over dead men' (HC, 201). Left unchecked, violence is capable of destroying the political space in which power appears. But power can also be a *corrective* to violence.

It is indeed possible for one person to possess sufficient implements of violence to command all others to obey. But power itself, Arendt argued, cannot be 'stored up' and saved for later use as if it was a piece of property or a weapon 'kept in reserve for emergencies'.[13] Power is a potentiality and not a measurable thing; it 'can only be actualized but never fully materialized' (HC, 200). *Pace* Mao, the essential fact about power is not found in the workings of command and obedience, 'of giving and executing orders'.[14] What political philosophy normally discusses as power, power *over* people, is more accurately understood through the concept of rule, the rule of one person or group of people over others. Such a view, Arendt argued, 'has always presupposed someone in command who thinks and wills, and then imposes his thought and will on a thought- and will-deprived group—be it by persuasion, authority, or violence' (OT, 325). If that were so, then power would indeed grow out of a gun. And the bigger the gun the more power to be had. But as Mao well knew when he initiated and wrote about guerrilla warfare during the Chinese Civil War (1927–50), power cannot be 'possessed' in this way. There is no one in 'command' of power.

Arendt conceived of power as something which 'springs up between men when they act together and vanishes the moment they disperse ...; to an astonishing degree [it is] independent of material factors, either of numbers or means' (HC, 200). In contrast, violence cannot be understood without reference to its instrumental character. Violence always relies on implements.[15] It is dependent upon material means such as weapons, tools, things used for inflicting harm against bodies and buildings. The utility of force is simply that it is a means to achieve some political end. It is not the case that Arendt *only* understood violence as instrumental (cf. Habermas 1983; Hanssen 2000: 24–7) or unrelated to individual subjectivity and everyday life, such as interpersonal physical violence. Rather, her point is that political violence can never be completely dissociated from instrumentality even if we must also pay heed to the historical, social, and symbolic structures within which all acts of violence take place.

Consider the distinction between power and violence in relation to the development of the modern nation-state. Organized violence is habitually assumed to be the essence of power. Max Weber defined the state in terms of its monopoly of the legitimate use of violence (1946: 77–8). But, for Arendt, violence itself is not the *essence* of the state-form of government. 'Everything depends on the power behind the violence' (CR, 148). The state became the dominant site for politics and also took possession of the means of violence. But this force, Arendt reminds us, was derived from the organization of space and technological innovation. The growth in the means of destruction at the beginning of the twentieth–century was so 'monstrous...' Arendt argued,

because political, public space had itself become an arena of force both in the modern world's theoretical self-perception and in its brutal reality. This alone made it possible for technological progress to become primarily progress in the possibilities of mutual mass destruction. Since *power arises wherever people act in concert*, and since people's concerted actions occur essentially in the political arena, the potential power inherent in all human affairs has made itself felt in a space dominated by force (PP, 147, emphasis added).

It is power that sustains the state; violence is secondary. Bureaucratic administration and developments in technology led to an enormous expansion in the means of force available to the state (Mann 1986; Shaw 1988). For Arendt, it was the grouping of the state apparatus, the means of violence *and the public*, political realm that has been generative of so much destructive violence. Institutions such as the state are the material manifestation of the prior coming together of people into a political space.

Like war, violence in general is defined by its means; the means of war are always violent instruments of destruction. The *fact* of its instrumentality means that violence is 'ruled by the means–end category'. Like all things that rely on instruments it is governed by the categories of ends and means and requires justification in terms of the ends it pursues. Its instrumentality signals that (unlike power and political action) violence cannot be an end in itself. As Arendt wrote, 'what needs justification by something else cannot be the essence of anything'. Again, the point is to distinguish power from violence.

Power 'needs no justification, being inherent in the very existence of political communities'; it is 'the very condition enabling a group of people to think and act in terms of the means–end category' (CR, 150, 151). As a political category, power is an absolute. Arendt compared it with peace. The end of war, she suggested, must be either 'peace or victory; but to the question And what is the end of peace? there is no answer. Peace is an absolute, even though in recorded history periods of warfare have nearly always outlasted periods of peace' (CR, 150).[16] Arendt's account of the difference between power and violence is a preliminary step in our task of deriving the beginnings of a political theory of war from Arendt's thought. The next step is to establish the meaning of—and the distinction between—politics and war.

THE DISTINCTION BETWEEN POLITICS AND WAR

When Arendt referred to politics as such or the public realm 'properly under-stood', she was not referring to politics in the everyday sense of government and party politics. As others have argued, the 'definition of the political can be obtained only by discovering and defining the specifically political categories ... to which all action with a specifically political meaning can be traced' (Schmitt 1996: 25, 26; Mouffe 2005*a*). This is also true for Arendt, though she usually spoke in the lexicon of the 'public realm' and 'politics, properly speaking', rather than 'the political', and we will follow her lead. Arendt under-stood politics as having its own meaning, distinctions, and separate logic. 'For political thought', she wrote, 'can only follow the articulations of the political phenomena themselves, it remains bound to what appears in the domain of human affairs; and these appearances, in contradistinction to physical matters, need speech and articulation' (OR, 9). The meaning of politics is the freedom to appear among a plurality of equals and to engage in speech and persuasion.

The concept of plurality is central to Arendt's understanding of political action. It is the ontological basis of all politics; 'the fact that men, not Man, live on the earth and inhabit the world' (HC, 7). Given this plurality, political action is necessarily conflictual, filled with disagreement, discord and con-testability. Yet while this politics may occur in wartime it is not in itself violent. Political action signifies 'that men in their freedom can interact with one another, ... as equals among equals, commanding and obeying one another only in emergencies—that is, in times of war—but otherwise managing all their affairs by speaking with and persuading one another' (PP, 117). The ultimate expression of Arendt's idea of politics is not Schmitt's struggle to the death between enemies. It is the ability to appear before plural equals and to debate and act to build a common world. The only foundation for politics is the words and deeds of those who build the common public world. There is an important spatial element. The political realm is literally the space for politics. When individuals come together to debate and to act they create this political realm between them.[17]

We have only just begun to get a sense of Arendt's understanding of politics and how it is related to our subject of war. Before elaborating on this—here and in other chapters—we need to pause to consider the meaning of war. War is an act of force.[18] It is the use of violent means to achieve political objectives. The meaning—and the 'only meaning' according to Arendt—that can be revealed through 'brute force ... is the immense power of compulsion in human intercourse' (PP, 198). The essential relationship between people in wartime is one of command–obedience; this is the meaning of war and it exists until hostilities cease. Because politics and war are both based on performance, their meaning is revealed only in the *acts* of politics and war. Their meanings are contained within themselves, revealed only as long as the activities persist. This understanding of the meaning of brute force in war is in accord with Carl von Clausewitz's sense of war as quite simply fighting. War is about killing and being killed. The medium of compulsion is physical force; the collision of two living forces is a form of strategic interaction.

The absolute expression of war, for Clausewitz, the innermost essence of war is violence. 'There is only one means in war: combat'; it is the 'strand that runs through the entire web of military activity and really holds it together' (1976: 96). As an advocate for a certain form of civil–military relation, the Prussian general could not conceive politics in the same way as Arendt. He wanted the political leaders of his day to subordinate war to state policy. Hence they had to be clear, in his words, that 'war in itself does not suspend political intercourse or change it into something entirely different. In essentials that intercourse continues, irrespective of the means it employs' (1976: 605).[19] Arendt is in agreement that war is a product of political relations. But she took the 'grammar' and 'logic' of politics and war to be fundamentally distinct. The meaning of war, even a war intended to create the possibility of 'freedom' or liberation, differs from the meaning of politics. Indeed, for there to *be* a meaning of politics, as already suggested, it assumes 'that political relations in their normal course do not fall under the sway of violence' (OR, 2). If Arendt's definition of politics is to hold, then we must be able to observe and theorize the activities of plural individuals speaking and acting, creating a common world between them, in a manner that is not essentially violent. In short, we must be able to distinguish between politics and war.

The distinction between politics and war is closely related to but definitely not identical with that between war and peace. The distinction between war and peace has been maintained by the Western political tradition since the ancient Greeks defined action in the polis as wholly based on speech and persuasion, not violence. This was captured through the organization of space in the city-states where the wall around the city was a fortress, protecting the free citizens inside. The Greeks believed, as do most moderns, that the military sphere has its own characteristics separate from the political. But as Arendt wrote, 'the Greeks separated struggle...from the military world of war, in which brute force has its original home, and in so doing turned struggle into an integrating component of the polis and the political' (PP, 171). Arendt wanted to hold onto struggle as a defining element of politics. But, as we will discuss in Chapters 3 and 5, she rejected the Greek solution to the distinction between war and politics. Here we deal briefly with Arendt's challenge to liberal thought in relation to this distinction. She has been described as 'disinterested' in liberalism (Villa 1999: 199–203). But this was not based on ignorance or prejudice. Arendt rightly viewed liberalism as fundamentally weak in its understanding of war. 'Wars and revolutions', she believed, 'not the functioning of parliamentary governments and...party apparatuses, have shaped the basic political experiences of the twentieth century' (PP, 191).

Based on the conduct of war in nineteenth-century Europe, Clausewitz suggested that the distinction between war and peace (in the form of a political settlement) was necessary to prevent a constant war of manoeuvre, continual small skirmishes for limited objectives. In his capacity as a political advocate for a new type of war (the decisive encounter), he argued that the military objective must be to defeat the enemy's armed forces as a prelude to the political settlement. One side would step back from battle by accepting the enemy's political demands. 'That acceptance might well be at the cost of freedom', Arendt noted, 'but not of life' (PP, 146). War occurred where negotiations ceased and its goals were also determined at this point, which meant that 'all ensuing military actions really were nothing but a continuation of politics by other means' (PP, 159). The political theory counterpart to Clausewitz's military history of this period is the liberal separation between the domestic and the international. Liberal civil society is understood as the place of peace. War is the exception. Only in the international sphere might war occur, with 'civilized' fighting defined as encounters between large armies on the European continent and 'barbaric' war in the colonies. Arendt's history of late-nineteenth-century imperialism forcefully showed how these distinctions are untenable. Liberal political categories obscure the transnational character of military power and the place of violence in modern society, past and present (Joas 2003; Barkawi 2006).[20]

Both Arendt and Clausewitz offer an account of the relations between war and politics that are historically more accurate and conceptually more

useful than those found in classical strategy and liberal political theory
(see Chapter 4). But Arendt's most direct engagement with Clausewitz, perhaps with even greater consequences for how we understand politics as distinct from war, is found in her writing on the nuclear revolution. Like so
many others during the Cold War, she suggested his classic formula of war
as the continuation of politics by other means had been reversed (Freedman
1981). In a hostile nuclear stand off the 'normal' conditions ceased to exist
because life itself was at stake. The spectre of nuclear annihilation meant that
war could no longer be the continuation of politics by other means. It seemed
to Arendt that technical developments had reached a level where no political
goal could be compatible with the destructive consequences of nuclear use.
Yet, while reversing Clausewitz's formula in the nuclear context, Arendt still
appeared to maintain that in principle the distinction between politics and
war could still hold.[21]

But is a simple reversal of Clausewitz enough? More recent writings on the
philosophy of war have called into question *any* distinction between politics
and war. In the words of Deleuze and Guattari, 'to be entitled to say that
politics is the continuation of war by other means'—as Arendt and many
others did during the Cold War—'it is not enough to invert the order of
the words as if they could be spoken in either direction' (1987: 421). It is
not enough merely to point out that national security policy in the nuclear
age is concerned with avoiding war rather than prosecuting it. And we must
go beyond the glib but true claim that the liberal freedoms enjoyed in the
West have been purchased at the price of the blood and sacrifice of our
own and other earlier generations and peoples. There is a new, broadly post-
structuralist literature which suggests that politics and war/violence operate
as part of a much wider field of relations in modern society: political power
operates through a continuum of violence rather than through a war/peace or
war/politics dichotomy. Rather than considering war as the continuation of
state policy by other (violent) means, the beginning of a 'counter-discourse'
(Hanssen 2000: 14) or literature of 'counter-strategic thought' (Reid 2006) has
started to emerge.

An important inspiration for this potentially fruitful move is the writing of
Michel Foucault. In *Society Must Be Defended*, Foucault proposed a model of
modern power relations 'essentially anchored in a certain relationship of force
that was established in and through war at a given historical moment' (2003:
15). This is also the view of much of the literature on the history and theory
of war to the extent that such work understands the intimate relationship
between war and society (McNeill 1982). But Foucault goes further. Liberal
'civil peace' must itself be understood as a secret form of war. War is 'both
the principle and motor of the exercise of political power' in general (2003:

18). Life in civil society is the 'displacement' of war itself; 'what is rumbling away and what is at work beneath political power is essentially and above all a warlike relation' (2003: 16).[22] Similarly, for Deleuze and Guattari, states have 'appropriated' the 'war machine, and having adapted it to their aims, reimpart[s] a war machine that takes charge of the aim . . . and assumes increasingly wider political functions' (1987: 421).

There is a flip side to this position for others, in which a pacified world where war becomes impossible is considered to be the death of politics. The ever-present possibility of war is necessary for basic political tension and 'antithesis', in Carl Schmitt's words, 'whereby men could be required to sacrifice life, authorized to shed blood, and kill other human beings' (1996: 35). For Schmitt, a world without the friend–enemy distinction, which he takes to be the fundamental political relation, would be politics' end.[23] For Baudrillard, from a position distinct from Schmitt, '*non-war is the absence of politics pursued by other means*' (1991: 30, 83). And for Virilio, 'the Total Peace of deterrence is Total War pursued by other means' (1997: 31).[24] The thrust of this recent research is to announce the death of pure politics and the triumph of war. The idea of a 'counter-discourse' of strategic thought is certainly compelling. In particular, it suggests the further limitation of liberal assumptions regarding the distinction between 'civil' society and 'external' war. But where does this leave Arendt? For, again, without a meaningful distinction between politics and war we cannot assemble from her work a *political* theory of war.

Central ideas of the so-called 'counter-discourse' of strategic thought were not at all alien to Arendt. This is clear from her writing on the Vietnam War and the Cold War more broadly. In particular, she feared that the subversion of world order would bring with it the subversion of the American republic. Quoting from the hoax parody of Rand Corporation (think tank) literature, *Report from Iron Mountain* (1967), she wrote,

To speak of 'the priority of war-making potential as the principal structuring force in society', to maintain that 'economic systems, political philosophies, and corpora juris serve and extend the war system, not vice versa', to conclude that 'war itself is the basic social system, within which other secondary modes of social organization conflict or conspire'—all this sounds much more plausible than Engels' or Clausewitz's nineteenth century formulas (CR, 111).

The *Report*, in Arendt's words, was 'probably closer to reality, with its "timid glance over the brink of peace", than most "serious" studies. Its chief argument [is] that war is so essential to the functioning of our society that we dare not abolish it unless we discover even more murderous ways of dealing with our problems' (CR, 107f).[25]

Arendt addressed these problems of the relations between war and society within an imperial frame and wrote of the 'boomerang effect', the 'unexpected ruinous backfiring of evil deeds on the doer, of which imperialist politicians of former generations were so afraid' (RJ, 271; also see Chapters 4 and 5).[26] The negative backlash was evident from the way in which imperial foreign policy brought with it the expansion of bureaucracy, 'an "invisible government" by secret services' (OT, xx). Arendt was critical of the notion that the establishment of a web of secret services in the early years of the Cold War was the necessary and inevitable reaction to Soviet espionage. It was the Second World War itself, and not the Soviet threat which 'had propelled the United States to the position of the greatest world power and it was this world power, rather than national existence, that was challenged by the revolutionary power of Moscow-directed communism' (OT, xx; Sparrow 1996). The danger was that this interventionism would simultaneously retard the development of democratic constitutions in the new states and weaken those that existed in the old.[27]

Clearly in such circumstances, the language of strategy and tactics is useful for understanding modern politics and the 'non-military functions of war'. Arendt viewed war as more than just the wielding of instruments. It was a form of social system in itself.[28] Perhaps most relevant to the possibility of a continuum, rather than distinction, between politics and war is Arendt's monumental history and theory of totalitarianism. In *Origins*, Arendt showed how this novel form of government was the political form of total war, the epitome of politics as war by other means. Both totalitarianism and total war, she wrote, used 'systematic terror to destroy all inter-human relationships' (PP, 159, 162). Totalitarian forms of rule are only able to countenance genocidal war. In such wars of annihilation the fighting goes beyond the obliteration of military assets. In Arendt's words, 'the entire world that has arisen between human beings' becomes a target and then politics itself is obliterated (PP, 162; also see Chapter 6).

The difference between Arendt and at least some of those in the 'counter-tradition' of strategic thought on the distinction between politics and war turns on an ontological question. It is a disagreement about what is and what appears in the world. Arendt consistently claimed that the fact of human plurality, of human difference and disagreement, was at the heart of politics. The ultimate expression of political action is plural equals coming together to build a public world. For writers such as Deleuze and Guattari, Baudrillard and Virilio *there is no* distinct public realm, no political world, as Arendt understood it. These thinkers simply reject her belief that she can observe and theorize this element of the human condition. It would be easy to respond that if everything is war then nothing is. But Arendt's fundamental difference with post-structuralism runs much deeper. This is not an epistemological question about foundations of knowledge, the existence of some rational truth as a way to adjudicate conflict (Villa 1992*a*). Nor is her position dependent on some objective sense of what 'peace' looks like or the liberal idea that war is the exception, an emergency and not a regular feature of modern politics. At issue is whether it is possible to recover from the past and observe in the present political events and experiences that are not forms of war in disguise. In the language of contemporary social science, this is simultaneously an empirical, historical, and theoretical question. On each of these counts, and drawing from a number of historical and philosophical traditions, Arendt argued for the integrity of a distinct public, political realm.

CONCLUSION

For some, any world without the possibility for war would signal the death of politics. It is not at all clear whether Arendt's political realm would also survive the 'paper wars' of perpetual peace.[29] During lectures at the New School in New York in 1970, Arendt told her students that in the work of the author of *Perpetual Peace* 'you will find repeatedly the notion of how necessary war, catastrophes, and plain evil or pain are for the production of "culture". Without them, men would sink back into the brute state of mere animal satisfaction' (LK, 26). Arendt rightly argued that this made Kant an 'odd kind of pacifist'. Kant encountered the same problem as Arendt. An initial reading of her writing may leave the impression that she was some kind of utopian writer on the subjects of power and violence (McGowan 1998). It may seem that her thought is ill-suited to the hard facts and realities of the political world. Arendt's goal was indeed to mark out a hopeful vision of the promise of politics after the horrors of the twentieth-century. The public, political realm appeared to her uniquely able to offer a mode of interaction that was non-violent. The short-lived moments and spaces of political freedom that she described throughout her work are the occasions in which humans temporarily escape the world of violence. But Arendt's writing was far from utopian. Her thoughts on war and politics were rooted in concrete historical analyses of modern society and political thought enabling critical analysis of war and the political world.

War and revolution remain the basic political experiences of our age, as they were for Arendt's. By repeatedly identifying the essence of free political action as taking place during times of war, Arendt's thought belies the notion that during periods of extreme violence men and women become little other than sheep. She understood political action to be identical with the freedom to act with others to bring something new into the world. And this could happen in times of both war and peace. This new beginning could involve the creation of the public political space or simply a specific change in public policy. But she always associated the political promise of this form of freedom with the ability to create something new (EU, 321). This faculty of action was rooted in Saint Augustine's concept of natality; the fact of human birth suggests that we are, in fact, new beginners (OT, 479; LK, 13).[30] Each new life is a new beginning and through political action with a plurality of others it is possible to make new beginnings throughout our lives. That we may begin the world anew, however, does not mean that we have the power to control it. Political actors rarely gain what they set out to achieve. Their goals are always overrun by the nature of political action where, just as in war, the totally unexpected is normal. Birth was necessary for new beginnings. But Arendt also believed that life itself was a threat to the integrity of the political world. She argued that 'politics is never for the sake of life' (HC, 37) and she had some praise for the 'basic credo' of soldiers—'that *life* is not the highest good' (1970*a*: xiv). What, then, is the relation of Arendt's understanding of politics and war to death?

3

Who Is Revealed in War? History, War, and Storytelling

The Western world has hitherto even in its darkest periods, granted the slain enemy the right to be remembered as a self-evident acknowledgement of the fact that we are all men (and *only* men). It is only because even Achilles set out for Hector's funeral, only because the most despotic governments honored the slain enemy, only because the Romans allowed the Christians to write their martyrologies, only because the Church kept its heretics alive in the memory of men, that all was not lost and never could be lost.

—Arendt, *Origins of Totalitarianism*, p. 452

To save your world you asked this man to die;
Would this man, could he see you now, ask why?

—W. H. Auden, 'Epitaph for an Unknown Soldier'

'They're digging up the dead' was widely said in Germany towards the end of the First World War. Bertolt Brecht's poem, 'Legend of a Dead Soldier', describes how a commission of military doctors stirred a soldier from his grave and declared him fit to serve. Brecht's early poetry was less about the experience of individuals in war, 'less the war itself', Hannah Arendt observed, 'than the world as it emerged from it'. The same is true for Arendt. The German defeat culminated in nothing less than the breakdown of traditional sources of social and political order in that country and across Europe. 'Politically speaking', she wrote, 'it was the decline and downfall of the nation state; socially, it was the transformation of a class system into a mass society; and spiritually it was the rise of nihilism' (MDT, 228; also see Weber 1946). Brecht naively viewed the war as having 'wiped the world clean. . . . It was as though, fleetingly, the world had become as innocent and fresh as it was on the day of creation' (MDT, 229). But this innocence cannot have lasted long, even for a poet. By the end of the 1920s, it was clear that the world had once again become a battlefield.

Although Arendt is rightly characterized as attempting to come to terms
with the Second World War, the rise of totalitarianism and the Holocaust,
the aftermath of the Great War is integral to her historical account of the
elements that 'crystallized' into the darkest days of European, perhaps even
world, history. The futility of modern warfare was most forcefully imprinted
on human consciousness with the mass carnage of the First World War. 'The
days before and the days after...' Arendt wrote, 'are separated not like the
end of an old and the beginning of a new period, but like the day before and
the day after an explosion'. She immediately qualified this image of explosion;
'the quiet of sorrow which settles down after a catastrophe has never come
to pass' (OT, 267). The 'uneasy' peace of the twenty-years-crisis witnessed
civil wars that had become more brutal than ever; the mass movement of
newly stateless peoples who could not be assimilated and who nobody wanted;
political hatreds, imperial policies, and a new wave of 'death-philosophies',
that all intensified in 'force and violence' (OT, 173).

Arendt wrote powerfully about the aftermath of the First World War, but
she also made a startling claim about the character of the war itself. What is
the meaning of the First World War? We have exemplary histories of the events
leading up to and during the war (Strachan 2001*a*). But for Arendt, it was not
until the appearance of William Faulkner's *A Fable* in 1954, over three decades
after the event that 'a work of art appeared which so transparently displayed
the inner truth'. What is this inner truth of the war? There is something about
Faulkner's novel that led Arendt to say 'Yes, this is how it was' even though
'very little is described, still less explained, and nothing at all "mastered"'.
Neither a military history nor chronology of the major happenings, Faulkner's
book instead leaves the reader with the 'tragic effect' of the war and 'the
shattering emotion which makes one able to accept that something like this
war could have happened at all' (MDT, 20). We cannot undo the event of a
war. But it is possible to become reconciled to it, to establish meaning, some
'permanent significance which then enters into history' (MDT, 21).

But what is this meaning? It cannot just be that war is tragic. We know
that for Arendt the meaning of war in general is brute force and compulsion,
killing and being killed. The implied insult to human dignity has always been
overlain, for some of the dead, in glorification; bearing witness to the 'great
deeds' of warriors is as old as human civilization. We come closer to the inner
meaning of the 'explosion' of the Great War when we consider the monuments to the Unknown Soldier erected afterwards. These monuments, Arendt
believed, 'bear testimony to the then still existing need for glorification, for
finding a "who", an identifiable somebody whom four years of mass slaughter
should have revealed' (HC, 181). This book began by noting the important
revelatory dimension to political action in Arendt's thought. Through acting

and speaking in public men and women can reveal something about themselves that even they would not otherwise have known. This 'who', someone's 'qualities, gifts, talents, and shortcomings', is contained in everything they say and do (HC, 179). What dignified 'who' could be revealed in the First World War? Remaining with poets, we might think of Sassoon or Owen, or with the commanders, Foch, Haig, or Ludendorff. For Arendt, the monuments to the unknown announce the most 'brutal fact' of all. The agent of the First World War, the unique 'who' that was revealed, 'was actually nobody'.

This is the Arendt most commentators know. In her ontology of political action 'who' an actor is must be distinguished from 'what' they are. Who somebody is, their unique identity, is constantly created and recreated and revealed in their actions and speech (HC, 179, 180). This is the 'specific uniqueness' of every single individual. 'What' somebody is is not an attribute of action and speech as such, but of physical fact and identity that may connect them to and define them against others. This 'what' is much easier to describe by reference to the qualities a person has in common with others. When we try to describe *who* a person is 'we begin to describe a type . . . with the result that his specific uniqueness escapes us' (HC, 181). We describe soldiers as brave, strong, dedicated but that is 'what' they are, not 'who' they are. And the answer to the question, 'Who are you?' is almost impossible to disclose. 'On the contrary', Arendt wrote, 'it is more likely that the "who", which appears so clearly and unmistakably to others, remains hidden from the person himself' (HC, 179).

Seen in this light, Arendt's seemingly strange suggestion that nobody was revealed in the First World War makes more sense. Modern warfare appeared as a hindrance to the full disclosure of the 'who' of an agent for two reasons. First, understanding the 'specific uniqueness' of a person is an outcome of humans 'being-together' in the full recognition of human plurality and difference (Arendt 2002: 295); 'we are all the same, that is, human, in such a way that nobody is ever the same as anyone else who ever lived, lives, or will live' (HC, 8). The revelation of this unique 'who' cannot occur, Arendt argued, when an actor is *for or against* the other. If a relationship is one of being for or against and not *with*, it becomes a means to an end. In modern war this is the end of killing and survival. As Arendt wrote, 'human togetherness is lost . . . where men go into action and use the means of violence in order to achieve certain objectives for their own side and against their enemy' (HC, 180). Violence is used, as Clausewitz understood it, as an instrument to achieve a political end or objective for the benefit of one side and 'against the enemy' (HC, 180). Deeds are violent; speech is 'mere talk' and no unique 'who' is revealed.

Arendt was referring to the particular circumstances of trench warfare; it was the men who fell in no-mans-land that remained unidentified.[1] For even in another (imperial) front in the same war, she wrote of T. E. Lawrence revealing much about his specific uniqueness. Famously, 'Lawrence of Arabia' fomented an Arab revolt against the Ottoman Empire so that they might fight on the side of the British. In an extended portrait we see Arendt's thoughts on modern identity, in this instance the imperialist character, occasioned by a 'hero' of Western war (OT, 218–21; also see Chapter 6).[2] We know Arendt viewed self-disclosure as possible through acts of political and military resistance in the Second World War, as discussed in Chapter 2.[3] Also consider the passage in *The Human Condition* in which she criticized Adam Smith's denigration of action and speech. This denigration 'is implied', she noted, 'when [he] classifies all occupations which rest essentially on performance—such as the *military profession*, "churchmen, lawyers, physicians, and opera-singers"— together with "menial services", the lowest and most unproductive "labour" ' (HC, 207, emphasis added). These are the very professions, 'healing, flute-playing, play-acting', to which the ancient Greeks pointed to as 'the highest and greatest activities of men'. But if we turn to the passage from *The Wealth of Nations* cited by Arendt, we find that he makes no mention of the military (Smith 1982: 431). Why does Arendt include this profession when Smith does not?

Arendt viewed war as an occupation that was based on performance. And she persistently turned to war to illustrate, and to show how others have illustrated, 'the highest and greatest activities of men' (HC, 207), as did the ancient Greeks. As we will discuss momentarily, they also believed that the 'who' of a person could be revealed through military combat. But how much of the Greek view was also Arendt's? Is it really the case that no 'who' is revealed in war? This chapter considers this question in light of the contemporary and controversial example of suicide bombing. In a recent book on Arendt, Elisabeth Young-Bruehl suggests that we should understand contemporary suicide bombers 'as those who do not reveal their *who* more thoroughly than any type of modern soldier. The suicide bomber is purely an instrument of violence—a bomb—programmed for self-destruction and the destruction of others; such people resemble pilotless drones, the kind of completely depersonalized shock-and-awe bombardier used by nations' (2006: 95).

Martyrdom through public suicide, including suicide attacks on civilians, is central to contemporary warfare but not all contemporary warfare is the same and neither are all suicide bombers. Can we interpret such acts differently and in Arendt's terms? 'Who', if anyone, is revealed? To answer these questions we turn to Arendt's reading of Greek political and military history out of which emerged a unique form of historiography with implications for how we might see the human in even those we take to be our enemies. Individual or collective acts of suicide bind an individual to a small group and the wider community for which the sacrifice is made. Seen in this light, it is possible that a unique 'who' is revealed. Dying for the sake of a political community is as old as politics itself, for as Arendt reminds us, 'men entered the public realm because they wanted something... they had in common with others to be more permanent than their earthly lives' (HC, 55). Arendt identified a form of historiography in the writing of Thucydides and Homer in which the meaning of an event is considered separate from its morality and from the criteria of victory or defeat. Arendt's writing suggests to us a mode of representing war in which we must describe both the noble and *evil* deeds of our side and the evil and *noble* deeds of our enemies. We must acknowledge the immortalization through commemoration of the enemy dead as we commemorate and immortalize our own.

THE GREEKS *AND BARBARIANS*: HISTORY AND THE REPRESENTATION OF WAR

One of the most frequent criticisms of Hannah Arendt is that it is hard to locate policy 'content' in her theory. She 'was never very clear', according to Judith Shklar, 'about what went on in that blessed "public sphere"' (1998: 371). Arendt wrote about the form that the political realm has, does, and should take in different historical periods. She hardly ever specified what political actors ought to do once the public realm had been established. Political action, speaking and acting in politics, was an end in itself. What are these great 'words and deeds' about? In a criticism of Arendt, Shklar pointed to the 'ferocious fighting between rich and poor and over who would conduct the next interpolis war, and in what manner' (1998: 371).[4] The suggestion is that Arendt's theory of political action inadvertently amounts to the glorification of violence (Kateb 1984, 1987; Shklar 1998). This charge is made in reaction to her effort to draw political lessons from the agonistic 'public realm' of the Greeks.

Arendt was in no way vague about the association between Greek politics and war. Her criterion for political action did not entail a competitive agonistic ethos as found in the Greek polis, the 'striving to prove oneself always and everywhere the best' (PP, 165; cf. Habermas 1983; Benhabib 1992*b*).[5] She was painfully aware that the greatest danger to political freedom, the ability to speak and act among peers, was the propensity for political disputes to turn violent.[6] Arendt valued political agonism and conflict. She wanted the tensions, struggles, ambiguity, and fragility of political action, but not through violent combat. And she knew that if left untrammelled any such political system could implode (Villa 1996: 156–7). Greek foreign policy was so brutal, Arendt wrote, primarily because the untrammelled agonal spirit 'made alliances between them well nigh impossible and poisoned the domestic life of the citizens with envy and mutual hatred... the commonweal was constantly threatened' (2004: 435; Canovan 1992: 210). To simply point to the intimate relationship between Greek political life and warfare as some form of criticism of Arendt is to miss her entire point. We must recall what Arendt was actually doing when she wrote about the Greeks.

Arendt was writing with the strong conviction that imperialism, world wars, and the rise of totalitarianism had left Western moral and political traditions in tatters. She believed that 'the pillars of the best known truths' such as God, faith in the promise of rationality and inevitable moral and political progress were no longer much assistance, nor should they be. Global and imperial wars had killed millions, produced and led to the criminal use of nuclear weapons, and the destruction of entire cities; literally, she wrote, 'we are standing in the midst of a veritable rubble heap of such pillars' (MDT, 10; EJ, 256). Arendt returned to the origins of the Western political tradition to help her think through the causes and consequences of this history without the conventional 'pillars and props' of religious or secular moralities. This is why she examined the political life of the Greeks. As Jean Bethke Elshtain has written, 'The Greeks are the "from" that sets in motion the "to" of the present *if* you are approaching questions of war discourse [in the West] as a political theorist. They invented [Western] political theory and politics, shaping tropes, offering metonyms, articulating various problems for thinking about and doing politics' (1987: 49). As Arendt put it, 'The Greek *polis* will continue to exist at the bottom of our political existence—that is, at the bottom of the sea—for as long as we use the word politics' (MDT, 204).[7]

The polis gave birth to the beginning of what would later be considered distinctly Western military practice, in particular war in the form of pitched battle (Hanson 1989). Changes in forms of agricultural production led to a change in the practice of war. The correspondence of the hoplite battlefield and the polis indicates the mutually constitutive relationship between war and society. The existence of a diversity of city-states and hence 'inter-polis' war was made possible by the absence of a common external threat to compel their merger. The use of force was the norm in inter-polis relations when any city-state, in Arendt's words, 'was threatened by the power of another community or because it wished to make others subservient to it' (PP, 129). For approximately 200 years prior to the fifth century BC, city-states agreed to resolve border disputes through one short explosive head-on collision of warrior-citizens (Dawson 1996; Santosuosso 1997).

Fighting between city-states was a special kind of 'war' restricted to local conflict between neighbours. Greek battles in this period were horrifying scenes but there was an unwritten rule. While the fighting was extremely brutal it was also comparatively quick. The phalanx system was an egalitarian affair. The soldier had a personal stake in the outcome of the contest and fought with others as part of a collective. Hoplite armies were small, normally from 6,000 to 10,000. It was egalitarian but was also not, strictly speaking, political. To issue commands and expect obedience is necessary in war. In Arendt's words, 'military decisions cannot be a matter of debate and persuasion'. For this reason, the Greeks viewed war as a 'nonpolitical sphere' for it 'invalidated the basic equality of citizens' (PP, 165). Nonetheless, it was this small-scale fighting which made possible the Greek ideal and practice of the citizen-warrior.

After battle, which sometimes only lasted a matter of hours, surviving warriors would return home. The glorification of these men was a central aspect of polis life. The ancients' estimation of politics was in large part a result of how the ethos of fighting and the perceived distinctiveness and greatness of citizen-soldiers appeared to be expressed in agonistic political action. The Greeks believed the public realm to be the site of excellence, of great speeches and new action, for performance and even aesthetic enjoyment. Accordingly, war was understood as not simply a way to fend off attack or acquire new territory. It offered a way to display unique character, a unique 'who'. The mental, physical, and moral qualities of the Greek citizen most praised were those best suited to the arena of battle. 'The polis...' Arendt wrote of the Greek view, 'this place of assembly is now permanent, not the campsite of an army that will move on after its work is done... [;] the polis at its height now hoped to engage in that same struggle without any use of brute force' (PP, 172). It was as if those returning from wars past permanently established the remembrance of 'their deeds and sufferings'. The political community of the Greeks is imagined to have originated as a form of organized remembrance and commemoration of the dead; their combat was the model for agonistic conflict, the lifeblood of the polis. The combative nature of the agonistic spirit, struggle, debate, and contestation, became institutionalized in the public space of the agora.

The roles of warrior and citizen were closely related and the form of warfare reflected the interests of the classes waging it. The privileges of citizenship were for the few. Foreigners, slaves, and women were excluded and were not allowed to fight. Judith Butler has suggested Arendt ignored how 'the boundaries of the public and political sphere [in the polis] were secured through the production of a constitutive outside' (2000: 82). But this is precisely Arendt's point. The political freedom of the citizens, she argued, *required* the institution of slavery and the practice of war. Slavery was not simply a part of Greek political life;

it was a necessary condition. Power was organized to facilitate 'the organized solidarity of the masters' over the slaves (CR, 149; 2002: 285). From the perspective of the all-male citizenry, the chief merit of their political organization was that it enabled 'citizens to act as bodyguards to one another against slaves and criminals so that none of the citizens may die a violent death' (Xenophon in CR, 149*f*). This solidarity was an integrative, 'constitutive' struggle. Citizens banded together to protect themselves against those whom they oppressed. Limiting access to the public realm restricted the nature and content of matters discussed, which in turn reinforced existing hierarchies in society, economy, and gender.

Freedom was a privilege acquired by a particular kind of Greek man as distinct from slaves, women, and barbarians. But this was not a God-given right. Freedom was solely an attribute of human organization, which in turn determined who was considered free; 'whoever is excluded is not free' (PP, 170). The Greeks saw the walls of the polis as delimiting the political arena, which Arendt understood to be central to the brutality of their foreign policy. The Greek definition of the political was spatially bound in a way that crucially shaped the conduct of inter-polis wars and also later and more importantly against 'barbarians'. In relations with other city-states 'the polis as a whole acted with force' and hoplite battle was therefore deemed unpolitical (PP, 164). But these were not wars of annihilation. The basic amorality was expressed in the idea that 'might is right' through the course of a short battle. But there were normative limitations on the fighting. The character and scale of inter-polis war has led some to ask whether they were really wars at all. Plato did not think so, according to Carl Schmitt. Battle 'among Hellenes', Schmitt wrote, were merely 'discords'. Real war was that 'between Hellenes and Barbarians only (those who are "by nature enemies")' (1996: 29).[8] The term Hellenes itself came to mean 'civilized' and 'barbarian' the uncivilized speaker of a non-Greek language.

Hoplite battle, though brutal while it lasted, served an important limiting purpose in wars or 'discords' between small city-states. However, with the Greco-Persian wars from around 500 BC, with invasions from the East and counterattack from the West, the character of Greek fighting changed. The limitations of traditional hoplite battle were exposed, in particular its lack of mobility. A new-found respect for cavalry, lightly armoured troops, and navies appeared. By the time Athens and Sparta, the two most powerful city-states came to blows in the twenty-seven year Peloponnesian War (431–404 BC) short hoplite battles could no longer be the norm; citizen-militias were no longer adequate for the task. Foreign nationals and mercenaries—non-citizens—were increasingly recruited into the ranks. The nature and social basis of the fighting had dramatically expanded with enormous consequences for the beloved Greek concept of the city-state itself. For if barbarians were able to join in the battle who and what was left to glorify? A new type of army emerged, an army much more suited to overseas expansion, an army that better reflected what would emerge as the Roman military and civic tradition about which Arendt also wrote (see Chapter 5).

When Arendt recalled Thucydides' telling of Pericles' Funeral Oration, his role in 'immortalising' the great wartime deeds of imperial Athens, she reminded her readers that this speech 'has always been read with the sad wisdom of hindsight by [those] who knew that his words were spoken at the beginning of the end' (HC, 205). The polis system was in decline. For the tradition of political philosophy, Arendt wrote, 'there has been no single factor of such overwhelming importance... than the fact that Plato and Aristotle wrote... under the full impact of a politically decaying society' (2002: 297). Arendt was unsentimental and not particularly nostalgic about the Greek polis (Tsao 2002a; Dietz 2002; cf. Habermas 1983). She explicitly wrote of the violent dangers of its agonal spirit 'which eventually was to bring the Greek city states to ruin' (2004: 435). In Chapter 5, we discuss Arendt's unfavourable comparison of Greek politics, law, and war with the understanding of the Romans with important consequences for how we conceive imperialism and the laws of war.

We know that elements of military combat were emulated in the reconstitution of the Greek city-states after war and that they became an inspiration for political agonism. Arendt's point concerned a particular kind of historical *representation* of war and its wider political role. Heraclitus famously stated that war is 'the father of all things'. Arendt took from this not that war is the origin of all politics. Rather, she argued that the method of making apparent the many-sidedness of things and the necessary diversity of perspectives makes its 'real appearance only in struggle'. Her example was the historical and poetic 'embellishment' of the Trojan War.[9] This legendary war between the Greeks and the Trojans was an historical–political event 'forced... to appear... in both of its originally opposing aspects' (PP, 175). Homer believed that the many-sidedness of things was 'inherent in man-to-man combat'. His literary glorification of this war was *the* topic for 'pedagogical embellishments'; both the Greek polis and later the Roman republic came to see it as 'the beginning of their historical existence'. More importantly for us, elements of Homer's epic tale are suggestive of 'what politics actually means and what place it should have in history' (PP, 163). It is nothing short of the historical counterpart to Arendt's ontological basis for plurality, that people, not one singular individual, inhabit the world; 'every topic', she wrote, 'has as many sides and can appear in as many perspectives as there are people to discuss it' (PP, 167). Only with these many perspectives is political discourse conducted in a manner that is tantamount to living in the real world.

This form of history was exemplified in Homer's method of 'grand impartiality'. He left as much space for the defeated as he did for the victor and he spoke of the noble and evil deeds of both. We lose sight of the importance of the many-sidedness of events if we condemn on moral grounds some of the words and actions that become manifest. The conflict between Hector and Achilles, the centrepiece of the war, was compared with the wars between gods to suggest the 'element of divinity on both sides' (PP, 166). This form of impartiality suggests that the historian is without the right 'to strike down and slay, so to speak', the losers 'yet a second time' (PP, 174). This is captured in the comparison Arendt drew between the experience of defeat in war with how 'speech itself' can be 'considered a form of action' by the vanquished (PP, 125). Most political action is carried out through speech and it is through speech that we make sense of the world. The 'blows of fate' that may come with military defeat might not be successfully resisted with force, but they can be responded to and resisted through speech. The words, of course, change nothing of the military outcome, but Arendt is adamant that 'such words belong to the event as such' (PP, 125).

Arendt was not advocating some form of value-free objectivity. It is impossible for the telling of history not to be shaped by values. Rather, she evoked Thucydides' effort to treat the different sides, the defeated and vanquished as well as the victor, with a degree of equality. It is to seek liberation from 'particular interests' and, more importantly perhaps, 'complete independence from the judgement of history' (PP, 163). This is a form of impartiality that attempts to reconstitute the concrete political dilemmas faced by the actors themselves in a manner that leaves the interpretation of those choices and events to the reader. In contrast, modern history in the West, Arendt suggested, places the criteria of victory or defeat as 'the "objective" judgement of history itself' (BPF, 51). The subject of history, Arendt otherwise invoked, is not a story of losers and (inevitably Western) winners but of actions worthy of remembrance. Events themselves become the subject matter of history and they are no less significant, no less meaningful, when they are removed from the need to situate them in 'engulfing' processes of historical movement (BPF, 64).

The justice of the cause of the combatants or the criteria of victory or defeat is not the measure of greatness. Like Homer, Herodotus wanted 'to prevent "great and wondrous deeds, some performed by Hellenes, some by barbarians, from being relegated to oblivion"' (PP, 164). As such, he offered a form of history in which the actions of the Greeks and *the barbarians* is remembered. Thucydides too wrote of the Peloponnesian War because, in his words, 'this was the greatest movement yet known in history, not only of the Hellenes, but of a large part of the barbarian world ... almost mankind' (quoted in BPF, 48). He knew that he had broken with 'normal standards' when he described both the good and the evil deeds of the Greeks (HC, 206). The greatness of these experiences, in the sense of reaching out into the extraordinary is not measured by intentions or success. It is the political realm itself and the poets and historians who argue over and determine this through their judgement. It is about actions deserving of remembrance, criminal or kind; actions that become the subject of poetry and history such that they become immortal; actions that are distinctive, that may reveal a unique 'who', and that are central to the immortality of the political community that commemorates them.

SUICIDE AND POLITICAL IMMORTALITY

We know that, for Arendt, violence—as the opposite of power—was most often the death of politics, not its birth pangs. Violence might be used in the founding of a new political realm, but she sought to end the seeming endless fascination with the idea that violence was necessary for a new political beginning. It was the fact of birth that made politics possible; 'men, though they must die', Arendt wrote, 'are not born in order to die but in order to begin'. She considered the fact not of *death* but of *natality* to be the ontological root of political action (HC, 246). Repeatedly, and in contrast to philosophy's obsession with death, we find in Arendt the new beginning and promise of freedom inherent in *birth*—humans as 'a being whose essence is beginning' (EU, 321). Contra Hobbes, it was Arendt's claim that 'no body politic ... was ever founded on equality before death and its actualization in violence' (CR, 165–6).[10] She gave the example of suicide squads, which throughout history 'often called themselves "brotherhoods" '. These small organizations were not themselves political, properly speaking. But what *is* the role of death, including death by suicide in Arendt's thought?

Arendt wrote of the importance of birth and new beginnings. Yet, as we have already intimated, she also believed that the 'politically most pernicious doctrine of the modern age' was 'that life is the highest good, and that the life process of society is the very center of human endeavor' (OR, 58). Is it not birth *and death* that makes politics possible? George Kateb has suggested that there is a 'dark underside' to Arendt's theory of political action. Her understanding of politics at its greatest is accompanied by self-sacrifice and in the end 'the readiness to die' (Kateb 1987: 616). He notes some irony in this. In the last page of *On Revolution*, Arendt conjured the legendary founder of Athens, Theseus, to suggest what it was that 'enabled ordinary men, young and old, to bear life's burden' (OR, 285). It was the political way of life. Politics put the lie to the sorry view that it is better never to have been born and next best to die young. But is Kateb right to say that 'whenever the threat of death is missing' Arendt's understanding of the best politics is also absent? Is this why Arendt preferred full and direct participation in public affairs to government by representation? Kateb infers that Arendt criticized representative government, the central function of which was the preservation of the life of citizens, because it attenuates any '*automatic* assumption ... [of] self-sacrifice' (1987: 612).

It is certainly the case that in Arendt's thought, and in the Western historical tradition, the ultimate sacrifice and sign of solidarity with others is to offer one's life for the political community. She wrote, 'man insofar as he is a citizen, an acting being [is] concerned with the world and the public welfare rather than his own well-being—including, for instance, his "immortal soul"' (BPF, 245). The actors Arendt praised, the men and women of the French Resistance, the Danish citizens who saved the Jews, and the Hungarian dissenters, all overcame the urge to retreat and do nothing. All put their lives at risk; some died. But how necessary to Arendt's theory of political action is this element of sacrifice to the point of death? We know that Arendt described death as an essentially anti-political experience. 'It signifies', she wrote, 'that we shall disappear from the world of appearances and shall leave the company of our fellow-men, which are the conditions of all politics' (CR, 164–5). And yet she also repeatedly turned to experiences in wartime as evidence of great political action.

Kateb recognizes in a different essay that Arendt did 'not demand heroism' from citizens (2000: 136). It is not readiness to die that Arendt is demanding. It is *courage*. In her words,

Courage is a big word, and I do not mean the daring of adventure which gladly risks life for the sake of being as thoroughly and intensely alive as one can be only in the face of danger and death. Temerity is no less concerned with life than is cowardice ... Courage ... is demanded of us by the very nature of the public realm ... It requires courage even to leave the protective security of our four walls and enter the public realm, not because of particular dangers which may lie in wait for us, but because we have arrived in a realm where the concern for life has lost its validity. Courage liberates men from their worry about life for the freedom of the world. Courage is indispensable because in politics not life but the world is at stake (BPF, 156).

The world is the space for politics. It is literally the in-between space that is constituted between political actors as they speak and act. For the sake of *this* world, Arendt argued, political actors have always understood that life cannot be the highest good.

Why is there this tension between human life and the political world? We have already suggested that for the Greeks it was knowledge of mortality that provoked them into political action, to seek 'immortal fame in deed and word' (CR, 165). They knew as individuals that they would die but the polis would outlive them. It was the 'body politic which was potentially immortal' (CR, 165). To engage in political action is to participate in founding and sustaining the common, political world that lasts longer than a natural human life. This world, Arendt wrote, 'is what we enter when we are born and what we leave behind when we die' (HC, 55). The fact of birth, of natality, means that each man and woman that is born has the ability to bring into being something new. They may begin something that will last beyond the limited time they have on earth. The very fact of human mortality can itself be a motivation to political action just as it may be the motivation for the creation of a new human life. Men and women are mortal but the body politic is potentially not. 'If the world is to contain a public space', she wrote, 'it cannot be erected for one generation and planned for the living only; it must transcend the life-span of mortal men. Without this transcendence into a potential earthly immortality, no politics, strictly speaking, no common world and no public realm, is possible' (HC, 55).

Arendt was clear that self-sacrifice in war or violent uprising against oppressive rule could grant an experience in which 'death is accompanied by the potential immortality of the group we belong to' (CR, 165). She was not seeking to glorify war, the solider or brotherhood on the battlefield. It is a fact, or rather an enormously powerful assumption, that it is on the battlefield 'where the noblest, most selfless deeds are often daily occurrences' (CR, 164). Such assumptions have inspired many to seek to model political communities on the experience of battle, the ancient Greeks with their agonism (Hanson 1989) and the inter-war fascists with their 'trenchocracy' (Mussolini). Individuality may disappear in forms of collective violence, but as soldiers have long claimed this can be replaced by a 'group coherence which is more intensely felt and proves to be a much stronger, though less lasting, bond than all the varieties of friendship' (CR, 164). In her introduction to Gray's *The Warriors*, Arendt singled out his description of the appeals of battle: ' "the confraternity of danger;" the "poignancy and intensity" of life in the face of death . . . the "light-heartedness" that comes from being "liberated from our individual impotence and [getting] drunk with the power that union with our fellows brings," a feeling akin to intense aesthetic pleasure . . . and we feel no longer "shut up within the walls of the self" ' (1970*a*: x).[11]

Death for the sake of a political community, and a certain way of community life, can be understood as a search for immortality. 'Immortality', Gray also writes, 'is not something remote and otherworldly, possibly or probably true or real; on the contrary, it becomes a present and self-evident fact' (1970: 46). This is death as a community event and when the most dangerous attractions of *collective* violence 'come to the fore' (CR, 164). From the perspective of the individual, death is 'perhaps the most antipolitical experience there is' (CR, 164). Yet Arendt was also aware that,

faced collectively and in action, death changes its countenance; now nothing seems more likely to intensify our vitality than its proximity...It is as though life itself, the immortal life of the species, nourished, as it were, by the sempiternal dying of its individual members, is "surging upward" [Fanon], is actualized in the practice of violence (CR, 165).

It is why, as we discussed in Chapter 2, Arendt was cautious of Franz Fanon's view of anti-colonial or any other kind of violence as 'an element of life' and creativity (CR, 166). Homi Bhabha has responded directly to Arendt's criticism of Fanon, to her idea that rather than bring new life, violence is the death of politics. We have already qualified this as Arendt's view. Fanon, Bhabha also writes, understood that 'violence...is part of a...search for human agency in the midst of the agony of oppression. It does not offer a clear choice between life and death or slavery and freedom, because it confronts the colonial condition of life-in-death. Fanon's phenomenology of violence conceives of the colonized...in a process of "continued agony" ' (2004: xxxvi).

Arendt too grasped the possibility of such an existence of life-in-death in her writing on the concentration camps and on suicide under such extremes. The political dimension of suicide appeared as a subject in her early essays on Jewish refugees in the Second World War and in *Origins*. Under the condition of totalitarian rule and the administration of the Holocaust suicide seemed to many a performance of freedom, 'its last and apparently still indestructible guarantee' (OT, 433). Suicide seemed like a kind of rebellion against 'superfluousness'. Detained in a camp at Gurs, France during the war, Arendt 'heard only once about suicide, and that was the suggestion of a collective action, apparently a kind of protest in order to vex the French. When some of us remarked that we had been shipped there "*pour crever*" in any case, the general mood turned suddenly into a violent courage of life' (JP, 59; JW, 268). The horror is displaced through the use of humour, but it was clear that for some in the camp this 'negative liberty' would be 'the last and supreme guarantee of human freedom'. This seeming exuberance on the part of the refugees was 'based on a dangerous readiness for death...[;] not being free to create our lives or the world in which we live', Arendt later reflected, 'we nevertheless are free to throw life away and to leave the world' (JP, 57, 59). The possibility of suicide as an act of resistance is linked to human spontaneity and the end of human spontaneity to the loss of the ability to take one's life.[12]

Historically, and in Arendt's political theory, suicide can be a way of affirming the kind of life you want to lead and the kind of community in which you wish to live. Drawing on Arendt, Roxanne L. Euben (2002) has suggested that we can understand elements of jihad, Muslim religious struggle, as a form of political action connected to the pursuit of *worldly* immortality. To believe one is fighting in the way of Allah does not necessarily involve suicide as a military tactic. The practice is controversial and is rejected by many Muslim clerics. But some armed groups have turned to acts of suicide bombing as part of a protracted campaign against the perceived foreign occupation of their land and claimed it as an act of jihad. Suicide terrorism possesses a compelling strategic logic as a weapon of national/cultural groups against foreign (usually democratic) occupation (Gambetta 2005). This is a profoundly *secular* not a religious goal and suicide bombing can be an effective strategic choice characteristic of the militarily weaker side. This is not suicide as Arendt described it, the last guarantee of freedom. The 'negative liberty' of suicide surely changes when it becomes a tactic in war and where the deliberate intention is to kill and maim an enemy. Indeed, we can question whether suicide bombers who target civilians are real warriors, those who risk their lives against other warriors.[13] But our question remains, who, if anybody, is revealed in such acts? How do we understand them, if at all, in Arendt's terms?

The notion that speech accompanies political action, that we verbally describe, explain, and justify what we do in the company of listening others, is central to the *subjects* of political action. Without this speaking subject, and the revelation of the unique 'who', Arendt suggested that most action could be achieved by 'performing robots' (HC, 178). If that were so, Young-Bruehl would be right. Suicide bombers would indeed resemble pilotless drones. If all human activity were conceived as a mere means to an end, if there was no sense in which certain human actions are more than that, it might indeed be possible and certainly more efficient for robots to perform all human tasks. We would not need the 'verbal accompaniment' through which an actor announces 'what he does, has done, and intends to do' (HC, 179). There is no *utility* in this disclosure of the 'who' of an actor; 'if nothing more were at stake here than to use action as a means to an end, it is obvious that the same end could be much more easily attained in mute violence, so that action seems a not very efficient substitute for violence' (HC, 179).

Arendt claimed that under conditions of industrialized mass slaughter, in an age that brought us the monuments to the unknown, the disclosure of the who, the distinct identity of unique agents in modern war could not possibly be revealed. With the rationalization of slaughter (Pick 1993), Arendt argued that soldiers might indeed become mere cogs in the machine of war, or performing robots (like the literal robots the Pentagon now hopes one day to send into combat (Coker 2004)[14]). Here speech for the cause of war is 'mere talk', a form of strategic action, a means to an end, 'whether it serves to deceive the enemy or to dazzle everybody with propaganda; here words reveal nothing' (HC, 180). The strategic language that accompanies war signals the end of the form of speech in the most meaningful sense. War is action, it is based on performance, and as we have seen it might itself become the subject of poetry and commemoration. But under the conditions of modern mass slaughter Arendt believed that no 'who' was revealed. The verbal justifications for suicide terrorism are also propaganda. These acts occur in the context of a protracted and deadly political–military struggle. But from the perspective of political community formation and commemoration it is clear that for many a definite 'who' is revealed in these bloody acts.

The religious justification that sometimes accompanies suicide bombing derives from the 'sacrificial myths' that always accompany acts of war (Pedahzur 2006). But the acts themselves cannot be reduced to these myths, nor can religion somehow be isolated as a sole cause. As Robert Pape has written, these religious myths are cultivated 'to mark an individual attacker's death as a contribution to the nation' (2005: 29). Ideas about politics and the greatness of immortality have been connected since the beginning of political communities. Some, though not all, acts of contemporary suicide bombing can be understood not as a perversion of religion, but as the pursuit of immortality in the context of political community formation.[15] The men and women who take their life are undertaking a profoundly *political* act that distinguishes them from others. In that sense, they are undertaking an act of greatness, in the morally neutral sense of the term. Without wider community support there would be no sense in which the individual attack was not only the killing of others but an act of martyrdom and the perception of a necessary sacrifice.

Individual motives for political acts of suicide vary from case to case. Many young men and women are manipulated to go to their death after extensive recruitment and indoctrination (Kurth Cronin 2003). 'Motives and aims', as Arendt put it, 'no matter how pure or how grandiose, are never unique; like psychological qualities, they are typical, characteristic of different types of persons' (HC, 206). Personal motives are less important than the willingness itself to die for a wider political world and the judgement of spectators. 'Greatness...' for Arendt, 'or the specific meaning of each deed, can lie only in the performance itself and neither in its motivation nor its achievement' (HC, 206). Such actions can be noble or wicked. The point is that the experience of suicide for the sake of a political community would be pointless unless it was hailed by the community as an extraordinary action. These actions would simply just be more deaths, 'unless they are talked about over and over again' (OR, 222). Both the suicide bomber and the political community can be represented in Arendt's terms as seeking to become immortal. The individual becomes immortalized in the act of public suicide and the subsequent community commemoration; the political community is itself maintained, made immortal, through these acts of commemoration and violence.

Understood in this context, suicide terrorism is martyrdom for the public world of the community and for its continuation. This is an uncomfortable conclusion. It can be painful for many even to recognize such men and women as human, and as one of the dead. The public acts of commemoration of martyrs, of suicide bombers who have taken the lives of enemy combatants and civilians becomes a form of public remembrance through which all political communities depend to the extent that they are concerned with immortality. In Arendt's terms, all political communities must be so concerned. This is not moral evasion. We must condemn suicide terrorism. Killing civilians is always wrong and if done deliberately is a breach of humanitarian law. But we are missing an important *political* element of this form of warfare, and we are evading reality, if we *only* condemn them as pure acts of evil, and then imagine that evil is the explanation.[16] The concept of evil cannot serve as an explanation for these actions.[17] Arendt teaches us that the concept of evil is descriptive, not explanatory; the difficulty of establishing what evil is becomes clearer with her observation that evil is empty and world-less; it 'is ontologically describable only negatively, in terms of what it destroys, and what it lacks' (Mathewes 2001: 168).[18] The only appropriate response to acts that we take to be evil is dedication to defend what they seek to wipe out. For Arendt, the destruction of plurality is the most evil of political sins. Whether a particular campaign of suicide bombing is an act in defence of or an attack on the condition of plurality is a matter for political judgement, no more but certainly nothing less.

CONCLUSION

Arendt explicitly—and repeatedly—illustrated that through violent resistance to perceived injustice men and women have not only established a new public space between them but also discovered 'who' they are, a discovery of a particular self that would not be possible in the absence of such constitutive action. 'Arendt conceives of the self as a singularity', as Gottsegen writes, 'whose uniqueness can only be revealed *in*, and *as*, the narrative of its own public becoming' (1994: 36). When Arendt spoke of the 'apparition of freedom' experienced by fighters of the French Resistance, it was not dependent on the cause against which they fought; 'the meaning of what they did...was beyond victory and defeat' (BPF, 6). As we noted in Chapter 2, it was not, 'to be sure, because they acted against tyranny and things worse than tyranny—this was true for every soldier in the Allied armies—but because they had become "challengers", had taken the initiative upon themselves' (BPF, 4). The meaning of what they did was contained within the event itself and not within our assessment of its morality.

At some point we have to make moral judgements and these judgements shape and are shaped by our political commitments.[19] But selfless deeds are no less selfless if they are for an end that we abhor. The meaning of historical events cannot be reduced to their causes or the motives of the principal actors. Each of these is important and Arendt addresses them throughout her work. But the meaning of an event is different from its place in any historical process or causal chain. It is possible, of course, to understand an event as part of an historical process. Political history is only superficially understood, however, when conceived as some unfolding struggle between good and evil or a progression of political developments from tyranny to democracy. Political history, and the history of war, may provide more illumination precisely *because* it is saved from the modern need to place everything that happens in some broader 'trend' of which the event is a mere example.[20] Arendt understood all historical and political processes as 'created and constantly interrupted by human initiative...Hence it is not in the least superstitious, it is even a counsel of realism, to look for the unforeseeable and unpredictable' (BPF, 170). The meaning of war or any event becomes clear only once we are able to relate what happened as part of a story, which also shapes history. 'No philosophy' Arendt wrote, 'no analysis, no aphorism, be it ever so profound, can compare in intensity and richness of meaning with a properly narrated story' (MDT, 22).

Arendt was a theorist but she was also an historian and her method and purpose has been compared with that of Thucydides (Disch 1994: 128).[21] Like him, she used the past to highlight the shortcomings and possibilities for the present. She liked to recall William Faulkner's statement that, 'the past is never dead, it is not even past' (BPF, 10; RJ, 270). Thucydides was a storyteller, the first writer of practical philosophy in the 'realist' vein. But, as Douglas Klusmeyer (2005: 126) has suggested, Arendt is more his heir than any of the so-called 'realists' of conventional international thought. Arendt identified a form of writing in Thucydides, and also Homer and Herodotus, in which the meaning of political events is revealed in the reflections of the political actors and the opinion of the judging spectators, the historians. Truth for Thucydides was determined by the plurality of judging spectators, the eyewitnesses to great events, with each one different and viewing the events from their unique perspective (Lebow 2003: ch. 3). Through the 'active nonparticipation' in historical events, the historian's judgement also becomes part of the story.

The social and political trends of the modern age are in the direction away from the conditions that make possible forms of impartiality and objectivity in the telling of history. Arendt, however, told stories to remind us that it is possible to tell a different kind of history and 'teaching by example'. The kinds of illustrations Arendt offered throughout her work were indebted to Walter Benjamin's method of fragmentary history, of reading history against the grain. 'What guides this thinking', she wrote, 'is the conviction that although the living is subject to the ruin of time, the process of decay is at the same time a process of crystallization, that in the depths of the sea . . . some things "suffer a sea-change" and survive in new crystallized forms and shapes that remain immune to the elements, as though they waited only for the pearl diver who one day will come down to them and bring them up into the world of the living' (MDT, 205–6).[22] Pearl-diving into history, telling the story of moments of political freedom—the spontaneous workers councils after the French Revolution, the rescue of the Danish Jews, the activities of the French resistance, the Hungarian Revolution—are disruptive fragments Arendt saw as breaking the hold of history as continuity, process, and certainly of progress.

4

The Boomerang Effect: On the Imperial Origins of Total War

Events brought out the undisguised facts in their brutal force, tumbling into a heap of rubble; for a moment, it looked as though all the chickens had come home to roost.

—Arendt, *Responsibility and Judgement*, p. 268

A central part of Hannah Arendt's effort to envision a post-totalitarian politics was to understand the elements that set Europe on its totalitarian path. Few things were more important than late-nineteenth-century imperialism. In *The Origins of Totalitarianism*, Arendt suggested how imperial aggression resulted in more than just useful adventures for European armies, an outlet for superfluous capital or strategic assets in great power competition. 'Lying under anybody's nose', she claimed, 'were many of the elements which gathered together could create a totalitarian government on the basis of racism' (OT, 221). Colonial violence acquired a dynamic of its own that belies the common assumption, then and now, that the vast majority of Europeans could safely ignore such wars. Colonial struggle was existential not only for the colonized. It unleashed a dynamic of violent and racist extremism, which in conjunction with other key elements of modernity directly prefigured the catastrophe faced by millions in the First and Second World Wars.

Arendt's ground-breaking work on the constitutive relationship between war in the empire and metropole, the links between colonial war and total war in Europe, has been central to subsequent empirical studies of these links (Bley 1996; Lindqvist 1996; Friedrichsmeyer et al. 1998; Bartov 2003; Hull 2003, 2005; Zimmerer 2004).[1] As such, Arendt is an important forerunner of emerging efforts to read the colonial and post-colonial into security and strategic studies (Barkawi and Laffey 2006).[2] Her history of the West is a global history. To date, however, the association between colonial and European total war has been neglected by classical strategic theory and military history. These fields comfortably draw connections between industrialized 'total' war in Europe and the social mobilization and technological advances of the 1860s evident in the American Civil War and the Prussian wars (McNeill 1982), but there is reluctance to explore the links between the conduct and justification of colonial war and degenerate war in Europe. In the words of Isabel V. Hull, 'Europe embarked on imperialism in the comforting illusion that the "civilized world" was insulated from the result. Military men (and too many military historians) continued to believe the myth that imperial warfare had nothing whatever in common with war fought in Europe' (2005: 332–3).

There are at least two explanations for this oversight in strategic theory and military history. The first is to be found in how these fields have interpreted the pre-eminent theorist of war, Carl von Clausewitz. Clausewitz was a product of his time. He held that European (civilized) and colonial (savage) wars were fundamentally different and largely unrelated. The world outside Europe was considered to be in a constant state of war; primitive peoples had an especially war-like spirit. 'Civilized' war between Europeans depended on the distinction between war and peace; it ended with the clear victory of one side over the other after a large-scale battle on the European continent. In contrast, the distinction between war and peace in the colonial context was never clear-cut. These wars did not end in any large-scale pitched battles between uniformed troops, but in massacres and scorched-earth campaigns. European armies often disdained any lessons concerning strategy that might come from colonial wars. In fact, there is little in Clausewitz's rich theory of war which should prevent analysis of the interconnections between war in the North and South. Nonetheless, civilized and savage wars, conventional European and 'small' imperial wars, were kept in separate boxes in nineteenth- and twentieth-century military thought.

The second reason why classical strategy and military history has underplayed the links between colonial and total war in Europe is that, in the language of post-colonial theory, these fields are Western 'ethno-texts'. In particular, the early canonical texts assumed the legitimacy of European colonial projects and are a product of imperial domination (Mahan 1895; Callwell 1896). More broadly, the academic discipline of International Relations has tended to underestimate the centrality of the 'periphery' in shaping global dynamics. Imperialism, almost by definition, is assumed to have relevance only outside Europe and few contemporary scholars of total war in Europe—'used to dealing with large armies, millions of victims and perpetrators, and warfare between modern states' (Zimmerer 2004: 50)—have taken up Arendt's call to think of its practices as connected to imperialism, and colonial in themselves.

Arendt's suggestive analysis of important processes and connections between imperialism and total war in Europe is certainly timely. Scholars and practitioners have sought to relearn the lessons of 'small wars' to apply to the

counter-insurgency campaigns in Iraq and Afghanistan and the debate about
the nature and possible consequence of a resurgent imperialism is ongoing.
'Contemporary historians...', once again, 'want to clothe imperialism with
the old grandeur of Rome and Alexander the Great'. The intention, of course,
as Arendt well knew, was to 'make all following events more humanly toler-
able' (OT, 132). But there was little humane about imperial rule, despite the
stories sympathetic European historians have always told (Ferguson 2003). For
'the only grandeur of imperialism', Arendt wrote, 'lies in the nation's losing
battle against it' (OT, 132).

Developing Hannah Arendt's work in this way also contributes to filling an
important gap in the secondary literature. There are few extended analyses of
Arendt's thinking on imperialism (but see Moruzzi 1991, 2004). In the words
of Seyla Benhabib, 'Arendt's attempt to locate in the European scramble for
Africa some distant source of European totalitarianism... is brilliant, although
it remains historically as well as philosophically underexplored', or perhaps
even ignored (2004: 51–2; Young-Bruehl 2006: 54–5). As Hans Joas writes,
'there is almost total silence about her claim that racism and bureaucratic
domination over foreign peoples are intimately intertwined with the history
of modern colonialism and imperialism... Arendt thus derived crucial traits
of the Nazi regime from the history of modernity... Arendt's position seems
to have remained completely unassimilable for decades' (2003: 165). The story
Arendt told about the rise of Nazism in Europe is not a German story, but a
modern one.[3]

One hindrance to reading 'Imperialism', the second part of *Origins*, is
that Arendt has frequently been read as hopelessly Eurocentric (Pietz 1988;
Serequeberhan 1994: 77; Norton 1995; James 2003). This is an easy criticism
to make. Consider her lack of understanding regarding the genocides in America and Australia, what she described as the 'comparatively short periods of
cruel liquidation because of the natives' numerical weakness' (OT, 187*f*). It is
callous to suggest that 'Canada and Australia... were almost empty and had
no serious population problem' (OT, 182). To focus solely on such statements,
however, comes at the price of missing the subtlety of Arendt's wider thinking
on total war and global politics. The moral problem of imperialism was not
only in relation to the conduct of Europeans in their domination of the rest of
the globe. Arendt argued that the defining facts of twentieth-century European
history—totalitarianism, total war, and the Holocaust—brought the horrors
of imperialism home to roost. Her Eurocentrism, this *focus* on Europe, as Ira
Katznelson writes, was analytical, 'not celebratory' (2003: 70).

Arendt's specific focus on totalitarianism means that the task of describing
in detail the relationships between imperial war and European total war was
left to later historians. She is the pre-eminent *theorist* of the political version

of total war that is totalitarianism.[4] She described the specific configuration of large-scale historical processes, those 'elements which crystallized into total-itarianism' (EU, 403), into something we had never seen before. But she was not a historian of imperialism; her account of its diverse practices and consequences is partial, incomplete, and Eurocentric. Nonetheless, her writing remains suggestive and insightful on the ideological and social–historical links between the colony and metropole in an era of total war. Her account of how late-nineteenth-century imperialism set off socio-military processes in the direction of total war helps students of international politics to rethink some of the foundational assumptions of classical strategy and strategic studies with enormous contemporary relevance.

The first section of this chapter describes the origins of the idea that late-nineteenth-century imperialism could have little impact on subsequent events in Europe. The focus is on the constraints imposed on classical strategy by the dominance of modern liberal categories of thought and how classical strategy has addressed one side of Clausewitz at the expense of another. Modern strategic studies focused on Clausewitz's idea that war is (or ought to be) the continuation of state policy by other means. But this has occurred at the expense of his ideas about the generative character of war, which nec-essarily bursts through the bounds set by discreet nation-states, as well as much strategic thought. The second section discusses Arendt's argument that important elements of total war in Europe were prefigured by imperialism. It is possible to discern three distinct but related threads to Arendt's claim: (*a*) the newly global reach of power afforded by imperialism; (*b*) the fostering and seeming proof of the validity of racist ideologies and the related growth of tribal nationalism and continental imperialism in central and eastern Europe; and (*c*) the institutionalization of degenerate military practices and tendency to final solutions. The final section evaluates the contemporary relevance of Arendt's ideas for the debate about the character of the detention camps used in the so-called 'War on Terror'. The conclusion notes Arendt's concerns about the potential dangers of imperial activism in the contemporary period, what she called the 'boomerang effect'. In an essay 'Home to Roost', which appeared in 1975, the year of her death, Arendt addressed the unintended negative consequences of expansive ideologies and aggressive foreign policies during the Cold War. She feared that twentieth-century proxy wars between the United States and the Soviet Union might eventually lead to a 'world-wide conflagration' (OT, xxi). But these were themes already central to Arendt's reading of the relationship between politics, imperialism, and war in her first major book. The danger is that global wars today might involve a similar lack of direction with disastrous results, a 'chain reaction' that is 'inherent in imperialist power politics' (OT, xviii).

WAR AS GENERATIVE

The word *strategy* is derived from the ancient Greek term for generalship. It is conventionally understood as the threat or use of military means to achieve political ends or objectives. As a 'system of expedients' (Moltke), it is concerned with the central issue in political ethics, the relationship between means and ends. Strategy secures the political end through war, although, as Arendt frequently pointed out, the end is always in danger of being overrun by violent means. What the political end is changes with time and place and is in constant dispute. Following Clausewitz's reading of the social and political conditions of his day, modern strategists usually view politics in terms of a trinity, composed of leadership, armed forces, and the population in a given territory. But what is the political end? Human societies have perennially used hideous means in the struggle over its determination.

Although the term strategy is Greek in origin, the 'classical' era of strategic thought emerged in late-eighteenth-century and early-nineteenth-century Europe in conjunction with the developing system of nation-states. The assumptions of classical strategy, much military history, and modern strategic studies derive directly from this period (Gray 1999). The political meant policy and policy meant national policy. Traditional strategy understood itself as the art of making war useful for the attainment of state goals. As a result, the strategic studies field begins with the assumption that states are the primary actors in world politics, and they are defined by their monopoly on the use of force. Armed forces generate violence that is instrumentally deployed to achieve state objectives. The military is a means for the continuation of politics, understood as the rational strategies of state officials. For Clausewitz, if states were to be sovereign, they had to subordinate war to an instrumental role in realising their political ends.

If the state is accepted as the legitimate possessor of the means of violence, then the significance of violence is assumed to consist in its instrumental deployment. This has led to a troubling blind spot in the study of war in strategic history and theory. There is little incentive to investigate the *transnational* constitution of force (Barkawi 2006). Territorially defined states, rather than transnational social forces such as imperialism, are considered to be the principal generators of military power. Yet, war, in Clausewitz's words, reflects 'the nature of states and societies as they are determined by their times and prevailing conditions' (1976: 586). War can be an act of state policy, but it is also more importantly an act of force that bursts through instrumental state-policy goals. Clausewitz understood that war needed to be domesticated, to become an 'act of policy'. If the state did not control military power the 'pulsation of violence' that is war would appropriate policy. The political aim, in his words, is not 'a tyrant. It must adapt itself to its chosen means, a process that can radically change it' (1978: 87; Reid 2006). It was therefore the *purpose* of the state to subordinate the phenomenon of war to the continuation of state goals.

Clausewitz's political advocacy for a new type of warfare between states (the decisive encounter on the European continent) depended on the distinction between war and peace and civilized and barbaric fighting. It was also a way to channel the force inherent in the combination of the people, the state, and the military arm after the social upheavals of the French Revolution. Clausewitz famously demonstrated how the transformation of the power of the state could also dramatically transform war. War became peoples' war for the first time and the mobilization of mass society for military endeavours in Europe would eventually culminate in the barbarity of industrialized total war. 'As policy becomes more ambitious and vigorous', he wrote, 'so will war, and this may reach the point where war attains its absolute form' (1976: 606). As a philosopher, Clausewitz fully appreciated the unpredictability of war: how violence itself can mutate from an instrumental means to an end into something that can become an extreme end in itself. Thus the classical rendering of Clausewitz as concerned only with state policy in the narrowest sense is misleading. The relationship between war and state policy was clearly a contingent, rather than fundamental relationship. War is generative of new social relations. It is an act of creation. Like Arendt's view of politics, war cannot be understood in purely instrumental, state-policy terms.

Classical strategic thought is clearly limited in its understanding of the relationship between war and the political. Subsequent to Clausewitz, strategic thinkers have been reluctant to pursue the rich theoretical framework he set out. They have narrowed questions down to those circulating around state policy and their military instruments, in which war is seen as a rational act of state policy rather than generative of new forms of social relations.[5] This failing, in part, derives from the dominant liberal understandings of politics and society in the West. War has not been a central analytical category in either liberalism or Marxism, the dominant traditions of Western social and political thought in which the principle driving forces of history are forms of government or economic structure (Shaw 1984; Joas 2003). Liberalism in particular defines itself in direct opposition to force and sees the ideal public realm as synonymous with civil society. War represents cruelty and arbitrary chance, the exception, not the rule. In constitutional democracies, the policy process is 'seen as controlling, guiding and even limiting war' (Strachan 2005*a*: 41). To this day, and exemplified in literature on the so-called 'liberal peace', war is considered a separate and distinct phenomenon from normal liberal politics and economy (Russett 1993; Owen 1997; cf. Barkawi and Laffey 1999).

Liberal thought downgraded the role of force as a social motor. It did so, in part, Arendt wrote, because in the (imperial) nineteenth-century liberals believed that 'the growth of force in the public, government sphere had, so to speak, taken place behind the backs of those acting in that sphere—during a century that might be counted among the most peaceful or, let us say, least violent in history' (PP, 148; HC, 130f; Angell 1913). The reasons for this strange view are well-known. In the imagination of many, colonial war came to be distinguished from European wars because they were 'small'. Wars of aggression in Asia and Africa did not count because small professional armies and native soldiers fought them; relatively few Europeans died. Small 'savage' wars were nothing like total war for Europeans (the phrase 'total war' had yet to be invented). Their tactics and morality were considered different from the rules of conduct in the civilized 'great campaigns' on the European conti- nent. The distinction was reflected in the emerging system of the laws of war from which non-Christian barbarians were invariably debarred (Koskenniemi 2001).

For liberal Europeans, it could truly appear as a paradox that the relative civil peace of the nineteenth-century was followed, in Arendt's words, by 'the greatest, most horrendous development of the means of force', culminating in the trench horrors and the death camps of two world wars (PP, 150). Of course, assumptions about the peacefulness of the nineteenth-century were only pos- sible by ignoring the 'never very peaceful exchanges of the treasures of the world' (OT, 186) and the frequency and scale of 'small' imperial wars.[6] Arendt mocked the liberal fantasy that after the appearance of a relatively peaceful nineteenth-century in Europe war would be constrained by civil society into the twentieth; the party system was supposed to reduce force to a 'minimum' (PP, 149–50). Rational, liberal policy, it was believed, would limit the excesses of war and perhaps even lead to its abolition. What liberals failed to recognize, Arendt suggested, 'was the specific combination of force and power that could arise only in the public realm of the state' (PP, 150). Arendt's proto-sociology of the modern state and imperial system suggests that the apparent 'decrease in brute force in the life of' European society ought not to have been 'equated with a gain in human freedom' (PP, 148).

The centrality of class to the relationship between society and the state, and eventually imperialism and the inter-state system, was clear. In Arendt's words, 'only a strongly centralized administration which monopolized all instruments of violence and power-possibilities could counterbalance the centrifugal forces constantly produced in a class-ridden society' (OT, 231). Arendt criticized the liberal-individualist, Hobbesian view of the rise of the nation-state that presented the Leviathan as ruling over individuals. It was not individuals as such, but classes that the state ruled (OT, 231). The nation-state-form as it emerged in Europe and was exported around the globe was as Marx described it, 'the instrument of the ruling class by means of which it oppresses and exploits' (BPF, 22). Indeed, imperialism originated as the quintessential bourgeois form of foreign policy. European respectable society, Arendt wrote, 'finally admitted its readiness to accept the revolutionary change in moral standards which Hobbes's "realism" has proposed' (OT, 156). In contrast to the conventional reading of Hobbes from inside out, from the domestic to the international, Arendt suggested that 'this process of revaluation ... began with the application of bourgeois convictions to foreign affairs and only slowly was extended to domestic politics' (OT, 138). The 'magnificence of Hobbes's logic' was revealed with nineteenth-century imperialism, when 'businessmen became politicians and were acclaimed as statesmen, while statesmen were taken seriously only if they talked the language of successful businessmen' (OT, 138, 139).

The major expansion of imperialism towards the latter stages of the nineteenth-century, Arendt argued, was initially caused by the gap between economic and industrial developments and the realities of the class-based nation-state system (OT, xvii). In other words, the apparent decrease in 'immediate domination of man over man' in Europe, the emancipation of the working classes, was directly linked to the increase in brute force elsewhere. Most of the rest of the world came under Europe's immediate domination when bourgeois economic interests came to dominate the national body politic. After a 'long period of false modesty', the bourgeoisie belatedly translated their position as the socially dominant class into organized political power (OT, 313). In the 'merry dance of death of trade' (Conrad in OT, 172), business interests and compliant state officials came to view the economic interests of a small group of men 'with national interests as such' (OT, 136). These 'modern imperialist schemers', Arendt remarked, then successfully appealed to the interests of the 'people and to hide their hideous faces under the respectable cover of nationalism' (OT, 167).

Arendt's account of the origins of imperialism was clearly shaped by the writing of Rosa Luxembourg (MDT, 39–40).[7] Although Arendt identified an original economic imperative, the imperialist doctrine of 'expansion for expansion's sake' acquired a political and strategic logic of its own (Owen and Sutcliffe 1972). The initial economic rationale behind overseas expansion was eventually abandoned when it was no longer 'driven by the specific appetite for a specific country but conceived as an endless process' (OT, 215). The power and violence implied by this philosophy of expansion inaugurated a new version of power politics. The centrality of violence to foreign affairs was not new. 'Violence', Arendt wrote, 'has always been the *ultima ratio* in political action and power has always been the visible expression of rule and government. But neither had ever before been the conscious aim of the body politic or the ultimate goal of any definite policy' (OT, 137). Conquest became the conscious aim and the ability to conquer seemed proof positive of the judgement of history. The superiority of European nations appeared determined by history-making acts, not only by the alleged physical differences between white and black; 'conquest alone, *fortune des armes*, determined the destinies of men' (OT, 164). In the end, 'expansion for expansion's sake' not only killed millions and retarded economic and political development in all corners of the globe, it also helped put Europe itself on the road to total war and totalitarian government.

THE IMPERIAL-TOTAL WAR CONNECTION

The relationship between imperialism and total war suggested by Arendt is characteristically not always easy to discern. Though her prose is often beautiful, as a writer Arendt did not always make things easy for her readers. It is possible, however, to draw out at least three direct links between imperial war and European total war in *Origins*; (*a*) at the global-ideological level; (*b*) the success of racist ideologies and experiments in race-politics in both overseas and 'continental imperialism'; and (*c*) the development of a military cultural tendency towards 'final solutions'. Taken together, these links belie the assumption that imperial and European total wars are unconnected.

Dreams of Global Rule

'Before the imperialist era', wrote Arendt, 'there was no such thing as world politics, and without it, the totalitarian claim to global rule would not have made sense' (OT, xxi). Imperial wars contributed to the ideological and material conditions that made industrialized total war thinkable and then possible. The most characteristic element of the imperialist form of power politics was the transformation away from the more limited goals of national interest that were local and largely predictable towards a 'limitless pursuit of power after power that could roam and lay waste the whole globe with no ... territorially prescribed purpose and hence with no predictable direction' (OT, xviii). Arendt identified the shift from the limited search for maritime ports for the expansion of trade towards a dedicated and more deadly policy of full-scale imperial expansion.

A similar expansion of means and goals was indicative of the coming era of industrialized total war in which enemies imposed no limits on the lives and resources used to obtain total surrender and victory. The brief appearance of moral limits to violent action in Europe, though always partial and imperial, were breached—'the destruction brought about by brute force must always be only partial, affecting only certain portions of the world and taking only a certain number' (PP, 160). The forced movements of populations and use of concentration camps central to imperial rule were reimported into the interior of European empires under martial law. Extensive domestic social mobilization also pushed aside the already fragile distinction between civilian and military spheres.

The totalitarian pursuit of global domination was presaged in the geographically unlimited search for imperial wealth. The ideological and material realities produced by imperialism were necessary for its potential realization. For Arendt, 'total domination is possible only under the conditions of world rule' (OT, 422). The states that began world war in Europe were empires as well as states; their wealth, their ability to prosecute world war depended upon resources and men extracted from colonial possessions. Competition in the great game of imperial expansion played no small part in bringing European nations into direct armed conflict. The legacy of this joining up of the world, the beginning 'of genuine world politics' (OT, xx), was still very clear in Arendt's day, as well as our own. During and since this era, the interstate system itself has 'proved incapable of either devising new rules for the handling of foreign affairs that had become global affairs or enforcing a Pax Romana on the rest of the world' (OT, xxi). As a result the abyss that divides the wealth of the West from much of the rest has grown with the end of formal empire. Even in Arendt's day, the gap was 'assuming truly alarming proportions' (OT, xxi).

The Success of Race-Thinking and 'Continental Imperialism'

The dynamic identity politics of race, what Arendt considered imperialism's 'main ideological weapon', linked imperial and European total war in a number of important ways (OT, 160). Unlike the tradition of international theory, Arendt placed the 'humanity-annihilating power of racism' at the centre of the development of the European society of states (OT, 162; Vitalis 2000). 'Race-thinking...' in her words, 'was the ever-present shadow accompanying the development of the comity of European nations, until it finally grew to be the powerful weapon for the destruction of those nations' in total war (OT, 161). Imperialist expansion necessitated the construction of a moral reality in which groups were distinguished from each other through racial and ethnic categories. Imperial rule was not possible without this differentiation. It was necessary to cement the difference between colonizers and colonized and colonial armies raised from the native population were divided (and ruled) in accord with a new racial-imperial hierarchy (Killingray and Omissi 1999).

The scientific 'research' conducted on the Jews of Europe to prove the superiority of Aryans was first tested in the form of medical experiments on black Africans to prove the superiority of whites. And it was German deliberations about colonialism that made popular much of the justificatory rhetoric of the Holocaust (Bartov 2003). The Nazis' racial doctrines, their crude admiration for the will-to-power, of violence and extreme cruelty, Arendt suggested, 'was preceded by the awkward and pompous "scientific" proofs of the imperialist elite that a struggle of all against all is the law of the universe, that expansion is a psychological necessity before it is a political device, and that man has to behave by such universal laws' (OT, 330; Holquist 2001: 123). Biologically-based accounts of politics were not only fashionable in Germany. At the end of the nineteenth-century British zoologists wrote 'Biological Views of our Foreign Policy', a guide for London's statesmen (OT, 180).

Arendt was scathing of the influence of organic and biological traditions on political thought.[8] Even the use of biological or organic metaphors, she believed, could 'only promote violence in the end'; no theoretical move has been 'more dangerous' than that in which 'power and violence are interpreted in biological terms' (CR, 172). The problem is that such thinking views power as expansionist by nature. Just as organic life must grow to survive, power, on this view, has an innate urge to grow, otherwise it will die. Such views spawned 'survival of the fittest' thinking, the 'old might-right doctrine', and the idea that 'a powerful struggle for existence dominates all living things' (OT, 178). Violence is thus easily excused and then later glorified as part of a natural process of destruction and creation. In the political realm, violence becomes a natural precondition for survival and the growth of political community. These so-called theories were not Nazi or German inventions. But the connections between eugenics and imperialism, the race-thinking perfected in the colonies and European anti-Semitism, appealed to the lower-middle-class social base of Nazi power.

The tribal pan-German and pan-Slav movements of Central and Eastern Europe borrowed the basic tenets of imperialist race-thinking and presaged Hitler's search for living space for the German race. Indeed, as Sven Lindqvist suggests, 'The extermination project's theoretical framework, the *Lebensraum* theory, is part of imperialist tradition. To this same tradition belongs the historical model of extermination of Jews: genocide in the colonies' (1996: 159). These tribal organizations emerged in Europe, especially after 1890 as advocates for 'continental imperialism', the right to establish land empires in the East just as the British and French successfully held empire overseas. With little or no hope of expanding abroad, the openly stated and rather popular goal of the Pan-German League was to treat Poles, Czechs, Jews, and others like the natives were treated in Africa. On the 'Dark Continent', Arendt wrote, proto-Nazis believed they 'had seen with their own eyes how people could be converted into races and how, simply by taking the initiative in this process, one might push one's own people into the position of the master race' (OT, 206; 223*f*).

The ideological claims of the pan-movements were expansionist by nature and hostile to existing political structures and borders, a dangerous form of identity-politics without limits. Such movements, Arendt argued, did not possess 'the vaguest notion of responsibility for a common, limited community' (OT, 232). Relatively stable civic–political boundaries and associations disappeared in the name of expansion and ethnic and racial self-assertion. State structures were dissolved in the interests of an ideological abstraction— the common interests of a 'people' as expressed through their tribal national consciousness. The totalitarian consequences are clear from the different forms of expansion attendant overseas and continental imperialism. Overseas imperialism rested on a distinction between homeland and foreign territory. But this was absent in continental imperialism with important implications for the role of the army.

The totalitarian emphasis on the power of the police, according to Arendt, corresponded to an apparently strange 'neglect of the seemingly greater power arsenal of the army' (OT, 420). The Nazi preference for police power over conventional military power and discipline can partly be explained in terms of Hitler's plans for global domination. He recognized no difference between inside and outside, between rule at home and what it would take to rule over foreign lands. In Arendt's words,

The military forces, trained to fight a foreign aggressor, have always been a dubious instrument for civil-war purposes; even under totalitarian conditions they find it difficult to regard their own people with the eyes of a foreign conqueror. More important in this respect, however, is that their value becomes dubious even in times of war. Since the totalitarian ruler conducts his policies on the assumption of an eventual world government, he treats the victims of his aggression as though they were rebels, guilty of high treason, and consequently prefers to rule occupied territories with police, and not with military force (OT, 420).

The paramilitary formations used by the Nazis and the principles of organization for colonial troops were in some ways therefore similar. The connection between ever-greater militancy and ever-greater loss of normality was clear to the Nazis as it was to the colonizers of Asia and Africa. So as Arendt described, 'the stormtroopers were never assigned to duty in their home communities, and the active cadres of the SA in the prepower stage, and of the SS under the Nazi regime, were so mobile and so frequently exchanged that they could not possibly get used to and take root in any other part of the ordinary world' (OT, 372).[9] In the end, the concept of expansion attendant a continental form of imperialism did not require geographical separation between metropole and colony. As such, no 'boomerang effect' needed to occur before the consequences of continental imperialism were felt in the European homeland. 'Continental imperialism', as Arendt remarked, 'truly begins at home' (OT, 223).

Military Culture and Institutions

The relationship between colonizer and colonized was itself a form of total war, involving similar techniques and occasionally the same men as industrialized total war in Europe. 'African colonial possessions', Arendt wrote, 'became the most fertile soil for the flowering of what later was to become the Nazi elite' (OT, 206). Heinrich Goering, first imperial commissioner of German South West Africa, was the father of Hermann Goering, leading architect of the Final Solution. Isabel V. Hull reveals some intricate details of one important part of the link between imperial and total war intuited by Arendt. In *Absolute Destruction*, Hull suggests the association can be found in the culture of the German military, 'whose practices in the imperial situation followed an internal dynamic that favoured final solutions...perpetuated in institutions...primed to follow this developmental logic' (2003: 143). Imperial Germany first used concentration camps for the Herero peoples of South West Africa. In the suppression of the Herero Revolt (1904–7), the German army moved from a policy of regular colonial warfare to extermination of the entire people (Gann 1977). The annihilation of the Herero was not the original goal of the military campaign; punishment for revolt in the colonies was always severe, but it did not usually involve a deliberate war of annihilation. Yet early military failures against Herero fighters unleashed a ruthless dynamic of extremism beyond all utilitarian standards.

Native resisters to colonial occupation often learned to avoid direct military confrontation with Europeans. The absence of a clear enemy, in turn, often led European armies to attack whatever they could hit with little or no regard for civilian life. All members of the group became the enemy. Arendt quoted T. E. Lawrence's description of the process of colonial 'pacification'. The British, in his words, fight their way... to their objective, which is meanwhile bombarded by artillery, aeroplanes, or gunboats. Finally perhaps a village is burnt and the district pacified. It is odd that we don't use poison gas on these occasions. Bombing the houses is a patchy way to get the women and children... By gas attacks the whole population of offending districts could be wiped out neatly; and as a method of government it would be no more immoral than the present system (quoted in OT, 134*f*).

Arendt did not condemn Lawrence. Indeed, she even suggested that British colonial warfare was often circumscribed within a limited territory and, on occasion, was conducted with a degree of 'moderation' (OT, 221).[10] The depiction of British actions as moderate is surely questionable. As Arendt herself pointed out, in South Africa their scorched earth policy and removal of Boer women and children into concentration camps led to over 26,000 deaths.[11] Roughly an equal number of black workers died as a result of disease, food shortages, and sanitation. Indeed, more died in South Africa as a result of British actions than died in South West Africa as a result of German.[12]

The picture Arendt painted of German atrocities was, however, quite different from that of the British. Examples of deportations, forced labour, and mass murder beyond even exaggerated military need were more common German practices in the colonies and in both world wars. Extreme violence characterized not only the 'instrumentalization of civilians' in the colonies but can also be traced to the German treatment of civilians in occupied Europe during the First World War (Hull 2005). Their obsession with a skewed vision of 'military necessity' further prevented German commanders from protesting with vigour against the Turkish genocide of Armenians, which was counterproductive to their allied war effort. The Turkish state continues to dispute that these actions amounted to genocide. Interesting in this context is that the genocide of the Herero by Germans not only contributed to the socialization of the future Nazi elite, in the words of Kurt Jonassohn, 'it also spawned the rise of a literature that first denied the genocide of the Herero, and later the facticity of the Holocaust' (1999: 66).[13]

Nonetheless, Arendt wholly rejected the view that totalitarianism was a uniquely German rather than *modern* phenomenon, along with all associated ideas of collective German guilt (EU, 121–32; also see Baumann 1989). Indeed, she occasionally appeared *not* to locate the seeds of the totalitarian movement that would sweep Germany in the military. She also exhibited misplaced faith in the restraint of the German army to resist the worst excesses of Nazi killing sprees. In her view, it was unfortunate that men from the regular army seemed 'at least as brutal as the SS' when deployed in concentration camps from 1944 (OT, 411*f*). While the members of the Reichswehr were happy for Germany to turn into a military dictatorship, and falsely believed they could use The

Führer as a 'stool-pigeon', Hitler's coming to power and method of rule went beyond them. More recent research suggests that by the end of the war junior officers from the lower-middle classes (Hitler's most active supporters) had already been exposed to Nazi ideology from youth and fought with great brutality on the deadly Eastern Front (Bartov 2001; Bessel 2004: 170–1).[14]

The justificatory principle behind all imperial wars of aggression, and related massacres, slavery, and camps was the idea that 'everything is permitted'. In contradistinction to the emerging legal and normative (though flawed) regulation of European warfare, there were far fewer perceived limits to transgress in the colonies. And yet as a general rule, military actions appeared to remain 'tied to utilitarian motives and self-interest of rulers' (OT, 440). The motives for the forced concentration of civilians, labour camps, and the killing of rebels were clear. They were tactical means to achieve the goal of suppressing rebellions in the colonies. As such, they were utilitarian, entirely useful for the purpose and therefore 'permitted'. That these actions were utilitarian is central to Arendt's argument about what changed when apparently similar practices rebounded back into Europe, especially in the latter stages of the Second World War.

By the end of the war, the Nazis had transcended the imperial principle that 'everything is permitted' into something much more radical, the belief that 'everything is possible'. Particularly towards the end, numerous of Hitler's actions were no longer limited by the utilitarian or self-interested purpose of military necessity. The brutally efficient running of the death camps was not interrupted by the usually overriding condition of a military emergency in face of total defeat. This was not simply due to Hitler's apparent personality and mental dysfunctions. When imperial violence migrated into the heartland of Europe and was allied with Nazi *ideology* its character and breadth changed. There was an association between the genocides in the colonies and the treatment of civilians in the European theatre of war. But the institutionalized practices that produced the former now spiralled out of control.

The Nazi death camps in which millions of Jews and others were tortured and killed en masse were entirely counterproductive and 'anti-utilitarian' from the perspective of the German state in total war. They served no economic, political, or military rationale. And yet they were made to function as 'normal' even in the wake of the defeat in Stalingrad and the danger of Germany losing the entire war (OT, 410, 415). Hitler requisitioned transport routes for the Final Solution in utter disregard of the Wehrmacht's pleas about diversion of resources and the serious loss of manpower for the real military effort. What was unprecedented about the Nazi camps was not the number of the dead. For Arendt, as we see in other chapters, it is not usually about the numbers. The unprecedented fact about the killings, in Arendt's words, was 'the ideological nonsense which caused them, the mechanization of their execution, and the careful and calculated establishment of a world of dying in which nothing any longer made sense' (EU, 243). This is why the camps were so difficult to comprehend in normal, common sense, categories of thought. The 'gas chambers', wrote Arendt, 'did not benefit anybody' (EU, 236).

As we have seen, Arendt understood violence as instrumental to political goals and not as intrinsically evil. Violence is not evil to the extent that it is used to achieve an end that may in some circumstances be justified. ('I do not mean to equate violence with evil' (CR, 155).) It is rational to the extent that it reaches goals that seem to justify it. Terror totalitarian style was different. Totalitarian terror, Arendt argued, 'was no longer a matter of calculated policy... [It] had become a kind of philosophy through which to express frustration, resentment, and blind hatred, a kind of political expressionism which used bombs to express oneself, which watched delightedly the publicity given to resounding deeds and was absolutely willing to pay the price of life for having succeeded in forcing the recognition of one's existence on the normal strata of society' (OT, 332). 'Normal' violence, even against civilians, can be a means to an end that may or may not be justified. But it always *seeks* justification. Nazi terror was different.

EVERYTHING IS POSSIBLE

Having drawn links between imperial and total war, Arendt nonetheless also wished to argue that there was a 'horrible originality' to totalitarianism. While contemporary political leaders often describe their enemies as the new Nazis, Arendt warned against efforts at 'deducing the unprecedented from precedents, or explaining phenomena by such analogies and generalities that the impact of reality and the shock of experience are no longer felt' (OT, viii).[15] The European death camps were unprecedented, but not because they were in Europe. Unlike those struggling against colonialism, who posed at least a nominal threat of resisting colonial rule, none of the Nazi death camp inmates posed a threat of committing a crime in the usual sense of the term. Nazi terror was accompanied by no provocation, 'its victims [were] innocent even from the point of view of the persecutor' (OT, 6). The exception to this rule was the inclusion of a few regular criminals, 'the aristocracy of the camps' (OT, 448).

The importance of Arendt's claims about the novelty of the Nazi camps is of some contemporary relevance. Consider the recent suggestion by the influential philosopher Georgio Agamben that the initial legal situation of the detainees in the camps established by United States at Guantanamo Bay, Cuba was in some way analogous to the Nazi death camps of the Second World War. Those captured by the United States were without legal status, he argued, 'thus producing a legally unnameable and classifiable being....Neither prisoners nor persons accused, but simply "detainees", they are the object of a pure de facto rule' (2005: 3). The only comparison, he suggests, is with the legal position of the Jews of Europe 'who, along with their citizenship, had lost every legal identity, but at least retained their identity as Jews' (2005: 4). A closer reading of Arendt suggests that this analogy is nonsense. 'There are no parallels to the life in the [Nazi] concentration camps' (OT, 444).

Arendt illustrated the difference between imperial and Nazi mass murder in terms of the animating principles behind them. For imperialists, everything is permitted. For the totalitarian ideology, everything is possible. To take seriously Arendt's argument suggests that the more appropriate analogy for Guantanamo Bay is the British camps in the Transvaal.[16] The Nazis did not invent detention camps. In general, as Arendt noted, they have been used 'for "suspects" whose offences could not be proved and who could not be sentenced by ordinary process of law' (OT, 440). The US government has argued that the detainees captured in the 'war on terror' cannot be processed by any existing system of law because they have already been defined as 'unlawful combatants'. Despite the circularity of this argument, it is nonetheless possible to make sense of the detention of those captured, even while strongly disagreeing with the legality and morality of their treatment. We can make sense of it because the actions of the United States remain guided by self-interest, political rather than military necessity (Kinsella 2005a). The claim of the Bush administration that to award legal prisoner of war status would be to acknowledge that these are soldiers fighting for a political cause which has legitimacy has been increasingly—and successfully—contested.

The principle behind this form of detention is the same as the principle behind imperialism; 'everything is permitted' in defence of US national security. Everything is permitted from the perspective of the Bush administration because it does not recognize international law as a constraint on what it may do in what it describes as a 'new kind' of global conflict. The detention camps are politically expedient. This idea is strengthened, rather than undermined, by the fact that even the Bush administration has expressed a desire to see the camps closed in the face of the worldwide public relations disaster that they represent. The fact that the executive branch of the US government refuses to accept any higher authority than itself for the determination of whether it has committed crimes in treating detainees this way does not undermine the principle that any abuse of those detained ought to be amenable to prosecution. In contrast, it was Arendt's belief that no law could cover the crimes that were committed by the Nazis, 'crimes which the Ten Command-ments did not foresee' (EU, 242). Arendt supported the post-war trials. But, she asked, 'What meaning has the concept of murder when we are confronted with the mass production of corpses?' (OT, 441).

There are no parallels to Auschwitz; 'all parallels' Arendt argued, 'cre-ate confusion and distract attention from what is essential. Forced labor in prisons and penal colonies, banishment, slavery, all seem for a moment to offer helpful comparisons, but on closer examination lead nowhere' (OT, 444).[17] To illustrate, Arendt distinguished between three types of concentra-tion camps, which she called Hades, Purgatory, and Hell, and which corre-spond to the dominant Western ideas about existence between life and death. The Nazi camps, as we have already suggested, resemble nothing short of Hell, where 'the whole of life was thoroughly and systematically organized with a view to the greatest possible torment' (OT, 445). They were labora-tories for conducting hideous experiments on human nature itself, 'trans-forming the human personality into a mere thing' (OT, 438). Though they would ultimately take more lives, she compared the Soviet labour camps with purgatory. The inmates were thoroughly neglected, forced into labour and millions died. The detention sites run by the United States resemble Hades and have been popular, Arendt noted, in 'non-totalitarian countries' for removing undesirables from public view and legal scrutiny. These camps, she wrote, are 'relatively mild' compared to the 'medieval pictures of Hell' (OT, 447).

In noting Arendt's crucial distinction between the principles that 'every-thing is permitted' and 'everything is possible', the point is not to defend the Bush administration. The Bush regime has done nothing less—but also nothing more—than to eliminate and degrade individuals for strategic ends. The United States has not undertaken an 'organized attempt . . . to eradicate the concept of human being' as such, which would truly mean that 'everything is possible' (AJ, 69). The effort to remove legal personality from those detained at Guantanamo Bay is *permitted* from the perspective of the Bush regime. Other lawmakers both inside the United States and without have fought against this interpretation, and with a limited degree of success. The juridical personality of those detained has not totally been destroyed, neither has their moral personhood as far as we can tell. The analogy between Auschwitz and Camp X-Ray does not hold. Unlike the perversion of strategic logic advo-cated by the Bush administration—the belief that everything is permitted—no sense at all could be made of the Nazi camps within normal frameworks of thought.

CONCLUSION

The connections Arendt drew between imperialism and total war in Europe are illustrative of the 'all-pervading unpredictability which we encounter the moment we approach the realm of violence' (CR, 107). For Arendt, both political action and war initiate processes that cannot be predicted by the principal actors themselves. The unpredictability and contingency of political action is frequently noted as one of the defining features of Arendt's thought. Yet, she wrote that, 'while the results of men's actions are beyond the actors' control, violence harbors within itself an additional element of arbitrariness' (CR, 106). This unpredictability is troubling for a foundational assumption of modern strategic theory that 'small' imperial wars and European total wars are distinct and largely unrelated. These links also have broader implications for how we might understand the relationship between political ends and violent means in the more recent past. The organization of violence (and prevailing ideas regarding its use) shape and condition world politics in ways more far-reaching than classical strategy assumes.

The links Arendt drew between imperial and European total war highlight the enormous disparity that can occur between cause and effect in the political and military realms. The imperial solution to Europe's economic problems, and the emergence of imperial competition, in the late nineteenth-century led to a transformation of worldwide political, economic, and moral conditions that could never have been predicted. Arendt's assessment of the meaning of imperial force, overseas 'coercion by violence', cannot be limited to an analysis of instrumental state policy, the achievement of security, wealth or self-aggrandisement. Just as we can never reliably predict the outcome of political action war is the realm of chance and contingency. The imperial logic identified by Arendt unexpectedly sparked a set of practices and ideas that contributed to driving 'respectable' European society to mass violence.

There were clear contradictions for Europeans in the accumulation of worldwide power through violence. The somewhat ironic result was the 'degraded' European, who became little more than a 'cog in the power-accumulating machine' (OT, 146). Swept up in what many European elites believed to be an inevitable historical process—and *progress*—of imperialism, individuals were without the power of political action at its greatest; they were left only with 'thoughts about the ultimate destiny of this machine, which itself is constructed in such a way that it can devour the globe simply by following its own inherent law' (OT, 146). The administrators of violence in the colonies were enormously influential back home and many of them feared that 'rule by violence in faraway lands would ... [mean] that the last "subject race" would be the English themselves' (CR, 153).[18] This never quite came to pass. But as Arendt wrote during the early stages of an escalating Cold War it was clear that the wider global social relations initiated in the imperial era had not evaporated with the so-called 'wind of change', the end of colonialism in Africa.

Arendt deplored the neglect of imperial social relations in most accounts of the Cold War for in many ways, she argued, it was a continuation of the imperial era. She took as evidence the fact that the United States and Soviet Union competed for influence in virtually the same parts of the world and in a not dissimilar manner to the Europeans. The term 'expansion', she argued, 'has disappeared from our political vocabulary' (OT, xix). The idea of an East–West confrontation had taken such hold that the very term imperialism had more or less disappeared 'except for the purpose of name-calling' (OT, xxi). And yet Cold War policies and ideological frameworks represented a 'backsliding' into imperialism. Taking a longer view of US foreign policy we might consider its actions during the Cold War—and post–Cold War period— as propelling forward rather than 'backsliding'. There were differences between the policies and methods of older European expansionism and the new order of power. The circumstances have changed and the language is different. But as Chapter 5 argues, the history and mentality of the United States is imperial through and through.

5

'How Dangerous It Can Be To Be Innocent':
War and the Law

You know of course that all our war criminals are 'not guilty'
—Arendt to Mary McCarthy, *Between Friends*, p. 278

Many opponents—and supporters—of recent US-led wars have suggested they were not only (or even) based on so-called 'humanitarian' or 'anti-terrorist' grounds. They were quests by the United States for strategic influence and in light of the current balance of power that could only translate into a form of imperialism, whether judged pernicious or benign. Debates about the effectiveness of international law in recent wars have therefore coincided with a trend in both media and academy to describe the emergence of a new form of imperialism. It has also been suggested by those writing on contemporary imperialism that recent breaches of international law by the United States are not in keeping with some of the oldest democratic traditions of the country.[1] Hannah Arendt's work suggests that the opposite may more accurately be the case. There is a close relationship between imperial foreign policy and the foundations of the law. It is a relationship that emerged at the very 'beginning of the Western world . . . as a *world*', that is, as the in-between space for politics (PP, 189).

Central to Arendt's explanation of the decline of the ancient Greek system of city-states was its inability to build a real empire. She located part of this failure in the Greek understanding of politics and law. Law established the boundary between political communities and political relations were deemed to end at the border. The law was both this wall-like structure and a system of 'precepts and prohibitions whose sole purpose is to demand obedience' (PP, 189). Greek conduct in war was often brutal, including the annihilation of the enemy, because no political relations and alliances with former enemies were deemed possible. In contrast, the Romans were more successful in building an empire because they understood law as relational, not just a boundary or a system of rules to obey (Taminiaux 2000). Treaties and laws instituted a relationship *between* peoples, including enemies that were first encountered in battle. The expansive alliance system of the *societas Romana* captured the new arrangement, Arendt wrote, 'in which peoples and lands were not only bound to Rome by temporary and renewable treaties, but also became Rome's eternal allies' (PP, 186).

Law was an important part of the expansion of the Roman Republic and its transformation into the Roman Empire. 'For the Romans', as Mills describes, 'there was no "conflict" of laws—Roman universalism demanded the integration of other territory as part of the empire, not mutual respect of different people and their legal systems. Given the Roman conception of justice as unitary, absolute, universal... international order was simply the universalization of the Roman order—a homogenization of law' (2006: 5). But the Romans also suffered as a result of their conception of law. While they were able to establish a system of alliances and ties, the system itself was also without limits. As Arendt described, it 'forced them against their own will—indeed absent any will to power or lust for domination—to rule [what they believed to be] the entire globe, a dominion that once achieved could only collapse' (PP, 187). Arendt's history of the constitutive relationships between power, law, and war placed imperial expansion at the centre of the analysis. Unfortunately, the centrality of power and the constitutive relationship between law, war, and expansion has been neglected in much international thought. In this field, such questions are usually framed in terms of the extent to which law articulates principles, norms, and procedures as a check on brute force. Law is either considered irrelevant by some schools of thought, and therefore unworthy of much consideration, or it is considered a constraint, and research accordingly centres on questions of compliance with the law.

For realists and post-Marxists, for example, powerful states only abide by international law when it is in their interests to do so. In the absence of a sovereign to impose its will, international law can be broken or cynically manipulated by the most powerful in the international system. Most other schools of thought, but especially liberal, constructivist, and international society scholars, suggest the power of law goes beyond this. Consider the legal injunction that states must distinguish between combatants and civilians and take all reasonable precautions to avoid targeting non-combatants. High levels of US compliance with this norm—even when dysfunctional in purely strategic terms—reveals the power of law in shaping war. We are frequently told of occasions where US commanders called off attacks on strategically important targets when the risk of civilian casualties was deemed too high.[2] In such circumstances, the United States is considered to be complying with the laws of war that protect civilians. In each school of international thought, the question of the relationship between power, law, and war has overwhelmingly been addressed as one of various degrees of compliance.

But what if we understood law as more than simply regulative or completely extraneous? Is it possible to consider law—and assumptions about compliance with the law—as productive of the social and political context that makes possible certain forms of war and certain relations of hierarchy (Kinsella 2005b)? Law is not simply irrelevant. Nor is it simply a limitation within which, for example, US wartime actions must comply to remain legitimate. The point is not to spend time arguing that the Founding Fathers were explicit that when America reached its full potential it would walk the world stage undaunted, though indeed they did (Marks 1987). Moreover, as Arendt wrote, European and later American imperialism was and is very 'different from national conquests in border-wars as it was from true empire-building Roman style' (OT, xvii). Indeed, the word 'imperialism', she argued, 'does not mean a thing if it is used indiscriminately for Assyrian and Roman and British and Bolshevik history', and American history we might add (EU, 407).[3] The imperial histories of the Roman and the American republics are different. Nonetheless, Arendt's account of the relationship between law, war, and imperial expansion suggests that perceived compliance with the law itself is partly productive of the global order in which contemporary war occurs.

Approaches to the relationship between law and power in international theory have been useful in capturing some important developments in the evolving system of the laws of war. Realist theory rightly argues that law alone can never be a match to political and military power (Carr 1939); international society approaches and constructivism suggest why states often comply with various legal norms governing war that may not be in their narrow strategic interests (Bull 1977); normative theory has suggested why the laws of war ought to be respected and has raised the practical question of how to strengthen the law to provide a check to political and military power (Caney 2005); post-Marxist scholars suggest that the law, when narrowly conceived, may be increasingly irrelevant given the resurgence of US imperial power (Barkawi 2006). However, while capturing some central features of the current system of military power in relation to law, most international theory is limited in its capacity to capture this relationship, in particular the *productive* effect of law—what law can do (Foucault 1984, 1995). In pursuing this path with Arendt, the chapter moves away from an understanding in which law is merely a constraint on pre-existing power. Instead, we address how law plays a role in producing not only imperial power relations, but also the subjects of the law, in particular the civilian casualties of Western military campaigns.

POLITICS, LAW, AND EXPANSION

The status of law in any society is always fragile. But law is necessary to provide an element of stability and regulation to the always unpredictable character of political action. Since the Greeks, Arendt argued, the tradition of political thought has 'understood that laws are the stabilizing forces', the only check on the inherent unpredictability and instability of all political affairs (PP, 186; OT, 467). There was nothing intrinsic to political action that was stabilizing and limiting. When left unchecked, it was the nature of political action—which after all emerges *in-between* people acting and speaking together and is not mediated by material things—to be boundless, to overrun existing rules, to bring about the new and unexpected. 'The stability of the laws', she wrote, 'corresponds to the constant motion of all human affairs, a motion which can never end as long as men are born and die. The laws hedge in each new beginning and at the same time assure its freedom of movement, the potentiality of something entirely new and unpredictable' (OT, 465).

The purpose of law was to offer some stability and form to what could otherwise seem so fleeting and transient, political words and actions. This was part of the greatness of political action and why boundaries and laws were so important.[4] Arendt analogized the law with territorial boundaries, which 'protect and make possible the physical identity of a people'. Laws similarly 'protect and make possible its political existence' (HC, 191). Law itself does not bring about change. It can 'stabilize and legalize change once it has occurred, but the change itself is always the result of extra-legal action', the result of politics (CR, 80). Law and territorial boundaries provided the main limits to political action, but, again, their capacity is limited; the 'limitations of law are never entirely reliable safeguards against action from within the body politic, just as the boundaries of the territory are never entirely reliable safeguards against action from without' (HC, 191). The concept of territory is itself a legal and political as well as geographical term.

International law is similarly a product of customs, treaties, and agreements between states.[5] To be enduring, any political space has to be 'hedged in by laws'. Without such conventions the world would truly be little more than a Hobbesian state of nature, or more accurately, in Arendt's words, a desert, a 'lawless, fenceless wilderness of fear and suspicion' (OT, 466).[6] In the absence of such laws the space in-between that emerges through political interaction would seem so ephemeral (Williams 2005). Arendt believed the territorial principle established by the European comity of nations was praiseworthy to the extent that it reflected that 'the earth is inhabited by many peoples and that these peoples are ruled by many different laws' (EJ, 264). These laws and boundaries served a limiting function to the extent that each member of the comity respected the principle of sovereignty. However, as Arendt's history of imperialism reminds us, this European comity and respect of plurality did not extend to the rest of the world and indeed made possible the expansion of overseas empires (Keene 2002).[7] Indeed, crucially for our later discussion, Arendt never identified the law of this comity of nations as embodying potentially universal and abstract norms that could be divorced from force and imperial power.

Arendt did not focus in detail on the role of law in her study of the history of European imperialism at the end of the nineteenth–century.[8] She presented this new form of expansionist power politics as law*less* and spent little time addressing the extent to which European lawyers had sought to make the power grab as orderly as possible (Koskenniemi 2001; Keal 2003; Anghie 2004). In her accounts of the ancient political systems of Greece and Rome, however, she did draw explicit links between politics and law, war, and imperial expansion. Recall the Greek model of politics and war as discussed in Chapter 3. Politics was understood as the realm of non-violent speech and persuasion among equals that reached its limit at the boundary of the polis and the doorstep of the home. This system emerged as their self-conscience solution to the problem of violence in human affairs. As Arendt put it, they sought to turn 'struggle into an integrating component of the polis and the political' (PP, 171) and simultaneously exclude war and brute violence from conduct between citizens. The limited space of the Greek polis was protected, indeed constituted, through the exclusion of non-citizens, slaves, and women who therefore had no formal protection from violence. Ideals of citizenship were modelled on the practice of hoplite battle by farmer-warriors who would return to the city after a short, sharp battle. All this, Arendt reminds us, was the peculiarly Greek response to the 'annihilating element of brute force, which destroys both the world and the political sphere' (PP, 171).[9]

Legislative activities involved in building a system of laws were considered to be pre-political. Law-making was necessary to secure the structure of the public realm within which political action could then occur.[10] But this law, as Arendt wrote, 'was neither the content of political action … nor was it a catalogue of prohibitions … It was quite literally a wall … This wall-like law was sacred, but only the inclosure was political. Without it a public realm could no more exist than a piece of property without a fence to hedge it in' (HC, 63–4). Law, the Greek word *nomos*, was understood as constitutive of all subsequent political speech and inter-action, a necessary precursor for the properly political to begin. But the building of the protective walls around the polis contained a different essence to that of speech and persuasion among free and equal citizens. There was 'something violent about it in terms of both its origins and its nature. It comes into being by means of production, not action' (PP, 181). The law is *made* and as such 'contains in itself the violent force inherent in all production' (PP, 181).[11] This is captured in the notion that citizens are subject to the *force* of the law.

The means used to form the institutional, legal element of the Greek polis was not considered political and neither was anything that went on outside the walls of the city. Law ceased to apply in interactions with other city-states. We have described the constitutive 'negative exclusion' of women, slaves, and non-Greeks. This exclusion was so radical that anything outside the polis was deemed non-political. This is clear from the brutality of Greek conduct in war, especially against barbarians. Thucydides' description of the brutal lessons the Athenians sought to impose on the islanders of Melos has always been cited by the realist tradition as evidence of the timeless and often brutal power struggle between groups (Gilpin 1986; cf. Lebow 2003). Clearly the Greeks waged war according to the principle that it is might that makes right. Foreign relations were necessarily violent. Moreover, in Arendt's words, 'negotiation and the conclusion of treaties [were] understood merely as the continuation of war by other means, the means of cunning and deception' (PP, 165). Such talk was not deemed to be political speech and no real 'ties and linkages' were believed to emerge out of them (PP, 181). The most important thing was the border, which was not a bridge that connected but a barrier that separated. Once the Greeks had annihilated their enemies they would retreat 'inside their walls, to be with themselves and their glory' (PP, 178).

The bulk of Arendt scholarship is now clear that the Greek model of politics (and war) was not Arendt's, though elements of political agonism were attractive to her (Tsao 2002a). Instead we find traces of a qualified endorsement of an alternative, though no less imperial, solution to the problem of war in politics and which emerged out of meeting in battle. The Greek solution to the problem was to define separate spheres and treat the legal boundary of the polis as the limit to authentic politics. But law can do more than secure boundaries and provide a structure of commandments that must be obeyed. Law can also institutionalize a relationship *between* people, that is, be constitutive of interaction in a newly public, political space. Arendt's alternative example is that of the rise of the Roman Republic, which from around 200 BC emerged as the most powerful political entity after the decline of the Greek city-states and which eventually evolved into the Roman Empire. The Roman word for law, *lex*, Arendt wrote, 'has an entirely different meaning; it indicates a formal relationship between people rather than the wall that separates them' (HC, 63 f). The spatial significance of law in relating what would otherwise be separate had enormous implications for the conduct of war and the earliest meanings of foreign policy in the West.[12] Indeed, Arendt argued that this alternative understanding was the beginning of what we now think of as foreign policy.[13]

The Roman army as an instrument of the republic was very different from the Greek hoplite force, and more adaptable to the needs of imperial expansion. The Roman legion-based system, in common with all military systems, reflected the society from which it emerged. Roman society was less insular and more diverse than that of the Greek city-states. Expansion into new territories provided economic resources and land to divert social conflict, and some power was shared between the aristocracy and lower classes. With a larger population a professional army was established and higher casualty figures could be absorbed. During the course of a campaign, one single battle did not necessarily bring a decision as it had done with the Greeks. 'The real strength of the Roman Republic', as Antonio Santosuosso writes, 'was the ability to remain at war until the enemy was exhausted, asked for a humiliating peace, or was utterly destroyed' (1997: 205). Vast expansion into new colonies ensued. The native aristocracy did not face inevitable annihilation. Rather, they were often placed in positions of power. It may have been humiliating, but it was a peace nonetheless, a peace with a treaty.

Greek and Roman foreign policy—which was imperial foreign policy— diverged in terms of their respective thinking about politics, law, and war. War was the beginning of Greek political existence. But this was only to the extent that they understood themselves as institutionalizing agonistic struggle in the polis; 'they became themselves', in Arendt's words, 'through conflict and then came together to preserve their own nature' (PP, 178). For the Romans, struggle with outsiders was not only an opportunity to discover the identity of the self. There was *recognition*, self-interested, imperial recognition, of the other.[14] Indeed, Arendt ultimately explained the demise of the system of Greek city-states in these terms. The Greek understanding of law and war as pre-political came with a high cost for they were unable to build an empire. They were unable to unite and join their colonies 'in a permanent alliance' (PP, 187). It was simply beyond the Greek conception of what they were doing when they fought. The failure to 'transform wars of annihilation into political wars', wrote Arendt, '… led to the ruin of the Greek city-states' (PP, 164).

What does Arendt mean by political wars? Anything political involves speech. She thus pointed to the Roman beginnings of the tradition of the 'just war' as the origins of Western wars accompanied by verbal rationalizations. Arendt is not writing in support of this tradition. The Romans, she wrote, 'drew no line between aggressive and defensive warfare. "The war that is necessary is just", said Livy, "and hallowed are the arms where no hope exists but in them"' (OR, 3). But the Greeks' sharp, definitionally and spatially enforced distinction between political and non-political life meant that violence needed no justification and few normative limitations. War was far less likely to be accompanied by the language of justice; violence was understood as purely instrumental, not the beginning of a new relationship. But the Roman concept of warfare, as Arendt described, was 'that unique and great notion of a war whose peace is predetermined not by victory or defeat but by an alliance of the warring parties, who now become partners, *socii* or allies, by virtue of the new relationship established in the fight itself and confirmed through the instrument of *lex*, the Roman law' (OR, 211). The end of the war and conquest of new territory resulted in the signing of a binding peace treaty, a lasting tie. Fighting a political war instead of a war of annihilation enabled the literal creation of a new political order, indeed a new world, a space in-between the former enemies. This political outcome was only possible because violent hostilities were ended before the complete destruction of the life and world of the vanquished.

Rather than annihilating the enemy, the Romans acknowledged them, Arendt argued, 'precisely when that adversary revealed itself as such in war'. This was not out of compassion, but 'for the sake of expanding Rome' (PP, 185). This relationship between alien peoples was not a relationship of equality.[15] The choice was between submission and destruction. The defeated could retain their life, and the Romans, in Arendt's words, 'gained... a new political arena, secured in a peace treaty according to which yesterday's enemies became tomorrow's allies' (PP, 178). As such, to meet in battle remained an encounter between people and a new political realm emerged, expanded and endured from a meeting which originally occurred 'as war' (PP, 183). Out of battle the creation of new lasting ties was possible. Law and legislative activity were the very things that secured these new relationships. Law itself indicated a 'lasting tie' and later 'contract'.

If for the Greeks to meet in battle meant the end of politics, then we might say that for the Romans it was the beginning; 'politics began as foreign policy' (PP, 183). This was the beginning of the Western concept foreign policy 'of *politics* in foreign relations' (PP, 189).[16] Law would assume different meanings throughout the centuries. But from the very beginning there emerged an association between politics, law, and war that still resonates. Law can be understood as a necessary check on the inherently unpredictable nature and boundlessness of political action. In the tradition of international thought this relationship is considered in the terminology of compliance (Scott 2003). How effective is law in restraining political action, especially the action of the most powerful state in the system? In contrast, Arendt pointed to an understanding of law that brings into being and justifies new power relations that did not previously exist. The tradition of international thought has been less good at asking questions about the productive or constitutive character of the law. To understand why this is the case we briefly review the dominant liberal assumptions concerning law that have shaped most international thought.

SOME PROBLEMS WITH INTERNATIONAL THEORY

The relationship between law and power in most international theory is fundamentally liberal. It mirrors the way in which John Locke and the liberal tradition positions law in domestic society as a 'constant and lasting force', derived from the command of society and not the Leviathan (1963: 343). Thomas Hobbes had asserted that Truth (state power) makes Law. With Locke and the emergence of liberal society, the origin of legal codes became de-institutionalized and set apart as the emblem of society and social interaction, not the state. The public sphere, the privileged realm of the law in liberal theory, is imagined as cohering around and deriving force from more general social norms. Norms of economy and politics come together within the public sphere as codified law and this process in turn instantiates a vast array of assumptions concerning public and private. 'In the "law", the quintessence of general, abstract, and permanent norms', interpreted Jürgen Habermas, 'inheres a rationality in which what is right converges with what is just; the exercise of power is to be demoted to a mere executor of such norms' (1991: 53).

Locke's influential model of power and law is based, in part, on claims about the emergence of liberal society in the United States. Locke had gone as far as citing America as the exemplification of the original state of nature. 'Thus in the beginning', he wrote, 'all the World was America' (1963: 343, II §49). His conception of democracy derived from social contract theory and as the process of manoeuvring government in the interests of society. But political order could only exist when the many 'freely' submitted to be 'ruled'. Locke reversed Hobbes's image of the Leviathan as the supreme lawgiver securing the necessary conditions for civil society to emerge. This alternative narrative—followed closely by the American Founders (and later international theorists)—begins with the people (or states) assembling first and then agreeing to representative government through the social contract (or norms of international society). In the international domain, the counterpart to this conception of the role of law is the founding moment of 1648 and the Treaty of Westphalia after which a system of international law developed in a new non-hierarchical society of independent sovereign states (but see Rosenberg 1994; Krasner 1999).

To be sure, the establishment of the legal apparatus in the United States was a major contributor to the democratization of sovereignty. Similarly, the collective association of common interests, values, norms, and legal institutions that developed in Europe served to limit some of the excesses of inter-state competition among Europeans. (This limitation on conflict facilitated imperial expansion into the rest of the world.) However, in both models the Lockean-liberal account of the origins of legal codes 'was less the law in any institutional form as it had in fact developed historically... and more the law now defined as general and abstract norms' (Somers 1999: 153). Liberal theorists could accomplish this feat of sociological revisionism because, as an historical point, constitutionalism in the United States was asserted in the course of rebellion against an executive foreign power. Yet law at once provided a positive rationale for political rebellion against the Old World and the perfect instrument of empire, patriarchy and slavery in the 'New', the legal institutionalizations of which still resonate (Ferguson 1984).

The American Revolution seemed to Arendt to offer at least a partial answer to *the* question of modern politics: How, in the absence of a king or god to impose authoritative principles on the public realm, could political freedom thrive and be stable? The most important act of the Revolution, Arendt believed, was in the 'necessarily relative' agreement of the Founders; 'those who get together to constitute a new government are themselves unconstitutional, that is, they have no authority to do what they have set out to achieve' (OR, 184). The trick rested in the act of instituting law without reference to any pre-existing authority. Accordingly, in Thomas Jefferson's famous words 'We hold these truths to be self-evident', Arendt emphasized the authority of the agreement 'we hold' rather than the 'self-evident' nature of the truth (OR, 92–4; cf. Strauss 1989; also see Chapter 7). With this conception, we see the productive force contained in the act of speech. The Declaration of Independence was 'the perfect way for an action to appear in words' (OR, 127; Honig 1993a). That its authority was contained within itself, that it derived its own legitimacy, meant that it met the dual yardstick of neither being autocratically enforced nor needing to appeal to grounds outside the political sphere.

At the moment of instituting a new legal system the law itself took on a powerful legitimating force. The liberal tradition, following Locke, was able to reinterpret the law as a 'constant and lasting force' originating from society as a whole and not a reflection of existing social and economic power, as Arendt always understood it. In the moment of founding this law, the institution of new socio-economic power relations appeared simultaneously. The new system of law and justice, therefore, did not appear as merely the product of pre-existing forms of domination, relations of force that could manipulate law to its own end and produce the subjects of law. Law itself took on the appearance of being the 'Immortal Legislator' (OR, 185) exterior to the prevailing distribution of power and control over the 'legitimate' means of violence. It accordingly became harder to criticize this and other forms of legally sanctioned 'violence since one cannot summon it to appear before the institution of any preexisting law: it does not recognize existing law in the moment that it founds another' (Derrida 1992: 40).

The liberal conception of this political history meant that the rule of law appeared at least in principle independent of political domination. Yet we know that in both domestic and international society, liberal norms of what it has meant to be a good citizen or a sovereign state did not simply arise out of a natural democratic disposition or the fiction of sovereign equality. Liberal norms had to be produced. In 'international society', a process of forcible socialization occurred before some societies—those outside Europe—were deemed fit to enter the society of states as equal sovereign actors (Koskenniemi 2001). In other words, law does not only regulate the behaviour of already existing individuals and states. It often violently constitutes individuals and states as legal subjects and makes some forms of violence appear legitimate.[17] The liberal vision obscures much of this sociological development of legal systems in both domestic and international society. But it has nonetheless been central to much recent legal theory. Indeed, such a vision enables the distinction between law and power necessary to pose the questions central to much international thought—how and in what way does law provide a check on political power and military force.

As indicated earlier, in international theory most legal thought focuses on measuring degrees of state compliance with existing legal norms or how state and non-state actors may break old norms and create new ones. Different sovereign states, distinguished by their relative material and/or ideational power, are generally understood to shape legal norms through their interactions in the society of states or international public sphere. Power in most international theory is understood as 'the ability, either directly or indirectly, to control or significantly influence how actors . . . behave' (Byers 1999: 4, 5, 35–50). Whether military, economic, or moral power is conceived as a possession, and depending on the particular school of thought, is held by both state and non-state actors. This power is then used to 'construct' the evolving standards and 'norms' of the international legal order (Barnett and Duvall 2005). The state with the most power in the system, the United States, is widely reckoned to be in the best position to break and create new norms with greatest ease. But this power is not unlimited even in the hard test case of war. Apparently strong US compliance with legal norms of non-combatant immunity, for example, has widely been attributed to the integration of 'humanitarian' norms into the law governing war (Finnemore 2003).[18]

Since the end of the Cold War, students of international relations have become more interested in law. The 'world', according to the editors of one text, 'is witnessing a move to law' (Goldstein et al. 2001: 1). There has been much talk about international punishment for war crimes. During the Bosnian conflict (1991–5), the International Criminal Court for the Former Yugoslavia was established at a relatively stunning speed, creating a supranational institution with independent decision-making powers to override Balkan state sovereignty. The permanent International Criminal Court (ICC) was established on 1 June 2002 at The Hague. The public event of a war crimes trial, even if the United States is immune, and the establishment or reestablishment of the rule of law can facilitate conflict resolution and for many bring about a sense of justice and finally peace (Minow 1999). Although the sheer scope of atrocities can sometimes make trials seem irrelevant, this has perhaps not been the case with a small number of recent conflicts. After the Holocaust, Arendt suggested that some 'are unable to forgive what [they] cannot punish and... are unable to punish what has turned out to be unforgivable' (HC, 241).[19] Several have analogized events in Bosnia, Rwanda, Kosovo, and Iraq with elements of the Second World War. One difference, of course, is that punishment has factored greatly in the international response.

Arendt was an early advocate for the establishment of a permanent international criminal court even though she believed Nazi crimes were so great that no legal system could ever mete out appropriate justice. The Nuremberg Trials after the Second World War were inadequate because Nazi crimes were not simply crimes of aggression and ruthless conduct—the expulsion, and murder of large numbers of people. None of these were unique to the Germans. Rather, Arendt argued that the Nazis had broken with 'that *consensus iuris*... the foundation-stone of international relations even under the conditions of war' (OT, 462). The supreme crime had been the effort to remove an entire people, not only from German territory, but from the face of the earth.[20] The Nazis rejected the territorial principle that different political and legal systems can exist.[21] 'Both moral judgement and legal punishment presuppose this basic consent; the criminal can be judged justly only because he takes part in the *consensus iuris*' (OT, 462).

The establishment of the ICC is clearly important. But Arendt's ideas suggest that some of its most fervent advocates set their sights too high. Lawyers have argued that the recent move to prosecute war crimes helps make possible 'the primacy of law over considerations of policy' thus constituting 'radical changes in the international constitutional order' (Weller 2000: 207, 208). Habermas is even more ambitious suggesting that such developments indicate a move away from the classical Westphalian system towards a 'cosmopolitan law of a society of world-citizens' (2000: 308). Arendt would have been wholly

suspicious of such claims (see Chapter 8). She believed that the purpose of
a trial could only be 'to render justice, and nothing else; even the noblest of
ulterior purposes... can only detract from the law's main business: to weigh
the charges brought against the accused, to render judgement, and to mete out
due punishment' (EJ, 253). Arendt's cosmopolitanism is far more modest than
Habermas's. Here it is sufficient to note that ICC jurisdiction is not recognized
by the United States and 'Laws that are not equal for all', as Arendt wrote,
'revert to rights and privileges' (OT, 290).

In such circumstances, accusations of victors' justice are easy to make. As
Arendt pointed out after the Second World War, Allied violations of The
Hague Convention were never examined or prosecuted. But she also recognized the 'understandable feeling on the part of the Allies that they "who had
risked everything could not admit neutrals"' (EJ, 274). In the context of total
war little else but victors' justice could be expected. Deliberate and inhumane
purpose was indeed found on the Allied side. The use of atomic weapons twice
against Japan, Arendt believed, was a clear war crime. While saturation bomb-
ings of German cities may have been provoked by the Nazis' aerial bombing
of London, Coventry, and Rotterdam, this was not an argument that could
be made to defend the nuclear destruction of Hiroshima and Nagasaki. The
very 'existence' of these weapons, Arendt argued, 'could have been announced
and demonstrated in many other ways' (EJ, 256). The issue of victors' justice
is obvious and clear, but is not the most 'potent' explanation Arendt offered
for the one-sided nature of the trials. 'For the truth of the matter', she wrote,
'was that... everybody knew that technical developments in the instruments
of violence had made the adoption of "criminal" warfare inevitable... Hence,
it was felt that... war crimes were only those outside all military necessities,
where a deliberate inhuman purpose could be demonstrated' (EJ, 256). The
very foundations of the laws of war and the definitions necessary to determine
war crimes had become obsolete—'the distinction between soldier and civilian, between army and home population, between military targets and open
cities' (EJ, 256).

The distinctions between these categories, like all legal distinctions, are
political. This has led to controversy over the extent to which Western states
in more recent wars have properly adhered to them, as well as debates about
the meaning of any such adherence (Kinsella 2005*a*). Again, the question is
usually framed in the language of compliance. For followers of realpolitik and
post-Marxism not much has changed (Barkawi and Laffey 2002).[22] International law is either instrumentally used by the United States when it suits
its strategic ends, or it is abandoned as outmoded when it does not. 'The
law...' in the words of E. H. Carr, 'cannot be understood independently of
the political foundation on which it rests and of the political interests which it

serves' (1939: 179). From this perspective, the language of 'humanitarianism' that invariably accompanies Western wars is mere rhetoric. The causes of war remain the pursuit of power in the national interest and/or imperial foreign policy.[23] The recently trumpeted idea that humanitarian intervention is a breach of sovereignty to protect human rights is nothing new. Throughout history, powerful states have frequently and hypocritically superseded the 'right' to sovereignty of weaker states (Krasner 1999). 'Modern power conditions...' as Arendt wrote, 'make national sovereignty a mockery except for giant states' (OT, 269).

The highly disputed legal justification for the invasion and occupation of Iraq appears to confirm some of the worst suspicions about the philosophy of the administration of George W. Bush in relation to international law.[24] In 2003, war was deemed necessary by the United States to uphold existing Security Council resolutions that mandated Iraq cease its development of weapons of mass destruction. Certainly, the function of the UN system in restraining the use of force has been dramatically weakened if unilateral action 'in support' of past resolutions is now deemed an acceptable *ex post facto* legitimation. Remnants of legalist rhetoric endure, of course, as one among many vehicles to legitimize grand strategy. But from a realist perspective, recent US wars—and any attendant rhetoric of humanitarianism—have been ruled more by geopolitics than any background rules of international (or even increasingly domestic) law (Scott 2004). The long-term political goal of the United States appears to be the diminution of the UN's legal authority to one of a number of policy instruments. While it is not in the US interest to undermine the fragile international legal framework governing war for all states, the United States may be seeking to have its desire for exceptional status codified in international law (Byers 2003). The legal claim of a right to preemptive war is the clearest indication of the imperial challenge to sovereign-state equality.[25]

Not all schools of international thought share the realist diagnosis of US compliance with the laws of war. Constructivists and international society scholars suggest that there is evidence that the existing fragile system may be robust enough to resist merely being used as a tool of the United States, and might even constrain imperial urges (Byers and Nolte 2003). The system of international law, including the law governing the use of force, exists as a legitimating normative structure that can be augmented in its own right. In principle, Arendt also held this view and quoted Justice Jackson from the Nuremberg Trials to this effect. 'Our own day', he said, 'has the right to institute customs and to conclude agreements that will themselves become sources of a newer and strengthened international law' (quoted in EJ, 273–4). Hence while the United States has taken great pains to avoid the appearance of needing to rely on international law to justify the right to fight, or *jus ad bellum*, it has also sought to avoid the admission that any of its wars are illegal. Law clearly remains central to the efforts to legitimate and de-legitimate apparent breaches of the laws of war (Kratochwil 1991; Clark 2005).

In the two most important recent test cases, the Kosovo and Iraq campaigns, the language of law enforcement was central to arguments for military action.[26] NATO claimed that it acted in Kosovo to avert a humanitarian catastrophe and this action was consistent with Resolutions 1160, 1199, and 1203 adopted under Chapter VII of the UN Charter.[27] Others have argued that even if such US-led actions were illegal they were still just (Wheeler 2000*b*). We cannot know what Arendt's position would have been on these specific cases. However, writing on the trial of Nazi war criminal Adolf Eichmann, she noted that his initial abduction from Argentina was 'a clear violation of international law... to bring him to justice' (EJ, 263).[28] Israel 'violated the territorial principle' that recognizes that different peoples are governed by different laws. However, Arendt also argued that 'he who takes the law into his own hands will render a service to justice only if he is willing to transform the situation in such a way that the law can again operate and his act can, at least posthumously, be validated' (EJ, 265). She cited the example of two interwar assassins who separately killed perpetrators of pogroms against the Jews and massacres against Armenians. Each assassin immediately turned himself into the authorities and insisted on being tried in a public court. The purpose was 'to show the world through court procedure what crimes against his people had been committed and gone unpunished' (EJ, 265; AJ, 415). Both assassins were found not guilty.

It is difficult to imagine the United States insisting on being tried in an international court to establish justice after admitting an illegal act of war. After all, it is the position of the United States, and the influential school of neoconservative thought, that wars in defence of peace, in the name of freedom and the spread of democracy need no further justification (see Chapter 7). On this view, wars waged by the United States are justified because they rid the world of demonstrably evil regimes. Even from the perspective of conventional international theory, it appears that the United States is on strong ground. From the realist perspective, might makes right. There is no need for further debate. Liberal, constructivist and international society scholarship can either concede to realism that power trumps law or agree with the United States that the cause was just, even if technically illegal. They can also point to the US effort to abide by the norm of non-combatant immunity. Realists are sceptical of the power of *jus in bello* norms to rein in fighting in the heat of battle.[29] But these other schools point to strong US compliance with international laws governing conduct *in* war, especially high standards of compliance with the founding principle of international humanitarian law, the distinction between combatant and civilian.

ACCIDENTS AND CIVILIAN DEATH

During recent military campaigns, US commanders and politicians have made frequent pledges to spare innocent lives; 'due care', '*great* care' is always taken to prevent civilian death. American soldiers are trained in the laws of war, which in any case do not impose obligations to absolute civilian protection. The law only requires commanders to take reasonable precautions and to discriminate between civilian and military targets. Lawyers are consulted. Strict 'collateral damage' avoidance rules produce frequent occasions when targets are avoided, reviewed again and again, or even cancelled at the last moment. This apparent compliance with non-combatant immunity is a product of both technological advances in precision weapons and the evolving normative framework. But what is this normative framework, and what is its relation to imperial power and the law? Are Western wars simply becoming more humane? (Finnemore 1996; Coker 2001; Thomas 2001) Can we question the too easy association between ethical practice and apparent compliance with non-combatant immunity? What forms of identity construction are maintained by the current application of military power and assumptions about its legality?[30]

The United States must be able to present its wars as more humanitarian, more clinical, and more civilized than the violence of its enemies. The deaths caused by the US military are seen as *fundamentally* different from the deaths caused by terrorists and rogue regimes. An important distinction has been constructed as almost beyond question or doubt—between the deaths inflicted accidentally by the United States which are aberrations in contrast to those that its enemies inflict deliberately. The comparison between the 'due care' taken by civilized states and the indiscriminate killing by others has been constructed as so obviously valid as to be almost beyond question or doubt.[31] Speaking of the war to topple the Taliban from 2001, then Secretary of Defence Donald Rumsfeld claimed he could not 'imagine there's been a conflict in history where there has been less collateral damage, less unintended consequences'.[32] Only military assets (at worst 'dual-use' sites) are targeted and thus if on occasion they kill civilians in error, the United States surely cannot be blamed.

Rumsfeld has rightly echoed William Sherman in saying that 'war is hell', that civilians always die in war. It is both an admission and a justification of wars' detrimental effects. But it also serves as an authorization. It plays on the narrow sense of liability disconnected from common notions of moral responsibility—the idea that we are responsible for the reasonably predictable consequences of our actions. With the removal of accountability from the equation the risks of warfare are justified because no one in power saw nor wanted their consequences. It is as if, to borrow Arendt's words, 'blessings and doom are meted out ... according to accident and without any relation what-soever to' anyone's actions (OT, 296). Holding the United States responsible for its deeds during wartime seems less important than the charitable han-dling of victims through generous promises of reconstruction aid. It appears less expensive to be lavishly generous to the target society, or appear to be generous, than to tolerate open international adjudication of the actions of the US military.

Rather than frame questions about law and war in the language of compli-ance we can ask how civilian deaths are legitimated and under what guises does this legitimation occur. How does it become possible that the humanity of Western-style war, rather than the savagery of all war, is reinforced by this con-struction of accidents? Widespread judgements about compliance with non-combatant immunity, made possible by advances in war-fighting technology, construct the deaths that do occur as 'accidents'. They appear like some ideal of an accident, where neither the victim nor the agent could possibly have been aware of the pending calamity. The issue at stake is not about compliance with law or increasing or decreasing civilian casualty rates. The laws of war admit the possibility of collateral or unintentional damage, as they have since St Thomas Aquinas first wrote of an act 'beside one's intention' (1988: 228). Rather, the intention is to raise questions about the very idea that some acts are 'beside intention' and what this idea allows.

Martin Shaw (2002, 2005) has convincingly written of the 'militarism of small massacres', military actions leading to the death of thousands of civilians but in discrete pockets of tens, twenties, and even hundreds. Accidental small massacres of civilians are legitimated through assumptions about compliance with international law and advances in weapons technology. Civilian casualties are made *more* not less permissible when constructed as 'accidents' and shown to be in accord with the law. Admission of responsibility for civilian deaths can perhaps never be fully declared. To accept liability would be injurious to the pre-emptive wartime spirit that sustains the current war on terror with-out end. The number of 'accidents' involving civilian death may increasingly be known. The potential of high-tech warfare to produce disaster may also be recognized. But 'accidental' small massacres of civilian populations have nonetheless—and perhaps necessarily—become normalized as part of the post-9/11 discourse of pre-emptive war.

CONCLUSION

Max Weber is widely considered to be the exemplary theorist of bureaucracy, or rule by rules. The rise of modern bureaucracy led to increasing efficiency, but it was soulless and inhumane, producing 'specialists without spirit' (1976: 182). Yet it was Hannah Arendt, more influenced by Franz Kafka, who identified bureaucracy with something potentially more frightening than rule by rules. Bureaucracy was 'rule by nobody'. In *The Human Condition*, she argued that this was 'not necessarily no-rule; it may indeed, under certain circumstances, even turn out to be one of its cruelest and most tyrannical versions' (HC, 40).[33] In its extreme form, individuals are dehumanized, becoming mere 'functionaries of men, mere cogs in the administrative machinery' and the 'intricate system of bureaus' (RJ, 58; CR, 137). Donald Rumsfeld's powerful claim that the United States and its allies are not responsible for the predictable deaths of thousands of civilians—in wars of choice not necessity—is underpinned by what Arendt described as the imperial 'philosophy of the bureaucrat' (OT, 213).

Bureaucracy, Arendt argued, is 'characteristic of all imperialist enterprise' (OT, 213). It was central to European imperialism in the late nineteenth-century as a 'principle of foreign domination ... [and a] substitute for government' in the colonies (OT, 185). The British administered their outposts with brutal and racist violence but also with bureaucratic administration, a form of rule that 'grew out of a tradition of military discipline' (OT, 186). With the rule of bureaucracy in far and distant lands there was at once the appearance of order and also 'an atmosphere of anarchy and hazard ... the daily accidents of incompetence and inconsistency' (OT, 246). It would indeed appear as though 'the Accident', as Arendt put, was 'the true Lord of Life' (OT, 246). There are many differences between the means and character of the administrative massacres of European colonial rule and the militarism of small massacres of more recent wars. But the administration and justification of these latter deaths—and the effect of the refusal to admit responsibility—is reminiscent of the mentality of the imperial bureaucrat that Arendt so powerfully described.

The soulless, technical specialists that ruled Empire by violence had nothing with which to identify, Arendt wrote, except some 'superstition of a possible and magic identification ... with the forces of history. The ideal of such a political body will always be the man behind the scenes who pulls the strings of history' (OT, 216).[34] Prior to his removal from the Department of Defence, Donald Rumsfeld said, 'I'm not a lawyer and I'm not in to that end of the business'.[35] But life and death for many was nonetheless decided by his decree. In the bureaucratic chain of command it *appears* 'impossible to localize responsibility and to identify an enemy' (CR, 138). 'In governments by bureaucracy', Arendt wrote, 'decrees appear in their naked purity as though they were no longer issued by powerful men, but were the incarnation of power itself and the administrator only its accidental agent' (OT, 244). Bureaucratic rule makes possible the thoughtless use of public power and diffuses responsibility. Although nobody is held responsible for such deaths, this 'nobody' still rules. All that remains, the 'one thing that counts [is] the brutal naked event itself' (OT, 245), the event of thousands of civilian deaths.

6

Rage Against Hypocrisy: On Liberal Wars for Human Rights

There is a great temptation to explain away the intrinsically incredible by means of liberal rationalizations. In each one of us, there lurks such a liberal, wheedling us with the voice of common sense.

—Arendt, *Origins of Totalitarianism*, pp. 439–40

As real in England as the tradition of hypocrisy is ... a tradition of dragon-slayers who went enthusiastically into far and curious lands to strange and naïve peoples.

—Arendt, *Origins of Totalitarianism*, p. 209

Michael Walzer begins his defence of the just war tradition with a claim about hypocrisy. The exposure of hypocrisy, he argues, 'is ... the most ordinary, and it may also be the most important form of moral criticism' (1992: xxix). Wherever hypocrisy is located moral knowledge is also found: hypocrites presume 'the moral understanding of the rest of us' (1992: 29). Unmasking the hypocrisy of politicians and generals, putting their words to the test of 'moral realism', he suggests, can uncover the moral reality of war. But is it always right to do this unmasking? Does hypocrisy matter, and how much? What happens when hypocrisy and rage against it become central to public debate? The rancorous debates about the invocation of human rights as part of the justification for recent Western wars can be analysed as a debate about hypocrisy. Hypocrisy is the practice of claiming to have higher standards or beliefs than is the case. Should we reject such wars because Western states evoke human rights hypocritically, that is, while also taking actions that abuse human rights? What does it mean for normative theory to accept the reality of hypocrisy?

In an article titled, 'Hannah Arendt on Human Rights and the Limits of Exposure, or Why Noam Chomsky is Wrong about the Meaning of Kosovo', Jeffrey C. Isaac suggests that there are good reasons for supporting 'human rights' wars even if the human rights justification is hypocritical. At a minimum, he suggests, Hannah Arendt's thought provides reasons for *not* condemning these wars on the grounds of hypocrisy alone. As the title suggests, this argument is made through an attack on prominent anti-war critic Noam Chomsky's exposure of Western hypocrisy (1999, 2000). Isaac does not challenge the content of his argument.[1] Of the 1999 Kosovo intervention, he writes, 'Chomsky effectively demonstrates that the policy and its rhetoric *are* hypocritical. The policy serves other interests, and its official rationales are typically self-serving...Chomsky proves this' (2002: 524, emphasis added). Instead, he condemns the cynical tone of Chomsky's writing as well as his alleged failure to offer a viable alternative to military intervention in cases of systematic abuse and ethnic cleansing (also see Brown 2003).

Following other liberals such as Judith Shklar (1984), Isaac ranks vices. In *Ordinary Vices*, Shklar suggested that the real strength of liberal political thought was not the glorification of rationality or progress, but that it offered a way to rank human vices in an imperfect world. The first and worst vice to avoid is physical cruelty. Robust action must be taken to avoid it; 'the world's most profound problem is not...hypocrisy. It is the infliction of harm and suffering on humans by other humans' (Isaac 2002: 518–19). As a result, other vices might need to be tolerated. Isaac extends this idea to the Kosovo intervention to suggest that the vice of Western hypocrisy is less bad than Serb-nationalist ethnic cleansing of Kosovo–Albanians. Moreover, to root out hypocrisy in this instance may increase human cruelty if the entire human rights regime is weakened. The exposure of hypocrisy is worse than the vice because without the vice the amount of human cruelty would increase. Some forms of hypocrisy, on this view, facilitate human rights. The logic is that the *exposure* of hypocrisy is a bigger danger to human rights than the hypocrisy itself and, by extension, the wider system in which hypocrisy appears to thrive. Merely exposing hypocrisy without offering any real alternative, Isaac claims, is 'fallacious' reasoning, 'politically irresponsible', and 'a particularly egregious example of what Arendt considered "unworldly" thinking' (2002: 535).

The purpose of this chapter is to evaluate the alleged limitations of the exposure of Western state hypocrisy in relation to human rights. Chomsky is well able to defend himself against the strange charge that his writing 'merely' reveals Western hypocrisy and produces a cynicism that undermines the very idea of human rights. Our interest is in the appropriation of Hannah Arendt's thought to bolster support for wars hypocritically justified in the language of human rights, what she once called the 'standard slogan of the protectors of the underprivileged' (OT, 293). What should we make of this effort to appropriate Arendt's work into a familiar liberal paradigm? As Norma Claire Morruzzi (2004) has pointed out, there is a danger that contemporary readers of Arendt's *Origins of Totalitarianism* ignore the centrality of the second part, the heart of the book, which is on imperialism. Doing so leaves a more conventional analysis of Arendt that understands hypocrisy as an occasional liberal convention, which is obviously less terrible than cruelty.

It is certainly true that Arendt believed there were greater sins in the political realm than 'hypocrisy's conceits' (CR, 163). She also noted more than once that truth telling has never been counted as one of the political virtues and that lying was 'one of the tools in the arsenal of political action'. She was also too astute to embrace the views of those who cynically depict the discourse of human rights as '*nothing* but the prejudice, hypocrisy, and cowardice of liberals' (Isaac 2002: 511, emphasis added; Power 2004).[2] With the exception of a few passages in *Origins*, she hardly referred to human rights as such, favouring instead the categories of action, opinions, freedom, and plurality to refer to the politics in which rights would make sense (Isaac 1996). For all the talk of the inalienable 'Rights of Man', history had taught Arendt that it was precisely at the moment when these human rights were needed most they were usually no-where to be found. There have been a number of positive developments in international humanitarian law since Arendt's day. But political rights remain wholly dependent on human conventions, the recognition of the 'right to have rights . . . to live in a framework where one is judged by one's actions and opinions' (OT, 296–7).[3] More pointedly, Arendt spent a lot of time illustrating the dangers of wars on hypocrisy (CR, 163*f*). Nonetheless, there are severe limitations to the idea that Arendt would have condoned systematic hypocrisy if it meant a reduction in cruelty.

Isaac believes that the greatest political sin is to fail to grasp the opportunity to prevent human cruelty. He believes this is the 'deepest reason' (2002: 519) Arendt did not denigrate 'human rights' as such. But the weighing of wrongs was an anathema to Arendt's political thinking. She was unsentimental about the pervasiveness of hypocrisy, 'to shine with something that is not' (OR, 100). But she was also unsentimental about the reality of human cruelty. Her political theory was humanist. 'Strictly speaking', she nonetheless wrote, 'politics is not so much about human beings as it is about the world that comes into being between them and endured beyond them' (PP, 175). There are firm grounds to argue that in Arendt's thought hypocrisy, when normal and even expected, brings about something worse than cruelty. When hypocrisy and wars on hypocrisy become defining features of public life they destroy 'the sense by which we take our bearings in the real world. . . . And for this trouble', she wrote, 'there is no remedy' (BPF, 257). Knowledge of political facts, including the hypocrisy of Western states, is the condition of possibility for a public world to exist. And without a public world, literally the space for politics, as Arendt frequently argued, human rights are impossible.

The pollution of political life by hypocrisy and hatred of it makes it easier for societies to slip into violence. Indeed, it was Arendt's startling claim that 'If we inquire historically into the causes likely to transform *engagés* into *enragés* it is not injustice that ranks first, but hypocrisy' (CR, 162). Hypocrisy produces rage and rage produces violence. This relationship appears in Arendt's work on at least four occasions and we will take each in turn. *Origins of Totalitarianism* describes both T. E. Lawrence's escape into empire and the post-First World War front generation who nihilistically came to celebrate cruelty. In the essay 'On Violence', we see hypocrisy and violent rage linked in her account of the celebrations of anti-colonial violence by the radical Left. *On Revolution* offers the most extensive discussion of hypocrisy in the analysis of the French Revolution and the Reign of Terror. From each discussion we see that Arendt clearly understood 'how justified disgust can be in a society wholly permeated with the ideological outlook and moral standards of the bourgeoisie' (OT, 328).

While Arendt understood rage against hypocrisy, she was also critical of political action to unmask it. Arendt's criticism of such efforts was not because anti-hypocrites fail to offer a viable alternative. Wars on hypocrisy are danger-ous and potentially more violent than hypocrisy itself because they tend to become a search for ulterior motives. Arendt understood the political as an artificial space of appearances where only words and actions can be judged because only they can appear. As we shall see, the public search for innermost motives, because it is impossible, 'transforms all actors into hypocrites; the moment the display of motives begins, hypocrisy begins to poison all human relations ... When we say that nobody but God can see (and, perhaps, can bear to see) the nakedness of the human heart, "nobody" includes one's own self' (OR, 92, 93). The effort to 'unmask' hypocrisy is to misunderstand the nature of political identity (Moruzzi 2000: 32–7). To speak in public is to wear a kind of 'mask', the mask of a public persona that is 'given and guaranteed by the body politic'. Arendt railed against both hypocrisy and wars on hypocrisy. But it is clear from her work that any exposure of the conceit must be based on an assessment of the gap between words and action, not words and motives. We are also not without grounds for acting against genocide, what Arendt called 'wars of annihilation'. The criterion, however, is not to be found in the defence of human rights as such, or a response to human cruelty. Rather surprisingly, hypocrisy is destructive to politics for the same reason. Both hypocrisy and genocide destroy a portion of our common, worldly reality.

HYPOCRISY AND THE TEMPTATIONS OF VIOLENCE

Hannah Arendt thought and wrote an enormous amount on the origins of the social, economic, and political conditions that led to the rise of fascism in Europe and ultimately to the carnage and genocide of the Second World War.

An important part of Arendt's story is about hypocrisy. It played a large role in fomenting the alienation from existing political institutions and increased the attractiveness of cruelty among the post-First World War front generation. Hypocrisy was the essence of polite and conformist bourgeois society. The European bourgeoisie, Arendt wrote, 'claimed to be the guardian of Western traditions and confounded all moral issues by parading publicly virtues which it...did not possess' (OT, 334). Indeed, she understood hypocrisy to be a particularly liberal vice and the sympathy she expressed towards many of those who rejected it was part of her distaste for liberalism more generally. 'Liberal concepts...' she wrote, 'express the bourgeoisie's instinctive distrust of and its innate hostility to public affairs' (OT, 146).[4] Arendt was scathing in her criticism of the invocation of human rights by European nation-states while those very states pummelled the colonies and treated millions of their own like second- and third-class citizens. Here Arendt's thought is a clear precursor to Franz Fanon's, as suggested in Chapter 2. Europe, he wrote, was 'where they are never done talking of Man, yet murder men everywhere they find them...in all corners of the globe' (1963: 311).

Arendt understood the rage of those sickened by the divergence between what European states said in relation to human rights and what they did. But *Origins of Totalitarianism* showed how rage against hypocrisy was part of the intellectual context of imperialism and ultimately fascism. The moral desire to expose hypocrisy by unveiling the dislocation between words, actions, and 'real' motives is consistently linked with violent rage in numerous places in Arendt's work.[5] She understood (without condoning) the disdain of those outside the constraints and conventions of respectable 'society', their desire 'to discard the uncomfortable mask of hypocrisy' (OT, 335); to go against everything bourgeois society claimed to value and represent. Anything that seemed to contradict respectable society was attractive if it meant 'the ruin of this whole world of fake security, fake culture, and fake life' (OT, 328). Proto-fascist groups that openly threatened to destroy the fabric of respectability came to play an increasing public role. Yet Arendt did not restrict her analysis of the relationship between violence, rage, and hypocrisy to the origins of totalitarian movements. The hypocrisy of respectable European society attracted men like T. E. Lawrence to imperialism, a precursor to totalitarianism, and added to the fascination with violence among the post-Second World War thinkers of the anti-colonial Left.

At the height of European imperialism, men like Lawrence (of Arabia) felt they could escape bourgeois hypocrisy into exotic and far-flung lands and reinvent themselves among strange foreigners. In doing so, Lawrence articulated a theory of guerrilla insurgency that still resonates.[6] He sought to transform his identity through fighting wars in the service of British imperialism; he identified with the greater, history-making cause of Empire. Lawrence's

public and private story appeared to fascinate Arendt.[7] He rejected the conventions and accessories of respectable society; he 'experimented fearlessly
upon himself'. To fulfil his role as a functionary of some greater historical
movement, as a secret agent in the Great Game, Lawrence delighted in altering
'his whole personality' (OT, 218, 219). Disgusted 'with the world as well as
with himself', he sought to shake off all the trappings of society in favour
of the more powerful 'stream of historical necessity' (OT, 218, 220). Arendt
suggested that Lawrence was a prototype of the man who consciously let
himself 'be used and abused by imperialism for the sake of glorious careers'
outside the 'world of dull respectability' (OT, 227, 318). Lawrence never quite
fell into a state of violent rage, though his role in empire was certainly violent.
The liberal in him meant it was important to hold onto some sense of personal
decency, to believe that he did the right thing. 'The real pride of Western man',
as exemplified by Lawrence, in Arendt's view, was that 'he pushed the right
way' (Lawrence in OT, 220). He could ally with the larger forces of history
and, in that, gain some satisfaction. After all, the curious view still persists
that European and especially British imperialism did more good than bad for
the modern world (Ferguson 2003; cf. Davis 2002).[8]

Lawrence's imperial beliefs in the impersonal laws of history directly prefigured the claims of totalitarian ideologies about laws of historical necessity. The
difference, however, was that in the aftermath of the First World War, the new
statelessness of millions further 'shattered the façade of Europe's political system to lay bare its hidden frame. . . . The very phrase "human rights" became
for all concerned—victims, persecutors, and onlookers alike—the evidence of
hopeless idealism or fumbling feeble-minded hypocrisy' (OT, 267, 269). Given
this burdened history, Arendt rarely referred to the concept of human rights
unless it was to criticize the hypocrisy of democracies in the interwar period;
such notions 'had become a mockery' (OT, 289). As discussed in Chapter 4,
the moral limits to violent action to which the modern age at least paid lip service appeared to be irrevocably broken. To be sure, the decision about places
and numbers of the dead was always partial and imperial and 'it has happened
often enough in history that the world of an entire people has been leveled'
(PP, 161).[9] But from the Eurocentric perspective, the Great War was shocking
because many wished to believe that war itself was on the wane (Angell 1913).

With such illusions dispelled it seemed as though the worsening plight
for increasing numbers of innocent civilians 'was like a practical demon-
stration of the totalitarian movements' cynical claims that no such thing as
inalienable human rights existed' (OT, 269). Open propagation of cruelty
and amorality in such circumstances seemed far more honest than the pre-
tence of 'respectable society'. A growing number of writers and intellectuals,
Arendt suggested, eventually 'elevated cruelty to a major virtue because it
contradicted society's humanitarian and liberal hypocrisy' (OT, 331). There

was clearly something appealing in this rebellion, something satisfying, even enjoyable, in the righteous anger accompanying the exposure of those in power who publicly paraded fake morality. The problem was that this delight in the unmasking 'could not even be spoiled by Hitler's very real persecution of the Jews' (OT, 335). The point is not that anti-Semitism was itself a *product* of liberal hypocrisy; far from it. Rather, Arendt frighteningly suggested that 'aversion against the philosemitism of the liberals' among the disenchanted elite was more important to some than actual hatred of the Jews.

The First World War destroyed the ease of escape into empire by the next cohort of young malcontents.[10] The desire of the generation of the 'Front' to lose themselves in violence was different to the experience of older men like Lawrence, but disgust at the conventions of bourgeois society remained. They found that they lacked that potential freedom from conformism. But they too wanted to lose themselves in something bigger, perhaps more Nietzschean than the Great Game of Empire. Many survivors of the trenches believed themselves to be more passionate and authentic in their suffering than the imperial adventurers; they 'had been more deeply touched by misery, they were more concerned with perplexities and more deadly hurt by hypocrisy' (OT, 331). Indeed, the corruption of European political institutions as a result of their use and abuse by the bourgeois imperial elite led greater numbers to be attracted to the claims of groups that were even more radical.

Ideas about war as the movement of world history with a will of its own came to nourish the 'antihumanist, antiliberal, antiindividualist and anticultural instincts of the front generation' (OT, 330). Many had joined the colours in the Great War to preserve the old order, others in the anticipation 'that everything they knew, the whole culture and texture of life, might go down in its "storms of steel" ' (OT, 328). Several among this cross-European generation thought they had finally found something 'to separate them definitely from the hated surroundings of respectability' (OT, 328–9). The experience of trench warfare was a treasure for these new 'worshippers of war'; the very fact of survival 'constituted an objective criterion for the establishment of a new elite' (OT, 329). The celebration of the cruelty of extreme violence appeared in no way reduced by the experience of war in a mechanical age. Writers such as Ernst Jünger did not idealize such violence, but revelled in its monstrousness. As Arendt noted, he was among 'the first to concede that war in the era of machines could not possibly breed virtues like chivalry, courage, honor, and manliness, that it imposed on men nothing but the experience of bare destruction together with the humiliation of being only small cogs in the majestic wheel of slaughter' (OT, 329; cf. Ashworth 1980).[11] Totalitarian movements would later build on such ideas, eradicating human individuality far beyond that achieved by conventional military training for the 'moment of collective heroic action' of the Second World War.

With the exception of the small German communist movement, for the generation of the interwar period there was little incentive to expose bourgeois hypocrisy in the interests of a more progressive cause.[12] The bourgeois was simply 'the other' against which fascist anti-liberals might contrast their own more honest celebration of violence and cruelty. However, there is a third group that we may include in Arendt's analysis—what she called 'the radical left' in the post-Second World War era of decolonization—that developed a progressive strategy of resistance around tearing away the West's hypocritical mask. Arendt engaged frequently with what she saw as Marxist-inspired glorifications of violence. Here we are concerned with the role of hatred for and violent rage against bourgeois hypocrisy in the thought of Georges Sorel, Franz Fanon, and Jean-Paul Sartre, a rage that distinguished the radical from the conventional Left in Arendt's mind.

The picture of the typical Western bourgeois citizen in the writing of Sorel (1999) was very close to that of the 'death philosophers' in the interwar period, 'peaceful, complacent, hypocritical, bent on pleasure, without will to power, a late product of capitalism rather than its representative' (CR, 167).[13] For Sorel, 'strikes and the violence associated with them are legitimate not because they are a means to social reform, but because they enable the oppressed to experience the process of becoming conscious of themselves' (Joas 2003: 41). And yet Arendt understood the political and strategic logic in the anti-colonial writing of Fanon as very different from the fascists. Here the incentive was to unmask and expose the lies and deceits of the imperial enemy 'that permit him to rule without using violent means, that is, to provoke action even at the risk of annihilation so that the truth may come out' (CR, 163). The conceit of colonialism was that it was mostly benign, for the benefit of the colonized as well as the colonizer. *The Wretched of the Earth* advocated returning to Europe its true nature, 'that violence which is just under the skin' (Fanon 1963: 71).

Fanon and Sartre understood anti-colonial violence as bringing agency to the oppressed, the rejection of passivity, almost like a life force in itself. We know Arendt did not share this view of violence as a bringer of life or promoter of 'causes'. She was critical of the depiction of anti-colonial violence as ' "man recreating himself", that it is through "mad fury" that "the wretched of the earth" can ' "become men" ' (CR, 114). But neither did she condemn such violence as 'beastly' or 'irrational' (CR, 160). This is clear from the essay 'On Violence' in which she linked rational violence to rage, including rage against hypocrisy. In Arendt's words,

That violence often springs from rage is a commonplace, and rage can indeed be irrational and pathological, but so can every other human affect.... Rage is by no means an automatic reaction to misery and suffering as such.... Only where there is reason to suspect that conditions could be changed and are not does rage arise. Only when our sense of justice is offended do we react with rage (CR, 160).

Arendt understood how difficult it could be to respond reasonably to hypocrisy. 'Words can be relied on', she wrote, 'only if one is sure that their function is to reveal and not to conceal. It is the semblance of rationality, much more than the interests behind it that provokes rage' (CR, 163). The point is also made in Arendt's description of Herman Melvilles's novella *Billy Budd*. The young sailor, Billy, is only able to answer the lying Claggart with a lethally violent blow (OR, 77–82). The lies of Claggart were perceived as so outrageous that 'without counting the consequences' only violence appeared as the appropriately swift and exacting response.

Arendt understood violent rage at the West's 'ideological policy of quaint humanitarianism' (Fanon 1963: 67). But she was hostile to the violence provoked by wars on such hypocrisy. The point is that behind the 'white mask' of Western hypocrisy, Fanon (1967) expected to see the more honest and pure 'black skin' of the Third World. It is common to hear the exposure of hypocrisy described as a process of 'unmasking'. The hypocrite wears a mask; by ripping it off the true face appears. As we shall see, this became the assumption of the leaders of the French Revolution as well as Sartre and Fanon. But the idea of the mask has another meaning in Arendt's political thought. This other meaning suggests an alternative reading of hypocrisy properly attentive to the constructed, artificial nature of the public realm. The mask that Arendt had in mind was not a disguise to hide one's true self. It represented a public *persona*. What was important was what the mask displayed—public citizenship—not what was hidden. This idea was not explicitly addressed by Arendt in her discussion of Fanon. But it suggests that we ought to reject any search for an honest and pure authenticity of self as a counter to hypocrisy. For a proper understanding of why Arendt ultimately rejected the idea of tearing away the politically enabling mask of the public *persona* we turn to her discussion of the war on the hypocrisy of the French court and genteel society in 1789. The problem, she wrote, was that 'by the unending hunt for hypocrites and through the passion for unmasking society, [the revolutionists] had...torn away the mask of the *persona* as well' (OR, 104).

POLITICAL IDENTITY AND THE LIMITS OF UNMASKING

In *On Revolution*, Arendt singled out one central trope of the French Revolution, that it would finally mean the tearing away of the mask of hypocrisy from 'the face of French society... exposing behind it the unspoiled, honest face of the *peuple*' (OR, 102). The corruption of the *ancien régime* led to an appeal outside the aristocracy for a new source of political authority. The true inner heart of the people stood against the rotten façade of the life of the rich. As such, Arendt suggested, 'the very concept of *le peuple* received its connotations from an outrage of the "heart"... against the corruption and hypocrisy of the salons' (BPF, 200). The idea is clearly expressed in the writing of Jean-Jacques Rousseau, who out of disgust for the heartlessness of the salons had valorized the unaffected sentiments of those uncorrupted by high society (Davidson 1997). With the Revolution, it finally seemed as though the true face of *le peuple* would no longer be ' "artificially" hidden behind any masks' (OR, 105).

Arendt recalled a different metaphor of the mask derived from Greek theatre, but its real significance is found in Roman politics and law. In her words,

The mask... had two functions: it had to hide, or rather to replace, the actor's own face and countenance, but in a way that would make it possible for the voice to sound through... The distinction between a private individual in Rome and a Roman citizen was that the latter had a *persona*, a legal personality...; it was as though the law had affixed to him the part he was expected to play on the public scene, with the provision, however, that his own voice would be able to sound through (OR, 102).

The mask made possible the public voice of the citizen. The artificial *persona* was the legal, public personality. This is not a mask of hypocrisy. On the public stage, to appear is to be. And to appear in public is to wear a sort of mask.

The meaning of the mask here is best understood, not as a defence of presenting oneself as otherwise, but in relation to the conditions for political agency. Arendt's idea is captured in Richard Sennett's description (1976) of theatrical conventions that emerged in the public discourse in European cities in the eighteenth-century (also see Villa 1999: 147–54). The focus, like the actor on the stage, is on the content of the political act, the gesture or word rather than the political identity of the agent behind. Such social codes provoked sentiments in others without compelling one to define oneself to the other. The mask enabled a degree of impersonality and alienation from self for the integrity of the public realm. By creating a distance between the actor and the act, individuals could express opinions as public personalities and to act 'as a sounding board for truth' (OR, 103). In turn, others could disagree with such opinions without demonizing the essence of the individual behind the mask. These conventions were essential to opening up communicative spaces for individuals to appear and express opinions in public.

The war on hypocrisy conducted by the French revolutionists failed to heed the importance of the public *persona* as the foundation of citizenship. Again, there was rage, 'the rage of misfortune pitted against the rage of unmasked corruption' (OR, 106–7). However, in contrasting the honest dignity of the poor with the filthiness of the rich the revolutionists apparently felt obliged to emancipate *le peuple* not as citizens but *qua malheureux*. The ordinary suffering poor would be freed from enslavement, but as *the poor*, as the needy, as men, rather than as equal citizens before man-made law. Unmasking the machinations of the Court was to reveal 'the "natural man"—that is, a human being ... indicating someone outside the range of the law' (OR, 103). But the possibility of liberation and equality was destroyed because the revolutionaries had no conception of the public personality 'given and guaranteed by the body politic'. As Arendt stated in *Origins*, 'Men are unequal according to their natural origin, their different organization, and fate in history. Their equality is an equality of rights' (OT, 234). Thus while hypocrisy did not distort the 'faces' of the people, neither did any 'legal personality' protect them (OR, 105). The human being *qua* human being, as Arendt frequently pointed out, is a *politically* irrelevant being.

To be political, to speak and act in the public realm, is to wear a mask 'as the rules of the political game demand, as a sounding board for the truth' (OR, 103). The bourgeois hypocrites so hated by Rousseau, Lawrence, the Front generation and Fanon, did not follow this rule, but used the mask 'as a contraption for deception' (OR, 103). But the anti-hypocrites each failed to understand that in the hunt for innermost motives, in seeking to tear away the mask of hypocrisy to reveal some other truer, more honest face, risked destroying the sense in which politics is itself an artificially constructed 'space of appearances' (HC, 199).[14] Arendt shared with Machiavelli the view that in the political realm it is impossible to judge anything but appearances—the words and deeds of political actors, not their innermost motives. For Machiavelli, it famously mattered only that the actor appeared good to others; only God, who was 'beyond the realm of appearance', could judge the goodness of a human heart. There was a necessary gap between how the actor appeared to others and to any 'transcendent Being'. This is not a defence of hypocrisy (cf. Grant 1997: ch. 2). It is a statement about the possibilities of knowledge and what constitutes the political world.

The public is constituted by a plurality of others speaking and acting and judging what is only visible in the 'space of appearances'. But we cannot verify innermost motives, no matter how authentic they may be. The inner motives of action, because they are located in the human heart and are not seen, cannot be judged. Moral clarity and the strength of conviction cannot be openly, publicly scrutinized or be beyond doubt; 'it is impossible ever to know beyond doubt another man's heart'; it 'becomes an object of suspicion rather than insight ... behind which again other, ulterior motives may lurk, such as hypocrisy and deceit' (OR, 91; OT, 430), or rather they should. For what is the guarantee of virtue? How do we verify the authenticity of the leaders' political convictions? In response, the resolute leader must expose the suffering that alone can make self-evident the virtuousness of the motive to act. The result is the glorification of suffering, 'hailing the exposed misery as the best and even only guarantee of virtue' (OR, 107).

Machiavelli taught, in Arendt's words, ' "Appear as you may wish to be", by which he meant: "Never mind how you [really] are [on the inside], this is of no relevance in the world and in politics, where only appearances, not true" being, count; if you can manage to appear to others as you would wish to be, that is all that can possibly be required' (OR, 97). To think through the political relevance of this idea with Arendt does not leave us without grounds for condemning hypocrisy. On the contrary, it provides a stronger basis from which to condemn the gap between words and actions so indicative in contemporary politics. The real problem is that in a perversion of Socrates' belief that we must be true to ourselves, the hypocrite behaves as though there is a unity between the public presentation of the self and the innermost motives of the heart.

This is the essence of the conviction politics so prevalent in the current political scene, which seeks support for political action based on the good intentions of morally inspired leaders (Runciman 2006). For the sake of authenticity, such a leader must pretend that the public and private selves are totally at one. It is also why the charge of hypocrisy is so easy to make against those who wear their moral convictions on their sleeve. 'The test applying to the hypocrite', Arendt wrote, 'is indeed the old Socratic "*Be* as you wish to appear", which means appear *always* as you wish to appear to others even if it happens that you are alone and appear to no one but yourself' (LM, 37). To be sure, as Arendt suggested, Socrates possessed an 'unquestioned belief in the truth of appearance and taught "Appear to yourself as you would wish to appear to others" ' (OR, 97). But in Andrea Nye's useful suggestion, the hypocrite 'no longer engages in the inner self-questioning which Arendt identifies with [Socratic] thought. To be "true to oneself" is not to appear to be someone identical with a real inner self. It is to think, to engage in a constant questioning of words and actions that results in a degree of consistency in words and actions' (1994: 146; LM, 36–40).

Arendt criticized both hypocrisy and wars on hypocrisy for failing to respect or understand the importance of the politically constructed *persona*, the mask that was necessary to provide the artificial built spaces in which each actor's voice is 'able to sound through' (OR, 102) and for breaking a promise. In her words,

It has been said that hypocrisy is the compliment vice pays to virtue, but this is not quite true. All virtue begins with a compliment paid to it, by which I express my being pleased with it. The compliment implies a promise to the world, to those to whom I appear, to act in accordance with my pleasure, and it is the breaking of the implied promise that characterizes the hypocrite (LM, 36).

Hypocrisy threatens the very sense in which the public is an artificial realm of what appears. The plurality of voices, each acting as a 'sounding board for the truth' is constitutive of worldly reality. Without hearing the many voices, the political facts and competing truths that make up the political world are lost. Arendt always discussed truth in a manner that placed the perspectival as central. Hypocrisy is therefore a problem of the first order when the factual truths about the gap between words and actions are concealed. The mask matters to Arendt because it enables the kind of political agency that focuses not on who actors are, or what their inner motives might be, but on the words that they utter and the actions that they undertake.

WORDS AND ACTIONS, NOT MOTIVES

Must the politics of exposing hypocrisy always become an obsession with motives? The foregoing analysis of the artificiality of the public realm as a space of appearances suggests that motives are impossible to expose and the effort itself is dangerous. This is not to suggest that motives do not matter. All political actors have intentions; most believe in a cause; without human motives such as greed, power, or greatness there might be no politics at all. Arendt's point relates to political judgement and knowledge. How do we judge political action? We can only judge words and actions—not motives— because words and actions are the only phenomenon that appears in the political sphere. Political engagement with hypocrisy becomes exposing the gap between words and actions, instead of words and motives. To illustrate we return to the debate about the hypocrisy of Western human rights wars.

Jeffrey C. Isaac argued that the hypocrisy of contemporary Western states does not disqualify human rights wars because the alternative is worse: cynicism and the possible destruction of the human rights norms we already have. He condemned Chomsky's exposure of hypocrisy and condemnation of the 1999 bombing over Kosovo. Wars like Kosovo, Isaac argued, could 'create a precedent for future human rights interventions...even if those officials who advanced the policy did not take human rights seriously at all' (2002: 535). Even insincere human rights rhetoric can in the long term increase the amount of human rights. The short-sightedness of this position has become evident since the 2003 invasion and occupation of Iraq. In the absence of the discovery of weapons of mass destruction, this action was defended in terms of 'regime change' and the human rights and freedom of the Iraqi people (Wilson 2005). That the war, occupation, and inevitable resistance have been a human security disaster for the people of Iraq, not to mention a blow to the international law governing the use of force, suggests the errors of conceiving the 'Kosovo precedent' as benign.

The rhetoric of human rights does a lot. This is why Arendt's lack of naivety—'politics is not like the nursery' (EJ, 279)—would lead her to be far less sanguine about the abuse of its powerful rhetoric. The language we use to justify political action is at the heart of how Arendt understood politics and its power. 'Wherever the relevance of speech is at stake, matters become political by definition', she wrote, 'for speech is what makes man a political being' (HC, 3). It is not the denigration of the moral authority of Western states that produces the cynicism dangerous to human rights (Rieff 2002, 2005). The 'peculiar kind of cynicism' that may result from the normalization of hypocrisy is a 'refusal to believe in the truth of anything' at all (BPF, 257). The hypocrite possesses no integrity; 'only the hypocrite is really rotten to the core' (OR, 99).

Arendt was a fierce defender of the primacy of factual truths in politics (see Chapter 7). This makes it difficult to believe she would have criticized the exposure of hypocrisy to justify an act that was itself hypocritical. Arendt can only be evoked to condemn the exposure of Western hypocrisy by ignoring almost everything she said about the dangers of concealing political facts. There is a thin line between the hypocrite and the liar. Both obscure or invent facts to conceal reality. The misinformation and half-truths of the hypocrite are so common in wartime propaganda that we can legitimately include hypocrisy among the 'many genres in the art of lying' (CR, 7). Hypocrites present themselves as other than they really are; they say one thing and do something else. The United States presents itself as a defender of human rights, but has been consistently shown to act in ways that despoil rights (Mertus 2004).

Arendt was highly critical of the elevation of motive, of good intentions, to the principle basis for judging political action. But this has been the very ground on which many Western state leaders ask to be judged. (Arendt identified the reduction of political matters to questions of motive as central to the success of political domination. It consisted in the 'ability immediately to dissolve every statement of fact into a declaration of purpose' (OT, 385).[15]) If the search for 'real' motives is ruled out, on what basis might the charge of hypocrisy be made? It might well be in the nature of Western war to be concerned with extending and maintaining hegemony rather than any serious concern for human dignity. But this theory can only be established through the detailed recounting of human rights abuses, that is, by deeds, through which hypocrisy is revealed. It requires an examination of the past and present track record of those who place human rights and the spread of freedom as central to political rhetoric. This is the only way to judge whether human rights rhetoric is misjudged and dangerous for *human rights*. To not undertake such an examination is to assume what is to be explained—the correlation between 'human rights wars' and the spread of human rights.

The stakes of the debate about the dangers of hypocrisy—and wars on hypocrisy—are great. Georges Sorel's influential image of the Western bourgeoisie—decadent, hypocritical, shallow—is a trope that retains enormous power.[16] In a statement immediately after the 9/11 attacks, Osama bin Laden divided the world into hypocrites and non-hypocrites. In his words,

if the sword falls on the United States after 80 years, hypocrisy raises its head lamenting the deaths of these killers who tampered with the blood, honour, and holy places of the Muslims....They came out to fight Islam in the name of terrorism....They bombed Iraq and considered that a debatable issue. But when a dozen people of them were killed in Nairobi and Dar es Salaam, Afghanistan and Iraq were bombed and all hypocrite ones stood behind the head of the world's infidelity...namely, America and its supporters....These incidents divided the entire world into two regions—one of faith where there is no hypocrisy and another of infidelity.[17]

History suggests that such a narrative has power. It also suggests that those who wish to challenge the violence that sometimes accompanies such claims ought to not fall into violent rage as well.

After the 9/11 attacks, President George W. Bush has implicitly acknowledged the hypocrisy of past US foreign policy. In his words, 'For too long, American policy looked away while men and women were oppressed, their rights ignored and their hopes stifled'.[18] This agenda for a 'new Middle East' claimed to disavow past support for friendly autocracies in favour of the spread of 'freedom'. The implication is that past policy backfired on 9/11, that this hypocrisy was indeed part of the 'root cause' for the terrorist attacks (Hitchens 2003). There is also the implication that with a new aggressive spread of democracy, freedom, and human rights the United States can no longer be accused of saying one thing and doing something else. But still, as a 2004 Department of Defence report on 'Strategic Communication' notes, 'when American public diplomacy talks about bringing democracy to Islamic societies, this is seen as no more than self-serving hypocrisy'.[19]

Polling suggests that anger at the United States across several Muslim societies is on the rise. If there are expressions of support for violence against the United States within these societies it can be explained, in part, as rage against the perceived hypocrisy of the West. Relative inaction regarding the

Palestinian situation, along with support for Israel in the occupation of Palestinian land, is contrasted with lofty talk of support for human rights and international law. Recall Arendt's suggestion that revulsion at the simulated philo-Semitism of European liberals overwhelmed any action against the very real Nazi persecution of the Jews. Today there is a danger that revulsion at the simultaneous hypocrisy of the United States and apparent unconditional support for Israel is in danger of leading some to stop short of condemning with equal strength violence against Palestinian, Lebanese, *and Israelis*. It must be possible to support simultaneously Palestinian resistance against Israeli occupation, the right to self-determination by the Lebanese and the right of *all* civilians, including Israeli civilians, not to be attacked.

We must resist the temptation to silence the exposure of hypocrisy in case it increases human cruelty. To do otherwise would be a denial of the reality of power politics as well as the reality crucial for the political world. We find Arendt's antidote to this political problem is a form of realism. As Deborah Nelson puts it, Arendt perhaps is the 'realist whose foremost obligation is to reality as such' (2004: 234; also see Nelson 2006). This is not the amoral realism that is caricatured in international theory, though Arendt did depart from Chomsky on the role of morality in politics. During a public debate on the Vietnam War she stated that 'Moralistic attitudes in politics tend to provide moral justifications for crimes, quite apart from leading into pseudoidealistic enterprises which are obviously to the detriment of the intended beneficiaries' (1971: 115).[20] In response, Chomsky argued that, 'it's quite true that American policy is often accused, as Dr. Arendt said, of being moralistic, that it tries to give a facade of legitimacy to acts that can't be legitimated'. Chomsky continued, however, that he was 'not in the least opposed to truly moral policies' (1971: 120). Arendt never explicitly framed her political ideas as leading to more 'moral' outcomes as such.

Machiavelli's writing was central to Arendt's ideas about the autonomy of politics with its distinct motives and principles for action. As we discussed in Chapter 3, Arendt believed that political action could not easily be measured in terms of conventional moral standards. She praised Machiavelli's claim that 'I love my native city more than my own soul'. It was the city itself not the people in the city that was the object of his affection. This 'was no cliché' and it was not a statement about the virtues of patriotism. It was a radical claim and against the grain of his time in protecting the political realm from the effects of Christianity. At issue, Arendt wrote, was 'whether one was capable of loving the world more than one's own self. And this decision indeed has always been the crucial decision for all who devoted their lives to politics' (OR, 290). Similarly, while Arendt was always clear that Jewish-ness was 'one of the indisputable factual data' of her life, she totally resisted becoming politically swallowed up in any love for a people. 'I do not "love the Jews", nor do I "believe" in them; I merely belong to them as a matter of course, beyond dispute or argument' (JP, 247). Anything else was too narcissistic. 'I have never in my life "loved" any people or collective ... I indeed love "only" my friends and the only kind of love I know of and believe in is the love of persons' (JP, 246).[21] Anything else was too vague and potentially dangerous.[22] Arendt preferred the love of the world.[23] Love of people and love of the world are not the same because the 'world and the people who inhabit it are not the same'. The world lies between people, and this in-between is literally the space for politics.

Machiavelli understood the kind of politics necessary for secularism, that is, in which the norms and rules of the political realm are separate from the doctrines of the Christian Church. 'It was for this reason', Arendt wrote, 'that he insisted that people ... learn "how not to be good", that is, how not to act according to Christian precepts' (OR, 29). This is not a call to become evil. It is an observation that what it takes to be good in the Christian sense of the term is unworldly and fundamentally opposed to the proper character of the political (BPF, 137; MDT, 236). Arendt was suspicious of the role of Christian ethics in politics, which she saw as an effort to fill with good deeds a gap in the sinful self.[24] It was about the self and not the world.[25] She wrote her doctoral dissertation on St Augustine, 'the greatest theorist of Christian politics' (BPF, 73) and observed the Christian effort to transform the self in the act of compassion and charitable giving.[26] Throughout Arendt's work we see why goodness, sentimentalism and Christian ethics more broadly are an anathema to the worldliness of politics, a threat to the plurality necessary for politics and potentially violent.

Arendt was not a realist who would reject the suffering of others. Indeed, it is the inability to be unresponsive, unsympathetic to it, that she wished to restrict its political power. She was not indifferent to suffering. As Nelson writes, Arendt was 'drawn to suffering as a problem to be explored and yet remained deeply suspicious of its attractions ... [its] anaesthetic' effect (2006: 88).[27] Arendt's was not a cold-hearted realism. But it was a cool realism of sorts, 'a characterological trait' (Pitkin 1998: 272). It was the tough-minded and 'attentive facing up to, and resisting of, reality—whatever that may be' (OT, viii). As Hanna Pitkin has put it, 'Action, freedom, and justice are as real for her as greed, cowardice, and selfishness, or as bread and air, barbed wire and bombs' (1998: 274). Arendt's realism involved a willingness to judge the meaning of events for one's own self and a belief that no matter what reality is it can also be resisted. 'The question', she wrote, 'is how much reality must be retained even in a world become inhuman if humanity is not to be reduced to an empty phrase or phantom' (MDT, 22). Arendt faced unpleasant facts head-on and refused to romanticize and feel pity for victims. She sought to moralize neither for nor against war.

This does not mean that we cannot find grounds for action, even military action, in cases of genocide. But Arendt's standard for action had very little to do with human rights and cruelty. R. J. Vincent formulated his influential defence of 'humanitarian' military intervention in terms of a 'basic right', the 'right to life—in the sense both of a right to security against violence and of a right to subsistence' (1986: 125). He took this to be a direct criticism of the principles he imagined Arendt might endorse. In Vincent's words, 'I embrace as a project for international society what Arendt called the "politically perni-cious" doctrine derived from Marx that life is the highest good' (1986: 126). He then contrasts this with an imagined case for intervention drawn from Arendt. Because Arendt praised the importance of democratic revolution, Vincent strangely claims she must therefore endorse military intervention to spread 'political liberty'. In contrast, he argues that international society works 'as well as it does by seeking to contain revolutions within the frontiers of states . . . Liberty upheld with revolutionary enthusiasm should exhaust itself at the border' (1986: 126). But as the conclusion will suggest, this was precisely Arendt's point.

CONCLUSION

Famously, Hannah Arendt's stated purpose in writing *The Human Condition* was to 'think what we are doing'. But if she were alive today, would she 'have been the first to press political theorists to place the question of what we are doing—*and failing to do*—at the center of our inquiries', as Isaac suggests? (2002: 507, emphasis added) We must doubt this. Arendt was a theorist of political experience, of events. It is not clear that she would have included thinking through what actors were *not* doing as a central task of political theorists. The absence of specific political action (or military intervention) was not central to her thought. There are few places where she calls for immediate, let alone violent, action to remedy specific grievances. That was not her 'style of thinking'. Neither was she motivated by an explicitly normative agenda. She wrote, 'It would be relatively easy to prove that Western civilization's political theories and moral codes have always tried to exclude a war of annihilation from the arsenal of political tools; and it would presumably be easier still to show that such theories and demands have proved to be less than effectual' (PP, 162).

It is nonetheless incumbent on those who criticize current practice to suggest an alternative and we can do so by drawing from Arendt. Witness to the worst atrocities of the twentieth-century, Arendt condemned the naivety of the interwar liberals and was a critic of the same liberal idealists that so provoked the wrath of post-war realist thought (Carr 1939). She considered idealism (the notion that anything was possible) as central to totalitarianism. But she also believed in the need for international institutions and a permanent international criminal court. Unlike many liberals, however, she did not conclude that the new category of crimes against humanity represented humanity's moral progress. (She preferred the term crimes 'against the human status' (EJ, 257).) However, Arendt did believe that the events of the Second World War were too immense to be satisfactorily dealt with in the setting of a national court. She argued for an international penal code that recognized Nazi crimes as not just a matter for the Jewish people to be settled in Jewish courts; 'the international order, and mankind in its entirety' was also 'grievously hurt and endangered' (EJ, 276) by the effort to wipe an entire people from the face of the earth.[28]

We have already suggested that massive human cruelty was not the greatest 'mortal sin of politics' according to Arendt (PP, 161). The greatest sin was genocide or 'war of annihilation'. But again this was not only because such wars involved extreme cruelty, the systematic abuse of human rights, or large numbers of dead. 'Suffering, of which there has always been too much on earth', she wrote, 'is not the issue, nor is the number of victims' (OT, 458–9). With genocide there is something even more at stake than human life 'and why, quite apart from all moral considerations, it cannot be allowed a place in politics' (PP, 175). Arendt condemned genocide as a crime against the human status given the consequences of the elimination of an entire people and 'their unique view of the world'.

Recall Arendt's argument that plurality was 'specifically *the* condition . . . of all political life' (HC, 7). She also argued that there was a direct relationship between plurality and our understanding of reality. In Arendt's words,

> If it is true that a thing *is* real . . . only if it can show itself and be perceived from all sides, then there must always be a plurality of individuals or peoples . . . to make reality even possible and to guarantee its continuation. In other words, the world comes into being only if there are perspectives . . . If a people or a nation, or even just some specific human group, which offers a unique view of the world arising from its particular vision of the world . . . is annihilated, it is not merely that a people or a nation or a given number of individuals perishes, but rather that a portion of our common world is destroyed, an aspect of the world that has revealed itself to us until now but can never reveal itself again. Annihilation is therefore not just tantamount to the end of the world; it also takes its annihilator with it (PP, 175).

Arendt's condemnation of genocide, and by extension her criteria for action to stop it, was for the sake of the political reality that only a plurality of human perspectives may bring to the world. Individuals are mortal. What does not necessarily die is the political reality and historical understanding that a plurality of people creates.

Wars of annihilation that aim to wipe out a particular group attack the basic fact of human plurality and violate the 'limits inherent in violent action'. With genocide we are not 'just' talking about large numbers of dead but something that is potentially immortal. The public, political world, the political constitution of a people, the outcome of a people's living together, and debating their common affairs is also destroyed with genocide. The real crime during the Second World War, Arendt believed, was not that the Nazis succeeded in killing millions. The point about genocide is that 'an altogether different order is broken and an altogether different community is violated' (EJ, 272). She believed that the order of mankind itself is threatened when an entire people is in danger of being blotted out. Such a war of annihilation was a crime against the very nature of humanity and not just a simple crime of war. Aggressive warfare is an old and common practice. But a war to annihilate an entire people, though old and still too common, is different 'not only in degree of seriousness', Arendt believed, 'but in essence' (EJ, 267).[29]

Hypocrisy is destructive to politics because it prevents us from hearing the plurality of voices and competing truths that make up the political world. Hypocrisy is an affect of authenticity and a denial of the constructed *persona*, the only mask that human voices are 'able to sound through' (OR, 102). The 'sounding board for truth' is always mediated by the interactions of a plurality of diverse individuals and groups, by the testimony of others, often, but not necessarily, in the artificial built spaces of the public realm.[30] Genocide may begin with the burning of this built space, of houses and hospitals, temples and mosques. But it breaches the limits on violence not because the human-made world is shattered, houses burned and towns destroyed. These can all be rebuilt. With a war of annihilation the 'historical and political reality housed in this world' is also wiped out. And, as Arendt feared, this is 'a reality that cannot be rebuilt' (PP, 161). What ultimately perishes with genocide is the world of speech and action. This system of relationships is less concrete than the world of fabricated objects. Words and actions, historical memory and knowledge, were never 'made' to begin with but when they are destroyed the human race has literally arrived at the end of the political world.

7

Beyond Strauss, Lies and the War in Iraq: A Critique of Neoconservatism

> I think commitment can easily carry you to a point where you no longer think.
>
> —Arendt, 'On Hannah Arendt', p. 308

Since the 1970s, neoconservative thinkers have argued that the foreign policy establishment in the United States, dominated by the realist mindset, is too risk-averse and, somewhat oddly considering its source, too *conservative*. Realism as a theory of world politics is viewed as too relativistic, uncomfortable speaking in the language of right and wrong. This damages the United States' moral high-ground and recognition of its own national greatness. In the past, neoconservatives argue, realists underestimated the wealth of moral righteousness that was necessary to sustain the sacrifices that eventually won the Cold War. The parched language of 'stability', 'balance of power', and the 'national interest' cannot rally the American people to a visionary commitment. Its political rhetoric is incapable of sustaining what President George W. Bush described as the 'distinctly American internationalism' integral to fighting the new global war on terror. Realist ideas are insufficient to mobilize the American public for the sacrifice of blood and money to keep the republic—and the world—safe *today* (Kaplan and Kristol 2003; Williams 2005a: 307–37).

Neoconservatism poses a powerful challenge to international theory. Its proponents speak of power *and* morality, credibility, interests, *and* values.[1] Liberal internationalist ideas about human rights are repackaged in a neo-Reaganite language of morality, US prestige and zealous patriotism. Unlike liberals, neoconservatives are not shy of unilateral military action; they embrace it. That 'ideas matter' is an obvious claim to neoconservatives. But the content of their world-changing ideas contains a different emphasis to liberals. They use the language not of international organizations and cooperation, but of patriotic moral clarity and the historic, universal values of 'America'. Neoconservatives share with realists a view of world politics as dangerous.

However, the world is not divided into competing states rationally pursuing interests. The human condition is defined as a struggle between good and evil. The fight against evil, as articulated by President Bush, is imbued with greater meaning through the citation of religious conviction and eschatology.[2] Neoconservatives are confident about the material and ideological power of the United States to shape the human condition. In a vein similar to more optimistic liberal-constructivist work, they believe in the power of ideas such as 'freedom' and 'democracy' to change the world when allied with American power (Wendt 2000).[3]

The dominant ideological justification for the US invasion and occupation of Iraq in 2003 was provided by neoconservatism. This is widely understood. But some of the claims about the connection between the ideas of Leo Strauss (1899–1973), the influential neoconservative philosopher, and the Iraq invasion have been truly grand indeed. According to one critic of the war, Strauss and his neoconservative followers provided the Bush administration with the politically useful 'philosophy of the noble lie, the conviction that lies, far from being simply a regrettable necessity of political life, are instead virtuous and noble instruments of wise policy' (Shorris 2004). Christopher Hitchens, influential supporter of the war, wrote that 'part of the charm' of regime change in Iraq 'is that it depends on premises and objectives that cannot...be publicly avowed. Since Paul Wolfowitz [then Deputy Secretary of Defence] is from the intellectual school of Leo Strauss...one may even suppose that he enjoys this arcane and occluded aspect of the debate' (2003: 17).[4] On this view, the secret premise behind the invasion of Iraq was that there were, indeed, 'root causes' behind the 9/11 attacks: the Cold War policy of supporting despotic regimes in the Middle East. The appearance of mendacity and misleading statements from the Bush administration, the bold misrepresentation of intelligence estimates about weapons of mass destruction, and dishonest arguments about links between Iraq and 9/11, provoked wild accusations of conspiracy and lies to justify an otherwise unjustifiable war.[5]

The implication of such claims is that lying in politics is a sin peculiar to neoconservatives and may even have been condoned by Leo Strauss (Weinstein 2004; Drury 2005; George 2005). What should we make of these allegations? There is an immediate temptation to dismiss such views. Indeed, we should. The Bush administration's notorious clash with factual truth in relation to Iraq had little to do with any belief in 'noble lies'. Certain of Strauss's works do indeed give the impression that political lying can be righteous, even 'noble'.[6] Strauss did not clearly set out his own political thought. Rather, others have sought to decipher his views. This has led to much confusion and infighting concerning what Strauss did and did not believe. While always noting the 'obscurity', difficulty, and 'alien character' of his writing, Straussians seem to take pride in the level of controversy provoked by his work; and, indeed, commentators observe that his writing 'continues to shatter respectable intellectual categories and rules' (Pangle 1989: vii). But lying in politics is not a sin peculiar to neoconservatives and would probably not have been condoned by Strauss (Strauss Clay 2003).

However, there is a need for further reflection on Strauss and the philosophical roots of neoconservative thought. It is possible to understand the contentious political debates surrounding the invasion and occupation of Iraq, including the appearance of mendacity, through a richer understanding of early neoconservative thought. The 'neoconservative persuasion' (Kristol 2003) and its political influence are based on more than a 'cabal' of influential men who are willing to lie on behalf of some greater cause.[7] It rests on firm and clearly set out theoretical foundations directly relevant to contemporary public policy and justifications for war (Deutsch and Murley 1999; Desch 2005). It is through understanding these foundations that we can begin to understand why neoconservative ideas became so popular in the United States after the 9/11 attacks and how they helped take the United States into an otherwise unjustifiable war.

Classical realists certainly offer a persuasive critique of the dangers and hypocrisy of moralizing international affairs and possess a more sophisticated vision of domestic politics than is often assumed (Carr 1939; Morgenthau 1960, 1970). These thinkers presaged some of the concerns contemporary foreign policy analysts have expressed about the neoconservative vision (Mearsheimer and Walt 2003; Gold 2004: ch. 9; Fukuyama 2006). But we should not content ourselves, as many have done, to return to classical realism in response to the failures of neoconservatism in Iraq (Gilpin 2005; Williams 2005*a*). The realist-'neocon' conversation will no longer suffice. We must turn to another interlocutor. In a very different language from that of classical realism, Hannah Arendt articulated a critique of the dangers of moralism in the political realm that avoids realist cynicism.[8] She is also better placed to challenge the neoconservative vision of international affairs, 'the automatic thought-reactions' of ideological conviction and their relationship to democratic society (OR, 225). She reminds us that there is a natural clash between factual truth and politics that is only exacerbated by the peculiarities of neoconservative ideology. To liberate Iraq was ideologically mandated; influential neoconservatives had their theory and strength of moral conviction 'and', to borrow Arendt's words from a different context, 'all data that did not fit were denied or ignored' (CR, 39). The origins of lying in politics are found in the nature of the political realm itself. It is tempting and even easy to lie in politics because the lie itself is a form of action. Almost by nature the liar is an actor because the liar wants to change the world from what is to what they want it to be.

In contrast to the repetitive and unchanging tasks of some other human activities, political action is the realm in which we are truly capable of changing the world. Given this ever-changing character, factual statements about what is the case are fragile. For as Arendt wrote, 'no factual statement can ever be beyond doubt—as secure and shielded against attack as, for instance, the statement that two and two make four' (CR, 6). Note the kind of truth to which Arendt was referring. She clearly distinguished between rational truth and facts. Rational truth is the business of philosophic speculation. Through rational argumentation (or simply faith) the philosopher (or theologian) may believe they have constructed the truth of claims such as 'all humans are created equal'. This is not a factual 'truth' of the kind political actors must establish to make proper judgements about the legitimacy of a particular war (BPF, 238; for a discussion see Nelson 1978).

Arendt's writing suggests that the fatal flaw of neoconservative ideology concerns its understanding of the place of philosophy in the public realm, the relationship between political thought and practice, ideas and action. These relationships do not tell us everything we need to know about the changing character of war and its relationship to democratic society. Nor do they tell us everything we need to know about the politics of foreign policy debates within the Republican Party after 9/11.[9] But we cannot fully understand the US decision to go to war in Iraq without understanding the basic ideas and principles, revealed in the public culture and rhetorical forms, shaping the political regime that started it. Arendt offers a systematic refutation of neoconservative ideas and its wider agenda in both domestic and international politics. A critic of all forms of 'hubristic radicalism' (Canovan 1992: 24), she offers international theory new grounds—and a new way to articulate—older realist concerns about the dangers of moralism, especially in wartime, and the arrogance of power that believes the world can change because it is so willed and ideologically mandated. Irving Kristol, so-called godfather of neoconservatism, once claimed that 'in the modern world, a non-ideological politics is a politics disarmed' (1983: ix). But for Arendt, it is in fact ideology that disarms politics.[10]

THE SEARCH FOR A NEW FOUNDATION

There are a number of resemblances between the philosophical roots of neoconservatism and the issues that concerned Hannah Arendt. German Jews in the early twentieth-century, Arendt and Leo Strauss began their intellectual journey from the same place and from similar traditions of thought. Indeed, they were acquaintances in the early years of Hitler's rule and much later colleagues at the University of Chicago. The Nazi takeover and destruction of European Jewry became the focal point of their thinking about politics, and what was necessary for 'the political' to have meaning in the post-Holocaust world. Both fled to the United States as a result of the Second World War and with their arrival, as Anne Norton writes, 'the study of the political returned to the American academy, and with a vengeance' (2004: 55). Both drew lessons from the politics and philosophy of Athens, though Arendt was far more critical of what she found there. Both were critics of positivist social science. Strauss's influence on political philosophy in the United States has arguably been greater if we take as evidence that 'a school formed around' him (Kielmansegg 1995: 5). Arendt and Strauss both wrote about the American Founding and in many ways accepted the idea of America's political experience as exceptional.

Yet, the differences between Arendt and Strauss are far greater than their similarities. This is the other motivation for initiating a further dialogue between neoconservatism and Arendt. Her name has frequently been invoked in the context of the recent resurgence of neoconservative thought, but as an inspiration and ally (Kristol 1983: 80; Pietz 1988; Podhoretz 1999; Williams 2005: 316). Several thinkers associated with neoconservatism point to Arendt's influence.[11] The story Norton (2004) tells about Leo Strauss is also, in part, a story told about Arendt (see also Scott-Smith 2002: 43–4). Diverse schools of thought, to be sure, legitimately claim Arendt's writing. She is one of a number of 'charismatic legitimators' (Jay 1993: 168). And the misreading of Arendt by Straussians is not without some justification.[12] But the association between Arendt and neoconservatism is superficial at best. They possessed entirely different evaluations of political action. For Arendt, political action is unpredictable in its outcomes. For Strauss and his neoconservative followers it is ideology that gives political action its certainty and political actors their moral conviction.

There are a number of ways to reconstruct Arendt's (usually hidden) criticisms of Strauss and the foundations of neoconservative thought (Beiner 1990; Villa 1999, 2001).[13] Here we highlight their differences over the relationship between politics and philosophy because it is at the root of a number of flaws in neoconservative ideological thinking about the recent past and the relationship between politics and war. Unlike Strauss, Arendt was strongly against the idea that ancient philosophy could invigorate modern democracy. Indeed, quite the reverse. She was highly critical of the anti-political character of Greek thought, preferring to draw lessons from their political experience.[14]

Strauss was far more attracted to Greek philosophy, implying that the many ought to (and do) consent to be ruled by the virtuous few. Some of his harshest critics have taken this to mean that one of the 'defining features of his work' was the 'rejection of liberal democracy' (Drury 1997: 4). This is over-stated and fails to take into account the complicated task Strauss believed he had undertaken to *save* liberal democracy from ruin.

Strauss's antipathies towards liberalism and democracy have been well-documented, but not so well understood. He rarely praised democracy itself fearing the disorder that it might bring. But he also defended liberal democracy as the least bad regime in the modern age. Indeed, the central problem of modernity, the basic political–philosophical starting point for neoconservative thought, is belief in the need for a new foundation for political order in the West. In the modern age, the single legitimate foundation for government is the democratic consent of the people. Liberal democracy places the people in the position of authority, not God or philosophy. The opinion of the democratic people, which for Strauss (unlike Arendt) was obviously inferior to philosophical truth, becomes the highest moral authority. However, for Strauss, the implied tolerance of all views risked degenerating into the belief that everybody's views, everybody's mere preferences, were equal. In the absence of older forms of religious and moral virtue, with the lack of authoritative truth, Strauss feared a dangerous vacuum had been created. As Irving Kristol, perhaps one of the most noted inheritors of Straussian thought, also believed, modern society was in a state of spiritual disintegration, afflicted by relativistic, 'nihilistic' decadence in which 'the individual must be free to create his own morality' (1978: 69).

Uninterested in true universal knowledge and authentic political action, the overriding concern of the modern individual, Strauss feared, was the pursuit of mere pleasure and wealth, a 'joyless quest for joy' (1950: 251). Since Max Weber, social science had argued that the ends of political life were without foundation. Since 'all these former illusions...have been dispelled', Weber wrote, 'the ultimate and most sublime values have retreated from public life' (1946: 143, 155). The consequences for modern politics and society were immense; the political and the ethical were now distinguished and the logic of each was 'governed by different laws' (1946: 123). Strauss viewed acceptance of this condition as a recipe for disaster and a denial of the true force of 'the political'. In the words of Kristol, 'one is led to question the validity of the original liberal idea that it is possible for the individual...to cope with the eternal dilemmas of the human condition. The moral authority of tradition, and some public support for this authority, seems to be needed' (1978: xi).

Strauss rejected the 'historicist' or 'relativist' argument that all value-claims concerning moral authority were contingent on particular historical circumstances. Conflict over values, Strauss believed, ought to be conducted through and expressed in 'universal terms', that is, of the 'political order which is best always and everywhere' (1989: 56). In *Natural Right and History*, he invoked the passage in the American Declaration of Independence related to self-evident truths and unalienable rights. This 'self-evidence', he suggested, is endangered by the 'retail sanity and wholesale madness' of relativism and historicism. Strauss wrote,

Political things are by their nature subject to approval or disapproval, to choice and rejection, to praise and blame. It is of their essence not to be neutral but to raise a claim to men's obedience, allegiance, decision, or judgment. One does not understand them as what they are, as political things, if one does not take seriously their explicit or implicit claim to be judged in terms of goodness or badness, of justice or injustice . . . To judge soundly one must know the true standards (1988*b*: 12).

Any effort to avoid value judgements about the fundamental questions of the human condition was an absurdity and affront to decency and morality.

Both Strauss and Kristol believed that the new foundation for the modern age was located in the first principles of the American regime. There are things 'essential to all political communities'. The most important is the founding of the political constitution, the 'permanent framework within which the right handling of changing situations by excellent politicians or statesmen can take place' (Strauss 1989: 53). Different regimes encapsulate and embody different answers to the profound questions of political organization as well as represent the particular, specific language, and customs of a community. Many of Strauss's ideas centre on the importance of political regimes and involve quasi-religious praise for the founding of the American republic. During this founding, philosophical statesmen displayed the 'most "architectonic" political skill that is known to political life' (Strauss 1989: 53). In this moment of political excellence wise men designed a political order to which the modern masses could consent.

In the past, 'noble' men acted with a dignity in politics now largely absent in the modern age. But politics itself, Strauss nonetheless argued, 'derives its dignity from something which transcends political life'. Defending Plato's hierarchical ordering of human activities Strauss believed 'political life was necessarily inferior to contemplative life' (1989: 64, 161). Where the former dealt with mere opinions, the latter activity was capable of discerning true standards; it was 'the ascent from opinions to knowledge or to truth' (Strauss 1950: 124). As such, the political philosopher is the 'umpire', who rules over and settles the political controversies of the unruly agora. Philosophical truth transcends the political realm of mere opinion. This is possible because the 'knowledge of the political philosopher is "transferable" to the highest degree'.

As evidence, Strauss cited Plato's frequent comparisons between 'political science and medicine' (1989: 54).

The privileging of philosophy over political action, truth over opinion, according to both Strauss and Arendt, originated in Plato's exasperation with democratic political action after the trial and death of Socrates. The philosopher-citizen, the questioner, was condemned for leading astray the Athenian youth. It was precisely the uncertainty and unpredictability of political action, the fact that the public was often arbitrary and irrational (to such a degree that Socrates is killed) which explains the long-standing desire of philosophers to escape from politics and eliminate its negative consequences. Arendt quotes Pascal: 'The most philosophic [thing] was to live simply and quietly. If they [Plato and Aristotle] wrote on politics, it was as if laying down rules for a lunatic asylum' (LK, 22). Before outlining the neoconservative solution to the dangers of unruly public action we must briefly pause to note Arendt's objection to Plato's hierarchical ordering of philosophy over politics, rational truth over democratic opinion, that so animated Strauss.

Arendt considered it in the very nature of philosophy to be hostile to politics. Philosophy requires withdrawal from the public world. She referred to thinking itself as the solitary internal 'dialogue between me and myself' (BPF, 220). In contrast to the worldliness of political action, thinking was 'unworldly'. The activity of the philosopher is essentially passive. Where thinking is done in solitude, politics always encounters a plurality of opinion; political knowledge is always perspectival. Though thinking importantly thrives on an anticipated communication with others, there is no unity between thought and political action.[15] Indeed, even if this were so it would not be fortuitous: 'You can't say A without saying B and C and so on, down to the end of the murderous alphabet' (OT, 472).

The anti-democratic and anti-political character of attempts to govern politics through ideology or philosophy was clear to Arendt. It was a principled dimension of her work that such endeavours were destructive of the very political freedom these blueprints sought, at least in theory, to render. Politics is such that no theory can adequately be 'applied' without destroying the very essence of political life.[16] To think and to act are not the same: 'all our categories of thought and standards for judgment seem to explode in our hands the instant we try to apply them' (EU, 302). The point, contra Strauss, is that politics involves 'matters of opinion and not the truth' (BPF, 247). Opinion and truth can be considered as almost opposites. Talking something through and forming an opinion, an 'opinion among opinions', is central to the formation of a political realm. For Arendt, opinion, *doxa*, is not 'mere' opinion, as it is for Strauss.

Like Strauss, Arendt believed that some forms of truth were an anathema to politics, but for an entirely different reason. Modes of thought and communication that claim truth, she believed, 'are necessarily domineering' because 'they don't take into account other people's opinions..., the hallmark of all strictly political thinking' (BPF, 241). Profound 'truth' needs no agreement. It simply is. As noted by Strauss, the American Declaration of Independence sought to enshrine certain principles, such as the idea that 'all men are created equal', as beyond dispute. This is why certain 'truths' were deemed 'self-evident'. But the statement of equality was not 'true'; it was a matter of agreed opinion. Contra Strauss, these opinions were held not because they were self-evidently 'true', but because they were *necessary* for democratic politics to begin; 'freedom is possible only among equals' (BPF, 247). Arendt emphasized the authority of the agreement 'we hold', rather than the 'self-evident' nature of the truth when Jefferson declared 'We hold these truths to be self-evident' (OR, 92–4). The significant revolutionary action was the 'necessarily relative' agreement. In the absence of 'transcending standards, everything remains relative' (Arendt 2004: 428; Honig 1991).

Since Plato, however, philosophers have sought to construct absolute standards, appropriate models for political conduct that could be applied to human affairs. Dana Villa nicely summarizes Arendt's diagnosis of the effect on almost the entire tradition of Western political thought: 'Throughout ... the faculty of reason is called upon to identify the idea or *telos* of justice, and to show how this idea can be realized concretely in the world. In Plato, Hobbes, Hegel, and Marx the "theoretical" analysis first isolates the (ideal) end, and then reveals the means by which it will be—or has been—produced (by philosopher-kings, a sovereign definer of rights and duties, world history, or proletarian revolution)' (Villa 1999: 94). Strauss, as part of this tradition, called for the subjection of political action and the vagaries of opinion to the authority of philosophical reason. Using Arendt's specific lexicon, we might say Strauss sought to transcend human plurality and overcome the 'fundamental relativity' of the 'interhuman realm' (MDT, 27).

In summary, Strauss held historicism and relativism to blame for the crisis of authority in modern society; the decadent amoralism of liberalism needed to be defeated. In praising the founding of the American republic, early neoconservatives drew attention to the dangers not only from outside tyrannies but from weakness within. As already indicated, a central flaw of secular liberal democracy, on this view, was the failure of modern individuals to believe that the good life rested on anything more than individual preference. To see how this is captured presently, we turn again to a modern day neoconservative thinker. One wholly 'negative consequence of the disestablishment of religion as a publicly sanctioned mythos', Kristol wrote, 'has been the inability of liberal society ever to come up with a convincing and generally accepted theory of political obligation' (1978: 64). If the good life can be found in private pursuits, what motive is there for public-spiritedness, public action?

The only salvation for the modern masses was to enter into mortal combat over values. Indeed, for Strauss, this was the essence of political life. The political was above all defined by the struggle for power, 'characterized by conflicts between men asserting opposed claims' (Strauss 1989: 51, 59). Strauss, like Carl Schmitt with whom he conducted a close dialogue, viewed politics as an antagonistic struggle to the death (see Meier 1995; Strauss 1996). Just as Nazi ideology had stepped into the breach in interwar Europe, the most ruthless and articulate men of action were destined to fill the spiritual and political vacuum created by liberal modernity. Strauss's project in the revival of political philosophy was to ensure the post-war moral and spiritual vacuum was appropriately filled.

In direct contrast to Strauss, Arendt frequently warned that the hierarchical ordering of philosophy over politics was a denial of the fundamental relativity of all political opinion and action. Rather than see the dangers in the loss of traditional authority, Arendt saw the contingency and relativity of political affairs as an opportunity. Unlike Weber, who saw modern humanity stranded in an 'iron-cage' of rationality (1976: 181), Arendt held out more hope for the promise of democratic politics. 'Even though we have lost yardsticks by which to measure', she wrote, 'and rules under which to subsume the particular, a being whose essence is beginning may have enough of origin within himself to understand without preconceived categories and to judge without the customary rules which is morality' (EU, 321). Rather than posing a nihilistic threat, Arendt believed that the abandonment of Plato's hierarchy bestowed a dignity on politics largely absent in the modern age; 'the abandonment of this hierarchy...is the abandonment of all hierarchical structures' (LK, 29; Canovan 1992: ch. 7).

At the same time Arendt's embrace of contingency required recognition of the limits of political action and the human capacity to change the world (including with violence) through the application of correct ideology. Neoconservative ideology embraces the use of violence to enact political change. But Arendt, like Clausewitz, fully understood the 'all-pervading unpredictability, which we encounter the moment we approach the realm of violence' (CR, 107). Arendt understood the limitations of using violence to achieve expansive political ends in a way that challenges the apparent ease with which many neoconservatives imagined they could achieve a military victory and then a stable political order in Iraq. Violence can remain rational only to the extent that it is aimed at achieving short term goals and any justification 'loses its plausibility the farther its intended end recedes into the future' (CR, 151).

For 'while the results of men's actions are beyond the actors' control', Arendt wrote, 'violence harbors within itself an additional element of arbitrariness' (CR, 106).[17]

War, like all forms of violence, Arendt argued, requires justification in terms of the ends it pursues. This justification, which always involves political speech to a judging audience, is the most important element—the most political aspect—of any political theory of war. Violence may be justified by appeals to the end that its perpetrators seek to achieve. Arendt is clear, however, that there are no objective criteria to judge whether a particular act of violence is or is not justified. It is wholly determined by the performative act of justification and the judgement of those who are being addressed. The task is to persuade the audience that the violence was necessary and it is the audience alone that may judge. Violence is always instrumental and can only be justified for short term ends due to the overwhelming tendency for violence to spiral out of control, to initiate unintended consequences, in short, to overrun any potential (perhaps even justifiable) end.

Both political action and war initiate processes that can never be predicted by the principal actors themselves. Efforts to contain the unpredictability of the political realm, the search for extra-political groundings, whether based on ancient philosophy or any modern political ideology, are self-defeating and almost invariably violent. In 1975, Irving Kristol wrote that ' "You can't beat a horse with no horse", and the horses of modern politics', in neoconservative thought, 'are ideologies and the social visions they embody' (Gerson 1995: 169). Returning to neoconservative justifications for the Iraq war, the next section argues that errors in its conception and execution, including the willful denial of a number of factual truths, can be explained in terms of neoconservative ideological passions. They ended up having a 'hypnotic effect' putting 'to sleep ... common sense, which', as Arendt reminds us, 'is nothing else but our mental organ for perceiving, understanding, and dealing with reality and factuality' (CR, 110).

THE PUBLIC AND THE POLITICS OF WAR

Neoconservative thinking about world politics cuts through several of the treasured theoretical distinctions upon which most international theory rests. Consider the literature on so-called 'humanitarian' military intervention, a literature dominated by liberals and constructivists (Finnemore 2003; Welsh 2003). The peculiarities of disciplinary theory-building, especially the effort to debunk a narrow view of realism, has led liberal and constructivist scholars to downplay US 'interests' in explaining 'humanitarian intervention'. Little or no engagement with the very different neoconservative defence of such wars has appeared in academe.[18] Neoconservatives say they want to change the world to one more favourable to human rights; they just believe that liberal arguments for 'humanitarian' war are based on faulty premises.[19] Neoconservatives describe the military interventions in Haiti (1994), Bosnia, and Kosovo as early examples of 'preemptive intervention', justified as the use of 'force to preempt harm to those nations' citizens and their neighbours when there was no direct threat to the United States' (Kaplan and Kristol 2003: 87–8). On this view, the pre-emptive war over Iraq was not a radical departure from US foreign policy practice or international norms regulating the use of force.

Recall the neoconservative criticism of classical realism as contributing to the problem of relativism. Uncomfortable grounding foreign policy in high ideals and moral crusades, realists counsel caution. They assume that states, even authoritarian regimes, are rational and even predictable, restrained by self-interest and the wish to survive. Classical realist scepticism of the high-rhetoric of world transformation and missionary zeal derives from gloomy assumptions about human nature, power, and the constraints of the inter-state system (Waltz 1959). Order and stability matter most for realists, despite the unfortunate human costs. Practitioners of realpolitik advocate action for narrow national interest, not abstract ideals. Morgenthau (1948) thought of 'interests defined in terms of power' and preferred order over unrealizable international justice. He understood the tragedy of the political, the undecided conflict. What was good today could be evil tomorrow.

From the neoconservative perspective, these classical realist views not only misunderstand the dangerous character of America's enemies. Realism misconstrues the nature of the political and is itself a reflection of moral decay. Its soulless philosophy is less an *American* Cold War strategy than an 'unsentimental realpolitik practiced by . . . *European* statesmen like Bismarck and Metternich' (Kaplan and Kristol 2003: 46, second emphasis added). It represents in the international realm everything that is wrong with modern politics. The political is defined by the struggle between good and evil. To deny this is to rob the modern individual of a vibrant source of moral purpose. The American people, Kristol wrote, 'really do believe that there is such a thing as the "public interest"—a *res publica* that is something more than the summation of individual interests' (1883, xiv–xv). To express this national–public interest in the international sphere is the goal of neoconservative international thought. Indeed, the domestic and the international are brought together into a coherent and powerful whole in a manner unmatched by realism (Williams 2005a).

Through a moral foreign policy with which the American people can identify the domestic and the international are united in a celebration of national
greatness. In liberating Iraq, America also potentially frees itself to pursue its
global mission. The biggest danger, however, even before the 9/11 attacks,
was that the American people would be afraid to utilize their unmatched
power to shape the world further to their advantage (Kagan and Kristol 2000).
Global peace and liberal democratic principles depend on it; the alternative
is the collapse of international order and the further disintegration of republican values. Foreign policy neoconservatives rework ideas about American
national origin and 'republican virtue' in an effort to mobilize a political base
around distinctive foreign policies supported by particular forms of public
rhetoric.[20] What are these values and rhetorical norms practiced in the ideal
neoconservative public? What is the content of public discourse and what is
its relationship to the politics of justifying war?

Strauss viewed religion as central to maintaining moral purpose in the life
of modern liberal citizens; neoconservatives tap into the religiosity of US society (combined with Jeffersonian republic-worship) in a way more naturally
secular liberals find more difficult. Indeed, especially in the domestic sphere,
a combination of religion and aggressive nationalism become the central
political ideology of the republic. The primary attachment of the majority of
citizens should be towards national greatness. A reverence for the Founding
Fathers, itself often approaching a religious fervour, supports neoconservative
ideas about American values being triumphant and universal, that certain
truths are 'self-evident' in nature, and in the moral character of the American
people. An overriding commitment to these national and civic values gives
meaning to the body politic, to the American regime.

Neoconservatives believe, or want the public to believe, that the founding
principles of the republic are self-evident truths applicable to all across time
and place. Yet political participation of only a certain kind is praised. Unruly
action in multiple and diverse public spaces is feared. Civil disobedience
and anti-war dissenters are treated with suspicion.[21] The ideal citizen votes,
is a patriot, holds traditional values about family and state; they shop and
follow their gut instincts. They are spectators, especially of foreign policy,
aroused to support the 'national interest' in an emotional way they know
to be right. Neoconservative leaders are men of action. But this is not government action to correct social ills related to class, gender or race. The
ideal civic engagement is 'faith-based' initiatives, a form of compassionate
conservatism rather than social-democratic action in favour of redistributive
justice.

The compassion of the 'American people' has traditionally been represented
as the political terrain of the liberal-left (Berlant 2004). But the sentiment

has more recently been appropriated in the popular language and ideology of the Christian Right. The moral tone of 'compassionate conservatism' revolves around the distinctly neoconservative symbolism of faith and social attachment to the (traditional) family, nation, and God (Olasky 2000). As Arendt might remark, President Bush has sought 'to raise compassion to the rank of the supreme political passion and of the highest political virtue' (OR, 70).[22] Compassionate conservativism is based on a moral clarity, explicitly billed as a corrective to the immoral, decadent, Clinton years. The religiosity of the Bush administration is not new to the United States or unique to the political right. And yet the political mobilization of the religious right has been central to the shift of compassion from a liberal to a conservative concept and has shaped both domestic and foreign policy discourse.

Central to this vision is the resoluteness, moral clarity, and good intentions of the President as a leader of the nation and Commander-in-Chief. As Strauss put it, the 'only thing which can be held to be unqualifiedly good is...not the cultivation of the mind...but a good intention, and of good intentions everyone is as capable as everyone else, wholly independently of good education' (1968: 22). In the absence of discovering weapons of mass destruction in Iraq, Bush not only evoked the higher political objective of 'freeing' the Iraqi people, but also his moral clarity. The emphasis on emotion and gut instincts, a disregard for facts in favour of statements about the 'march of freedom', is typical of a presidency famously dismissive of nuance, and makes more sense in light of neoconservative ideas.

In a rare prime time presidential press conference this question was asked: 'One of the biggest criticisms of you is that whether it's WMD in Iraq, postwar planning in Iraq, or even the question of whether this administration did enough to ward off 9/11, you never admit a mistake. Is that a fair criticism? And do you believe there were any errors in judgment that you made related to any of those topics?'[23] President Bush did not respond directly in the terms of the question. Rather he referred to America's new war-footing and how the 9/11 attacks could not have been predicted. On Iraq, he said,

The people *know where I stand.* I mean, in terms of Iraq, *I was very clear about what I believed.* And, of course, I want to know why we haven't found a weapon yet. But I still *know* Saddam Hussein was a threat, and the world is better off without Saddam Hussein. I don't think anybody can—maybe people can argue that. I *know* the Iraqi people don't believe that, that they're better off with Saddam Hussein—would be better off with Saddam Hussein in power. *I also know that there's an historic opportunity here to change the world.* And it's very important for the loved ones of our troops to understand that the mission is an important, vital mission for the security of America and for the ability to change the world for the better (emphases added).

The President's denial of the likelihood of error is made possible through accepting the logic of a world-changing idea, an ideology. The content of the ideology matters less than what ideology does to the mind and the kind of explanation that it allows.

The drive behind Bush's position, and the kind of thinking that enables it, was identified long ago by Arendt. It 'is based not so much on superior intelligence as on the correct interpretation of the essentially reliable forces in history or nature, forces which neither defeat nor ruin can prove wrong because they are bound to assert themselves in the long run' (OT, 349). The forces of history in neoconservative thought are men of action founding the right political regimes. History has proved them right and ideology is a means to this end. 'Its subject matter is history', Arendt wrote, 'to which the "idea" is applied; the result of this application is not a body of statements about something that *is*, but the unfolding of a process...They [ideologies] are historical, concerned with becoming and perishing...The "idea" of an ideology...has become an instrument of explanation' (OT, 469).[24] The instrument of explanation in neoconservative ideology, and expressed in Bush's rhetoric, is the self-evident truths established at the founding of the American regime, the superiority of American values and the inevitability of the march of freedom. The question of error or regret need not be addressed. Certain forms of public rhetoric enable troublesome facts to be downplayed. Indeed, certain ideological conviction need not admit of the possibility of a substantial mistake.

To change the world is ideologically mandated in neoconservative thought. When combined with a real capacity to act, when neoconservative ideas are listened to by the powerful and shape public rhetoric, there is a great temptation to exaggerate the possibilities for doing so. In 2003, Vice President Dick Cheney remarked that the early signs of widespread armed resistance to the US occupation were the last gasps of the defunct Baathist regime. But as Arendt wrote in the 1960s, 'To call such unexpected, unpredicted, unpredictable happenings "random events" or "the last gasps of the past", condemning them to irrelevance or the famous "dustbin of history", is the oldest trick in the trade; the trick, no doubt, helps in clearing up the theory, but at the price of removing it further from reality' (CR, 110). Great power is perhaps most likely to fall into this trap, as evidenced in the hubris of the Bush administration prior to the war in Iraq, the refusal to see, or admit to seeing, the real difficulties that would lie ahead.

For factual truths about the nature of Iraqi society, about the ambiguity of pre-war intelligence, about the limits of the power of high-tech warfare possess no inherent right to be as they are. In the political realm, all factual truths are contingent; they 'carry no inherent truth within themselves, no necessity to be as they are' (CR, 6). There was no necessary reason why Iraq did not pose an urgent threat to the United States. There was no necessary reason Saddam did not possess weapons of mass destruction. There was no necessary reason Iraq was not supporting al-Qaeda or seeking uranium from Niger. There was no necessary reason the invasion and occupation would not be a 'cake walk'. There was no necessary reason all Iraqis would not greet 'liberation' with flowers. There was no necessary reason why the first insurgents were not the last gasp of the defunct Baathist regime. But there is also no necessary reason why America should ultimately win.[25]

CONCLUSION

'Strangely...' Arendt remarked, 'the clash of factual truth and politics ... has—in some respects, at least—very similar traits' to the clash between philosophy and politics (BPF, 236). The whole purpose of political action is to bring into being something new. Action is 'the very stuff politics are made of' (CR, 6). For Arendt, this freedom requires an ability to imagine that things as they are may be different, to refuse to accept the 'unyielding, blatant, unpersuasive stubbornness' of what is (BPF, 237). Truth may be stubborn but factual truth, in particular, is the most vulnerable because it is easily outmanoeuvred by the constantly changing world. Political action and the lie have something deeply in common; 'the deliberate denial of factual truth— the ability to lie—and the capacity to change facts—the ability to act—are interconnected; they owe their existence to the same source: imagination' (CR, 5). In *The Neoconservative Imagination*, a collection of essays in honour of Irving Kristol, political engagement is presented as key to this practical philosophy (DeMuth and Kristol 1995). The goal is not only to advise statesmen. It is to effect dramatic social change. Thus we see the particular reasons why neoconservative thought appears to have trouble with factual truth.

Arendt was far from naive when it came to the place of lying in the political realm. In her words, 'the lie did not creep into politics by some accident of human sinfulness. Moral outrage, for this reason alone, is not likely to make it disappear' (CR, 6). Governments lie during wartime for a variety of reasons; it is endemic to the practice of war. In Arendt's words, 'lying as such is neither new nor necessarily foolish in politics. Lies have always been regarded as justifiable in emergencies, lies that concerned specific secrets, especially in military matters, which had to be shielded against the enemy' (RJ, 264). Indeed, following Machiavelli, the realist tradition is most often associated with deceit. To step from Strauss's exposition of what he took to be Plato's distinction between exoteric and esoteric writing to the gap between rhetoric and reality characteristic of the Bush administration fails to appreciate the inherent clash between politics and truth of every kind. It is not the idea of the 'noble lie' that should concern us. As Arendt once remarked, 'political secrecy hardly ever ends in anything nobler than the vulgar duplicity of a spy' (OT, 218). She dismissed Strauss's 'noble lie' reading of Plato without ever mentioning his name.[26]

The more general problem is not individual wickedness, or the content of any particular theory, but the nature of the political realm itself. There is an *inevitable* clash between politics and factual truth. But it is made even worse by the ideological assumptions of neoconservative thought. The point is not to argue that neoconservative policies are more likely to lead to public lies. Liberals also tend to defend 'human rights' wars, even when exposed as hypocritical. As we discussed in Chapter 6, hypocrisy, a form of lie, is sometimes condoned by liberals because the alternative is worse: human rights are revealed to be the conceit of the powerful. Neoconservatives similarly defend high ideals, even when hypocritically evoked, because they are necessary to give the public something to believe in and fight for. Both liberals and neoconservatives politically cheat for the same reason; they desire to change the world and believe in the power of ideas to do so. There is something particular about the neoconservative temptation to deny certain factual truths. But it is *also* in the very 'nature of the political realm to be at war with truth in all its forms' (BPF, 239). It is for this reason, not for any noble lie, that men and women of action appear to so easily trade in falsehoods.

An excess of moral clarity not only leads to bad foreign policy—the realists show us that—but the denial of political facts, Arendt also suggested, is destructive of the public culture necessary for 'freedom' and 'democracy' to make sense at all. The outcome of this conflict between Arendt and the neoconservatives holds important implications for the place of ideas and ideology in shaping political judgements about contemporary war. The danger, for Arendt, was that 'ideological thinking ruins all relationships with reality' (OT, 474). Ideology will not substitute for reality. As neoconservatives have learned in Iraq, reality has 'no substitute' and no ideology can substitute for thought. The world catches up because the ideological thinker 'can remove his mind from it but not his body' (CR, 36), or we might add the bodies of those in American uniform. Neoconservatives may be experts at selling war. They seem less adept at winning them.

8

The Humanitarian Condition? On War and Making a Global Public

On the other hand, humanity, which for the eighteenth century, in Kantian terminology, was no more than a regulative idea, has today become an inescapable fact. This new situation, in which 'humanity' has in effect assumed the role formerly ascribed to nature or history, would mean in this context that the right to have rights, or the right of every individual to belong to humanity, should be guaranteed by humanity itself. It is by no means clear that this is possible ... For it is quite conceivable, and even within the realm of practical political possibilities, that one fine day a highly organized and mechanized humanity will conclude quite democratically—namely by majority decision—that for humanity as a whole it would be better to liquidate certain parts thereof.

—Arendt, *Origins of Totalitarianism*, pp. 298–9

All political activity, whether local, national, or transnational, is constitutive of some form of public. The language of publics, to talk of public opinion, the public realm or various media of publicity is central to political theory and practice. However, the seemingly straightforward notion of a public is also one of the most ambiguous in common use. Different topographical locations (the park, the legislature) and fields of activity (child care, the law) are public in different times and places. Publics are constituted through a variety of media (print, radio, the Internet). And there are various rhetorical modes in which one can participate in public discourse (Warner 2002). Clearly publics need not be limited by the territorial boundaries of states. As the traditional state-centrism of international theory has eroded, for example, a literature has belatedly emerged on the relationship between publics and the international.

International theory has implicitly transposed different domestic models of public space—or lack of it—onto its various images of an inter-state public realm. Neo-realist international theory, drawing on Thomas Hobbes's account of the pre-political, pre-public state of nature, presents the international sphere as one of incessant competition and fight for survival in anarchy (Waltz 1979). The international society approach suggests that the society of states as it emerged in Europe relied on the distinction between public and private with respect for norms of non-intervention in the (private) affairs of other states and the spread of international (public) law (Bull 1977). Liberal international theory has extended Kant's notion of public justice to an international 'Society of Peoples' (Rawls 1999). Constructivist theorists have used the public as a category to understand social interaction between states (Lynch 1999, 2002; Mitzen 2005). And normative and critical theory has conceived publics as a tool for understanding the potential of global and institutionalized democratic forums beyond the nation-state (Habermas 1996, 1998*a*, 2006; Bohman 1997; Linklater 1998; Benhabib 2002, 2004; Cochran 2002; Payne and Samhat 2004).

The extent to which many of these critical and normative approaches have turned to the theory and practice of 'humanitarian intervention' for empirical support is striking. Relying heavily on German social theorist, Jürgen Habermas, a number of scholars have argued that a transnational, potentially global public has contributed to normative change in the Western use of military power (Habermas 2000; Habermas and Mendieta 2004; Linklater 2000; Wheeler 2000*a*; Crawford 2002; Lynch 2006).[1] 'Behind the advances in international justice and the increased deployment of troops to stop atrocities', according to Human Rights Watch, 'lies an evolution in public morality' (quoted in Kaldor 2001: 109; also see de Greiff and Cronin 2002). Normative and some critical literatures in international theory have turned to this discourse and practice of wars associated with human rights.

The military interventions of the 1990s, especially in Bosnia (1995) and Kosovo (1999), have formed an important part of the story many tell about what a global public of world citizens might be able to achieve in the future. Habermas and many of his followers supported NATO's Kosovo war not only because they wished to see an end to the perceived ethnic cleansing of Kosovo–Albanians by Serb-nationalist extremists. In the words of Andrew Linklater, some supported war 'because they believed that Kosovo might be the catalyst that introduces a new era of "cosmopolitan law-enforcement"' (2000: 493; see Kaldor 2001). Habermas made a similar claim after the Gulf War (1990–1), which he also supported (1996: 514). The global public regulation of military force for humanitarian ends is considered to be the most legitimate alternative to the current system of unilateral American power and assertion of moral leadership. The virtues and obligations of citizenship rights might be extended, especially to those near the periphery of Europe, through the armed intervention of 'cosmopolitan-minded militaries' (Elliott and Cheeseman 2004).

Consider Habermas's support for the US-led Kosovo war and his opposition to the 2003 US-led invasion of Iraq. The Kosovo war was justified, even without an explicit UN authorization, he argued, given the motives of some of the European states that participated in the intervention. Neither the United States nor NATO understood themselves as acting on behalf of a future cosmopolitan order, but Germany, France, and Italy supposedly did. In Habermas's words, they 'understood this intervention as an "anticipation" of an effective law of world citizenship—as a step along the path from classical international law to what Kant envisioned as the "status of world citizen" which would afford legal protection to citizens against their own criminal regimes' (2004: 3). With the Iraq war, however, the United States and its subordinate ally, Britain, merely imposed their desire for war on the rest of the world community and claimed 'the universalistic force of their own national "values"' (Habermas 2002, 2004). They favoured the 'moralization of international politics' over its 'juridification' (2006: 116). The 'pseudo-universalism' of American ideals is an insufficient grounding for military action. It undermines rather than strengthens the establishment of a democratic cosmopolitan order, the institutionalization of a global public sphere.

The establishment of a legal-cosmopolitan order was clearly not the dominant Anglo-American goal during the invasion and occupation of Iraq. And yet leading neoconservatives in the United States were resoundingly in favour of the 'humanitarian wars' of the 1990s (Kaplan and Kristol 2003). Several writers have claimed the Iraq war was an example of 'humanitarian intervention', a just war to rid the world and the Iraqi people of a dangerous tyranny (Hitchens 2003; Cushman 2005).[2] For Habermas, such a position is objectionable, not because it was a breach of international law, but because cosmopolitan, progressive values cannot simply be derived from the culture of the only remaining superpower. To move from 'power politics to cosmopolitan society' military force must be legitimated by an appeal to a source outside the traditional world of sovereign states, even of democratic states who believe themselves to be fighting defensive wars against global terrorist networks. On this view, it is only on behalf of the law of world citizens in a global public sphere that powerful states (still the primary agents of the use of force) may militarily act.

There is much at issue in the divergence between Habermas's version of critical theory and followers of neoconservatism. In the words of Ulrich Beck, 'distinguishing the national outlook from the cosmopolitan outlook and juxtaposing the two ... reveals new arenas for action and resources for power, but also explains what is ultimately at stake ..., namely the foundations for the legitimation of politics per se' (2005: 17). If the very basis of our vision of legitimate politics is at issue then we must interrogate Habermas's claims about the potential emergence of a global public able to regulate 'humanitarian' war.[3] Chapter 7 drew on Arendt to suggest the limitations of the neoconservative vision. But does war become more progressive when used by democratic states able to 'justify their actions before a critical international public', as Habermas and his followers suggest (Lynch 2006: 182)? Is it really possible that an emerging global public might be at the vanguard of a progressive transnational challenge to both the pervasiveness of war and US hegemony (Kaldor 2003)? Could an evolution in global public morality be constituted through debates about human rights and whether or not to intervene in a humanitarian catastrophe (Crawford 2002)?

Even to ask these questions we must leave aside the highly dubious suggestion that any global public played a direct role in the decision of powerful states to use military force in the cases most often cited as 'humanitarian interventions': Bosnia, Kosovo, and East Timor (1999). None of these interventions was directly caused by global public opinion as opposed to the interests of the states that conducted them. Nonetheless, even leaving aside this question we are left with a major problem. The global public sphere and associated law of world citizens does not exist. How can states legitimately act in the name of a non-existent global public? There is a 'dilemma', Habermas admits, 'of having to act as if a completely institutionalized cosmopolitan condition already existed, the achievement of which is supposed to be promoted' (2000: 315). If Habermas's ultimate aim is a republic of world citizens how can this global public be brought into being?

We can call this dilemma the problem of founding. The question of 'founding', what Hannah Arendt described as a 'setting of a new beginning' (OR, 31), is central to political theory. It locates the idea of 'the public' not only in (global) space, but also in time. Arendt wrote frequently about the possibility of non-violent political founding. Indeed, if we widen the engagement between the followers of Habermas and neoconservatives to include the voice of Arendt we come to an unsettling conclusion about Habermas's self-imposed dilemma. The paradox of founding is resolved precisely through violence. Habermas's public of 'world citizens' *requires* violent mobilization if it is to be produced as a social entity. In the effort to 'make' a global public we are seeing an explicit justification of 'humanitarian' war in the work of some critical and normative international theory.

What is meant by 'make' a public realm? As we have discussed throughout this book, Arendt understood the public realm as something which emerged out of political action. It is space, the realm in-between speaking and acting individuals. In contrast to this image of the public realm, Arendt identified a 'politics-as-making' tradition as one of the major fault-lines running through Western political thought (Saurette 1996: 11–13). By 'making', she was referring to the activities and mentalities associated with work, which is constituted by a world of objects and things governed by the categories of means and ends (HC, 139–40). There are real dangers, she believed, when the mentalities and configuration of work (the activities of 'making') come to dominate conceptions of politics. Political action is equated with shaping the human condition towards a preconceived end (a global public) in the way a carpenter might shape a piece of wood. To make this argument the chapter begins by outlining some of the more general problems with the relationship between publics and violence in Habermas's theory. Arendt's distinction between work and action is then outlined to suggest how Habermas and his followers have imagined the 'construction of the public space in the image of a fabricated object' (HC, 227). The chapter concludes with reflections on Arendt's complicated but rather more satisfactory relationship to cosmopolitanism. The shrinkage of the globe had occurred to such an extent that 'each man is as much an inhabitant of the earth as he is an inhabitant of his country' (HC, 250). But the reality of this new order, Arendt also believed, 'is far from being the consolation or recompense for all past history as Kant hoped it to be' (MDT, 93).

PUBLICS AND THE PROBLEM OF VIOLENCE

The most popular understanding of the relationship between publics and war in international relations is the notion of a liberal democratic *peace*. The domestic organization of publics in liberal democratic states is said to explain an important structural transformation of international politics—the absence of war between liberal regimes. Basic juridical respect for civil and political rights, the pacifying effects of trade, free and fair elections, few restrictions on freedom of speech and certain rights of protest and dissent are considered crucial features contributing to peaceful relations among liberal democracies (Doyle 1983). The assumed peacefulness of liberal states, certainly towards one another, is a key feature of international theory and this idea is mirrored in much contemporary political thought.

Our most influential political theories explicitly define 'the public' in direct opposition to force, violence, and war.[4] Liberal theory in particular treats the public as synonymous with civil society, which in Mary Kaldor's words, 'originally referred to the establishment of a domestic zone of peace, to the existence of legal, "civilized" non-violent ways of managing human affairs, in contrast to the barbaric war methods adopted externally' (1998: 93). War is considered a distinct phenomenon, separate from normal politics and liberal society. As such, political theory tends to be unmindful of how the national body politic is interrelated with the international and how modern liberal politics is intimately connected to justifications for war beyond the so-called liberal sphere of 'peace'.

Much critical theory similarly conceives the ideal public as devoid of forms of domination, including violence. 'The very concept of a "public sphere"', suggests Jim McGuigan, 'is to do with rational-critical discussion' (1996: 4). Habermas is famous for differentiating 'strategic action' from 'communicative action' oriented towards reaching mutual understanding. Strategic action is a form of 'systematically distorted communication' and can include the use of force. It is 'appropriate or inappropriate according to criteria of effective control' (2001*a*: 12). Communicative action, in contrast, is orientated towards reaching mutual understanding through language. It is dialogue aimed at consensus. In contrast to some forms of liberalism, where competition for public power occurs between rational actors and interests, Habermas posited that political legitimacy derived only from the communicative presuppositions of the political sphere itself.[5] The 'better' (more legitimate) argument will produce consensus in public only if the procedures for debate are fair. Undistorted conversation, Habermas argued, could be the means to political legitimation. A common commitment to dialogue and faith in publicity is considered the ideal mode of coming to terms with, if not settling, political disputes.

The category of the 'public' in Habermas's work is not just an abstract idea. It is also historical. In *The Structural Transformation of the Public Sphere*, he attempted a sociologically and historically grounded elucidation of the possibility for human emancipation through communication. In that book, Habermas famously identified the emergence of a critically reasoning bourgeois public in eighteenth-century Europe as the hoped for conduit of deliberative rationality. From the *salons* largely shaped by women to the male preserve of the coffee-houses and the world of letters emerged a public sphere, Habermas observed, among an elite avant-garde. Conversation on literature and art turned to matters economic and political. Significantly, this originary public was first and foremost a 'category of bourgeois society', as the subtitle of Habermas's work implies. This was the case not simply because the participants in public debate happened to be bourgeois. Rather one of the central political functions of the public was its role in forming the bourgeoisie's consciousness of itself *as* a 'society' (Warner 2002: 48).

Striking in its absence from Habermas's historical-sociology of the public that emerged in the salons and coffeehouses of Europe is its structural dependence on the global political context, in particular imperial relations of hierarchy and subordination. In marked contrast to Habermas, and as we discussed in Chapter 4, Arendt explicitly argued that the bourgeoisie's political emancipation—in Habermas's terminology, the formation of a critically reasoning public—was directly linked to the imperial international system. In *Origins of Totalitarianism*, she wrote, 'The bourgeoisie turned to politics . . . for it did not want to give up the capitalist system whose inherent law is constant economic growth, it had to impose this law . . . and to proclaim expansion to be an ultimate political goal of foreign policy' (OT, 126). The high-period of imperialism, she argued, was the first stage of bourgeois rule not the 'last stage of capitalism' (OT, 138). The public sphere of bourgeois debate that Habermas described—the historical evidence for his theory of communicative action— was brought into being, in part, in an effort to shape imperial foreign policy.[6]

Why is it significant that violent relations of imperial hierarchy were placed outside the historical sociology of the 'public' in Habermas's influential account? We have already noted the pacific bias in contemporary political the- ory and the more general failure of social theory to attend to the importance of military power and global social relations. Liberalism and some critical theories, especially those drawing on Habermas, locate violence outside the ideal public realm as barbaric and irrational. Why this fundamental separa- tion? We know that publics are intimately associated with and often dependent upon violence. Do more recent accounts of *global* publics, therefore, similarly overlook relations of global power and subordination in the effort to justify 'humanitarian' and cosmopolitan uses of military force? Arendt's insight con- cerning the imperial origins of the bourgeois public suggests we need to pay closer attention to the interaction between publics and contemporary Western war, often deemed a new form of imperialism by critics and supporters alike. The category of the public, as Habermas also recognizes, is not only a Western articulation of bourgeois forms of representation. It is constitutive of a social imaginary in which questions of war and peace are framed. Publics themselves can be founded in and through changing beliefs and practices about military force.

The emerging international theory literature on new forms of publics and political community is powerful and important. But we must ask what assumptions are drawn into the way in which international theorists under- stand politics (and war) when Habermas is considered the leading theorist of the public and when his ideas about cosmopolitan law-enforcement, the 'civilising' use of force in the name of humanity, is considered the best counter to US hegemony (Linklater 2005). Habermas's critical theory assumes that the public can only remain a place of rational communication as long as the use or threat of force is excluded. Otherwise discourse will be 'systematically distorted'. But Habermas's original historical sociology of the public ignored how the social conditions that made it possible depended on imperialism. His more recent construction of separate public spheres at the global level, one communicative (usually liberal-democratic and Western) and one strategic (usually undemocratic, barbaric, and non-Western) ought to be considered equally untenable.

The philosophical divergences between Arendt and Habermas have received a great deal of attention in political theory and do not require much further elaboration here (Canovan 1983). In 1969, she referred to Habermas as 'one of the most thoughtful and intelligent social scientists in Germany' (CR, 192n). He repaid the compliment by reading his own categories, not always accurately, onto Arendt's (Habermas 1983, 1996: 146–50).[7] But the concepts that she pointed to, violence and expansion, which Habermas and others have largely ignored when considering the 'structural transformation' of a global public, are precisely those useful for understanding the potential and actual violence of efforts to 'make' a global public realm.[8] Violence and publics are not radically divorced. Publics and the use of force should be considered as constitutively connected and historically codependent.

Recall the circularity of Habermas's justification for 'humanitarian war' over Kosovo in the absence of a fully evolved cosmopolitan morality. The use of force was justified because it was presumed to reflect the will of a rational global public debate on the issue. We must note some ambivalence in Habermas's endorsement of war. 'NATO's self-authorization cannot be permitted to become a matter of routine' (2000: 316). As he later put it, 'What from one angle appears to be progress on the path to the constitutionalization of international law, from another appears to be the successful imposition of imperial law' (2006: 180). Nonetheless, the Kosovo war had placed onto the 'agenda' the move from 'the "law of nations" into a law of world citizens' (2000: 307). How should we judge these claims about an imminent global public at the beginning of the twenty-first-century? That 'such a beginning', Arendt suggested, might 'be intimately connected with violence seems to be vouched for by the legendary beginnings of our history ... Cain slew Abel, and Romulus slew Remus; violence was the beginning and, by the same token, no beginning could be made without violence, without violating' (OR, 10; EU, 321). Do we find in Habermas continued adherence to these traditions? It does appear that the violent production of a global public, the founding *through war* of an imminent public at the global level, follows this 'politics-as-making' model. 'Humanitarian' war is justified in the effort to 'make' a global public realm.

POLITICS-AS-MAKING

To delineate more clearly Hannah Arendt's ideas about the dangers of conceiving politics as a form of 'making' we must review the conceptual distinction she drew between the activities of work and action.[9] We might best view

Arendt's phenomenological distinctions as ideal-types, a system she employed to think about politics and the mentalities and motives in which humans engage in the activity. Typical of Arendt, however, this was not phenomenological in the traditional sense that objects or phenomena can be analysed or reduced to their essence and experienced without the aid of prior theoretical commitments. Neither was her purpose to suggest that work and action constituted entirely separate realms of activity. Rather, she wished to suggest that when the activities and mentalities associated with one realm were transferred to the other they tended to institute their own ethic, their own reasoning and methods. There were real consequences of extending the mentalities appropriate to the realm of work, making and fabricating, to the ultimate measure of politics.

What did Arendt mean by 'work'? She described this as the human effort to create, to fabricate and make an artificial world of durable objects and things different from the natural earth. She built on the distinction between the natural environment of the earth, the lived place shared by all biological creatures, and the world, the space humans have made or constructed to inhabit. This is humanity as *homo faber*, a builder, a maker of things who 'conducts himself as lord and master of the whole earth' (HC, 139). *Homo faber* is creator of the human artifice. To engage in work is to rebel against the dictates of nature. *Homo faber* 'is master of himself' and the world (HC, 144). 'The human condition of work is worldliness' (HC, 7). The world occupied by humans includes cultural objects such as architecture and art. Arendt venerated the reification typified in works of art, which involved humans transforming the ephemeral into durable, worldly things (Frampton 1979; Steiner 2007). The artefacts that make the world our home are necessary to provide a place in which we then publicly appear.

The public represents two related but not identical things. First, in Arendt's words, it means 'that everybody that appears in public can be seen and heard by everybody and has the widest possible publicity' (HC, 50). This idea has affinities with Kant's writing on the critical use of public reason that was developed by Habermas in his theory of communicative action.[10] More importantly for Arendt, however, the public 'signifies the world itself, insofar as it is common to all of us and distinguished from our privately owned place in it'. She continued,

This world ... is not identical to the earth or with nature ... It is related, rather, to the human artifact, the fabrication of human hands, as well as to affairs that go on among those who inhabit the man-made world together ... the world, like every in-between, relates and separates men at the same time (HC, 52).

Political action is a specifically *worldly* and world-making activity. The sense of reality and stability accorded by the world is important if the political institutions and laws produced through political action are to endure. Without this 'space of appearance and without trusting in action and speech as a mode of being together, neither the reality of one's self, of one's own identity, nor the reality of the surrounding world can be established beyond doubt' (HC, 208). The world, as we have noted throughout this book, refers to the common space which is available for politics.

What is political 'action'? The ontological root of the faculty of action is natality, a concept Arendt borrowed from St Augustine's idea 'that a beginning be made man was created' (quoted in OT, 479). Humans are 'a being whose essence is beginning' (EU, 321). Arendt likened to a miracle this biological fact of human birth, that we enter the world as newcomers and begin a new world through birth. But this is a commonplace miracle; 'it is in our very nature to be beginners and hence to constitute beginnings throughout our lives' (LK, 13). These new beginnings are literally the political promise of freedom, the ability to bring into being something new. Arendt understood political action to be identical with freedom. More specifically, freedom is the ability to act with others to bring something new into the world, such as a new political space or public realm; 'without the fact of birth we would not even know what novelty is, all "action" would be either mere behavior or preservation' (CR, 179).

Political action has a definite beginning. But unlike 'work', it never 'has a predictable end' (HC, 144). We can never be sure of the consequences of our acts, dependent as they are on the actions and opinions of so many plural others. Action possesses a quality of unpredictability, changeability, and contingency. These are all characteristics of plurality, of the difference and human variability central to Arendt's thought. Political action requires a plurality of diverse actors and speakers. Through speech and action these men and women form a 'space in-between' them which can exist 'without the intermediary of things or matter' (HC, 7). As a form of work, the process of making is wholly shaped by things and matter, the material from which our worldly surroundings are built. But political action can occur unmediated directly between people linking them into a web of relationships. In this sense, it is also boundless and unpredictable; 'each relationship established by action ends up in a web of ties and relationships in which it triggers new links, changes the constellation of existing relationships, and thus always reaches out even further, setting much more into interconnected motion than the man who initiates action could ever have foreseen' (PP, 186–7).

Political action is episodic, fragile, and unpredictable and political actors rarely gain what they set out to achieve. The ability to begin something new, to initiate unprecedented processes means that (once set in motion) action cannot be controlled or predicted. The effort to control or predict is always overrun by the nature of political action, 'where', in Arendt's words, 'nothing happens more frequently than the totally unexpected'—the event itself (HC, 300). We can never reliably predict the future or predetermine what is going to happen because 'the world is daily renewed through birth and is constantly dragged into what is unpredictably new by the spontaneity of each new arrival' (PP, 127). There is something truly great in our capacity for political action and the creation of real spaces for public freedom. But there is also pathos, even tragedy. If political freedom to act and to create new beginnings is the essence of politics, then in few places do we 'appear to be less free than in those capacities whose very essence is freedom and in that realm which owes its existence to nobody and nothing but man' (HC, 234).

Given the unpredictability and frailty of human affairs, numerous philosophers have searched for a substitute for political action to avoid these frustrations. By conflating action with the activities and mentalities associated with work philosophy has sought to control it. Recall the previous discussion of Leo Strauss and his effort to construct universally valid grounds for political order (Chapter 7). This was possible, he believed, because the 'knowledge of the political philosopher is "transferable" to the highest degree' and he cited as evidence Plato's frequent comparisons between 'political science and medicine' (Strauss 1989: 54). Arendt traced forward from Plato to much of the so-called political philosophy tradition 'the consequences of seeing in *homo faber* the highest human possibility' (HC, 157). It is 'so-called' political philosophy because, for Arendt, many of its 'political standards were derived not from politics but from philosophy' (PP, 130).[11] Plato's displeasure with democratic political action after the trial and death of Socrates led him to seek higher 'true' standards to contain its unruly character.

The idea of true standards to eliminate the consequences of action was made possible through the imposition of the more solid and reliable categories associated with work which we use to build the human-made world. Work requires a model, an *idea*, to guide the effort involved in making and fabricating and from 'which the object is constructed' (HC, 140). The making involved in work offers an important element of enduring predictability in the world, even repetition and reality, compared with the changeability and unpredictability of political events. The activity of work, of making, also involves violence to things through their alteration or destruction. 'This element of violation and violence', Arendt wrote, 'is present in all fabrication, and *homo faber*, the creator of the human artifice, has always been a destroyer of nature' (HC, 139). This is why when we think of political action as a form of 'making' it is difficult not to view the political sphere as essentially violent. The effect is that politics has almost always been discussed by using the instrumental terminology of means and ends.

Work is determined by the relationship between means and ends. The ends justify the means. Indeed, as Arendt wrote, 'it does more, it produces and organizes them. The end justifies the violence done to nature to win the material, as the wood justifies killing the tree and the table justifies destroying the wood' (HC, 153). Politics itself can be seen as simply a means to an end. Rather than viewing politics as an end in itself, it is viewed 'in terms of an end purpose lying outside of politics' (PP, 152). The *ends* of an activity 'are as firmly defined as the model on which any physical object is produced and like it determine the choice of means and justify and even sanctify them' (PP, 193). Arendt understood political action as containing within it a unique meaning which exists for as long as the action lasts. But this meaningfulness is in danger of being overawed by the power of instrumentality 'whose meaningfulness', she wrote, 'ends the moment the end-product is finished: single events and deeds and sufferings have no more meaning here than hammer and nails have with respect to the finished table' (BPF, 80).

Arendt took the unusual step of rejecting the commonplace categories of means and ends, which places her at odds with the dominant conceptualizations of political ethics and war. Strategic theory believes itself to be ethical to the extent that it seeks to relate the practice of war to the ends of more or less legitimate state policy (Gray 1999). The just war tradition goes a step further, asking soldiers and statesmen to fight well by ensuring that the violent means are compatible with a just end.[12] Political realism conceives of the political in instrumental terms; to be political is to responsibly use violence when necessary to achieve already determined ends (Weber 1946).[13] Max Weber's sobering judgment is that the choice of end is ultimately arbitrary, but to have one's hand on the 'wheel of history' you *must choose* (1946: 115). This 'ethic of responsibility' holds that the political actor must accept the reality of dirty hands; to be political is sometimes to do evil. But the lesser evil must always be chosen and it should never be accompanied by self-aggrandizement or appeals to high-minded principles.

The ever-present danger that politics could degenerate into the sponsorship of evil was a constant preoccupation of Arendt's work. In the political sphere, she believed, it was the means that always count the most. 'Every good action for the sake of a bad end', she wrote, 'actually adds to the world a portion of goodness; every bad action for the sake of a good end actually adds to the world a portion of badness' (MDT, 148). Violence could be justified and was rational only for short-term ends, but she did not write about this in terms of being the lesser of evils (JW, 166–7); and she wholly rejected any criteria for weighing up the lives of the dead. 'This sounds to me like the last version of human sacrifices: pick seven virgins, sacrifice them to placate the wrath of gods. Well, this is not my religious belief' (quoted in Young-Bruehl 1982: 374). Arendt's divergence from the 'ethic of responsibility' had nothing to do with any support for an ethic of 'ultimate ends', however. Rather she believed that efforts to relate means and ends in the specifically *political* sphere fail to properly understand 'what politics is about'—the plurality of men and women coming together to talk and initiate action in concert. The danger of thinking about politics in terms of making, where there is an end *outside* the political realm including ends such as justice and equality, is that the end can be quickly overwhelmed by violent means. The moral and political results are disastrous: effective action is equated with violence.

It was Arendt's view that 'in the context of expedient action, where nothing counts except the achievement of postulated and fixed ends, brute force will always play a major role' (PP, 194). Political power, in contrast, is that which is constituted *in-between* people, the 'realm of appearances', not 'things' to be shaped, owned, or achieved as if it was a preconceived end. Power can never be possessed like a gun. It is *an end in itself*. In the political realm, nothing passes 'back and forth except speech, which is devoid of tangible means' (PP, 193). Even if non-violent political action, such as civil disobedience, fails to achieve its goal, for example of disrupting the use of a port for military purposes, the action is not without a point or a meaning. Political action has no other point than the action itself and therefore cannot be judged by the criteria of success or failure. Even if it fails, political action is never meaningless. Through the very action or 'back-and-forth of exchanged speech' a public space is created (PP, 193).

Conceiving political action as a form of 'making' has made ordinary the violence in politics. This is clearly demonstrated in the history of revolutionary political founding. There is an important relationship between Arendt's ideas about natality and new beginnings and the question of political founding, the establishment of a new public realm. It is evident in her writing on the French, American, and Hungarian Revolutions. She traced the origins of this practice back to classical Rome. 'The same linkage between being free and beginning something', she noted, 'is found in the Roman idea that the greatness of the forebears was contained in the founding of Rome, and that the freedom of the Romans always had to be traced to this founding' (PP, 126). Arendt also observed that it was Machiavelli, an admirer of the Roman achievement of founding a stable republic, who made the classic statement on the association between this form of political action and violence. Machiavelli viewed revolutionary founding as the central political act. He wrote of the experience of founding a new political apparatus in the absence of authoritative principles or god and famously believed 'that for this supreme "end" all "means", and chiefly the means of violence, were justified' (BPF, 139; OR, 29).

In linking violence to the greatness of political founding Arendt believed Machiavelli undertook a heroic but misguided effort 'to save violence from disgrace' (BPF, 22). For the violence involved in founding and maintaining the republic seemed inherently plausible: 'You cannot make a table without killing trees, you cannot make an omelette without breaking eggs, you cannot make a republic without killing people' (BPF, 139). Machiavelli's 'realist' contention that politics and violence were two sides of the same coin expressed *not* his 'so-called realistic insight into human nature', Arendt argued. Rather, it represented nothing more than 'his futile hope that he could find some quality in certain men to match the qualities we associate with the divine' (OR, 32). The 'Machiavellian' justification of violence derived from the revolutionary effort to found a republic in the absence of traditional morality or appeals to God. The justification of violence came from his search for a 'new absolute' (violence) upon which to ground politics. He showed 'the same combination of the old Roman enthusiasm for the foundation of a new body politic with the glorification of violence as the only means for "making" it' (HC, 228). Machiavelli identified the act of founding a new political realm with making.[14]

Much of Arendt's work can be read as a struggle against 'the age-old attempt to escape from the frustration and fragility of human action by construing it in the image of making' (BPF, 79). This conception underpins not only the effort of revolutionaries to found a republic. Habermas's search for a 'new absolute' upon which to ground world politics, a global republic of world citizens instead of US hegemony, similarly tries but has thus far failed to elide violence. 'Whenever we hear of grandiose aims in politics' Arendt observed, 'such as establishing a new society in which justice will be guaranteed forever, or fighting a war to end all wars or make the whole world safe for democracy, we are moving in the realm of his kind of thinking' (BPF, 79). Habermas's effort to found a global public of world citizens in the absence of traditional authority has led to an admiration for 'humanitarian' violence as one of the principle means to 'make' it.

'MAKING' A GLOBAL PUBLIC REALM?

Habermas's original theory of the public sphere was derived from what he took to be major social and political trends towards democracy in Europe. Similarly, he argues that the possible emergence of a new global public is connected to broader global trends, including the effort to regulate and justify 'humanitarian' military force. Social change in the global realm, he argues, may follow a path that largely replicates how political struggle developed in the democracies of the industrialized West. The growth of supra-territorial political spaces is 'simply the continuation of a process of which the function of integration performed by the nation-state provided the first major example' (1998*a*: 399). The history of European political development is certainly suggestive of the mechanisms by which it is possible to move from the era of classical power politics to a new era of world citizenship. The vital question is whether Habermas's interpretation of that political history is correct and complete. Any theory of emerging global publics must include an account of the changing character of war and mobilization of military power. But does Habermas go far enough in analysing the relationship between publics and war?

In the major European conflicts of the eighteenth- and nineteenth-century, the newly emerging power of 'public opinion' was mobilized in preparation for war. We know that the very idea of distinct territorially defined national-publics was itself partly constituted through the heightened patriotism attendant war-preparation (Giddens 1995).[15] The grounds for the political unity of peoples within nation-states went beyond merely pragmatic approval of the existing order. The cult of nationalism was far more effective in binding society together and individuals to the state. Arendt understood this political function and feared for the survival of political, public life independent from the 'tremendous business concern' that the national territorial state had become (OT, 17). She argued that political identification with the nation served to transform the potentially heterogeneous assortment of political opinions into a seemingly—though illusory—homogenous national interest. Here, once again, Arendt is close to Marx. She noted that ' "The Army", as Marx pointed out, "was the 'point of honor' with the allotment farmers: it was themselves turned into masters, defending abroad their newly established property...The uniform was their state costume, war was their poetry; the allotment was their fatherland, and patriotism became the ideal form of property" ' (quoted in OT, 229). Modern states mobilized citizens for war precisely in these national-patriotic terms.

Noting that the 'national institution *par excellence*' was the 'the army' (OT, 259), Arendt understood the importance of war in the formation of both states and national consciousness; 'the seldom-admitted stock-in-trade of national politics in the nineteenth and twentieth centuries', she wrote, was that it took 'the presence of the enemy [for] such a thing as *la nation une et indivisible*...[to] come to pass' (OR, 72). Hobbes, Machiavelli, and Rousseau all took for granted and required for their political theories a unifying common enemy. The fostering of this national consciousness was integral to the ability of states to mobilize for war, which in turn shaped the emergence of states as increasingly 'the total domain of the political' (BPF, 150). Popular allegiance to the nation—aided by multiple wars—would offset non-state fidelity to class. Rather than the labouring classes identifying themselves as such, modern society largely became 'identified', in Arendt's words, 'with a privately owned piece of the world . . . with a tangible, albeit collectively owned, piece of property, the territory of the nation-state' (HC, 256).

Arendt wrote of the 'conquest of the state by the nation' (OT, 230), of the defeat of potentially civic-republican institutions by notions of common origins. For Habermas, the establishment of 'post-national' constitutionalism, the seeds of a global public sphere, is equated with overcoming the patriotic and nationalist appeals historically needed to supplement democratic citizenship. The nation-state once offered 'a cogent response to the historical challenge of finding a functional equivalent for the early modern form of social integration that was . . . disintegrating. Today we are confronting an analogous challenge' (Habermas 1998a: 398). Where appeals to nationalism once served as a legitimating mechanism for binding individuals to the modern state and sending them off to war, nowadays 'republicanism must learn to stand on its own feet' (1998a: 408). If the territorial link between the nation-state and public is to be severed, then the search for a constitutional rather than a national patriotism is under way. The principle of 'humanitarian' war is significant because it represents how military power might be mobilized and regulated in a 'post-national' world.

The expansion of global public space has been accompanied by new demands for the legitimization and control of violence. Mary Kaldor, for example, has analysed how this process of legitimation and control may, in turn, require 'a far-reaching cultural transformation' (1998: 108). Absolutely crucial, she writes, is 'whether the capacity for regulating violence can be reinstated in some new way on a transnational basis and whether barbarism can be checked by an alert and active cosmopolitan citizenry' (1998: 109). Barbarism must be checked. For Kaldor and Habermas, this is why we need the global regulation of military force. The establishment of a global public is not only considered necessary to check the imperial urges of the United States and provide a foundation for 'humanitarian intervention'. Legally sanctioned, globally regulated police operations can counter religiously inspired terror networks. We need global law-enforcement of various kinds, not national war-fighting (Kaldor 1998, 2001, 2003: ch. 6; Habermas 2006: 184).

The emergence of global publics and the origins of 'humanitarian war' are understood as driven by struggles for 'post-national' republican citizenship and the end of ethnic cleansing. To fight a war in the name of humanity is to pursue not a nationalist, but a civic justification for the use of force. Such wars have been read as occasions in which violence is legitimated by the conscience of a global public, rather than the narrow interests and ideologies of hegemonic states. On this view, the Kosovo war, in particular, was fought for the civic goal of ending human suffering. So conceived, it constituted the first 'post-national' war (Beck 2002: 61), an example of 'good international citizenship' (Linklater 2000). As already suggested, this argument requires an extraordinary feat of revisionist history. It requires a reading of NATO's Kosovo intervention that the facts about the war do not support (Booth 2000; Bacevitch and Cohen 2001). Even so, it is worth investigating the *principle* for action as outlined by Habermas and others.

It has been argued that humanitarian intervention is justified as a response 'to acts "that shock the conscience of mankind" ' (Walzer 1992: 107). But how is this conscience manifest? There is a more unsettling possibility than the more common account of the power of global media to reveal worldwide suffering and conscience. It is possible that to come into existence, a global public sphere, like the national identities of nation-states, may actually *depend* upon violence. Civic patriotism in a global context might not only, or even, be the outcome of a sense of obligation to others and the commitment to end certain forms of human suffering. It is possible that such obligations are produced *through* the use of violence. Any global public, like the publics of nation-states before them, may require 'various forms of violent mobilization', as Arjun Appadurai suggests, 'in order to "produce the people" ', of the global public (1998: 447). You cannot 'make' a global public sphere, as Arendt might put it, without killing people.

Arendt's ideas pose a series of challenges to the visions of Habermas and others on the possibilities of reorganizing global institutions. However, the purpose of this questioning is not to suggest that we abandon all projects related to global political reform. Arendt was aware that the idea of humanity is no longer just 'a regulative ideal', as it was for Kant. It 'has today become an inescapable fact' (OT, 298).[16] But this is a warning as much as an opportunity. Consider the idea of a global police force. As early as 1957, Arendt imagined a world in which 'various armies with their old traditions and more or less respected codes of honor would be replaced by federated police forces'. The problem, she continued, is that 'our experiences with modern police states and totalitarian governments, where the old power of the army is eclipsed by the rising omnipotence of the police, are not apt to make us overoptimistic about this prospect' (MDT, 94). Habermas may object that his republic of world citizens would be very different in design and intent to the police state Arendt depicted. The question is whether the global regulation of military power would replicate sovereign domination (control over 'legitimate' violence) at the highest level of abstraction.

World government was not impossible, according to Arendt; it was indeed a matter of projecting the key functions of the state upwards. International Relations theorist Alexander Wendt shares this view and goes even further than Arendt. A world state, defined as possessing the global monopoly on the use of legitimate violence, is inevitable given the logic of international anarchy and the tendency for military technology to become ever more destructive (Wendt 2003). Arendt, too, believed that 'the most potent symbol of the unity of mankind' (MDT, 83) was the possible use of atomic weapons. But the formation of a world government in response, or for any other reason, may be almost as disastrous. '*No matter what form . . .*' it might take, Arendt wrote,

the very notion of one sovereign force ruling the whole earth, holding the monopoly of all means of violence, unchecked and uncontrolled by other sovereign powers, is not only a forbidding nightmare of tyranny, it would be the end of all political life as we know it . . . Politics deals with men, nationals of many countries and heirs to many pasts; its laws are the positively established fences which hedge in, protect, and limit the space in which freedom is not a concept, but a living political reality (MDT, 81–2, emphasis added).[17]

What does it mean for a political entity to hold the monopoly on the legitimate use of violence? Is this not the very definition of a world government or state?

For Habermas, the specific institutional design of any future cosmopolitan law should dispel such dangers and fears. The domestication of global politics is possible in a federal and multilayered world republic without all that is implied in Arendt's 'forbidding nightmare of tyranny'. A global political constitution, even one in control of legitimate violence, need not replicate 'the character of a state *as a whole*' and may still 'perform the vital but clearly circumscribed functions of securing peace and promoting human rights at the *supranational* level' (Habermas 2006: 136). But this is an assertion of a possibility. It demonstrates a *hope* that world government will not emerge when the capacity to regulate all legitimate uses of force is achieved. We will never know until the political experiment is tried. In the least, Arendt's writing suggests we ought to resist the urge to justify 'humanitarian' military force as part of a scheme to find out.

There is a clear overlap, but also an important difference, between Arendt's concerns about grand schemes of political transformation and the powerful warnings of Carl Schmitt. In 1951, she explicitly observed that by fighting a war on behalf of civilization or some other ultimate end, 'by applying the absolute—justice, for example, or the "ideal" in general . . . to an *end*, one first makes unjust, bestial actions possible, because the "ideal", justice itself, no longer exists as a yardstick, but has become an achievable, producible end within the world' (PP, 3). Schmitt issued a similarly powerful warning in 1932. War in the name of humanity, he wrote, 'is necessarily and unusually intense and inhuman because, by transcending the limits of the political framework, it simultaneously degrades the enemy into moral and other categories and is forced to make of him a monster that must not only be defeated but also utterly destroyed... [;] he is an enemy who no longer must be compelled to retreat into his borders only' (1996: 36). Both Schmitt and Arendt shared a belief that moralism in political and international affairs could only lead to disillusionment and the further intensification and brutalization of war. For Arendt, violence is only rational to achieve immediate and short-term ends, such as ending ethnic cleansing or genocide, not abstract goals of any kind.

Habermas believes such concerns can be sidestepped by turning the justificatory discourse of war away from the absolutist language of right and wrong. It must become a question of legal procedure. We must 'juridify' rather than 'moralise' war. 'Legal wars thereby take on the significance of global police operations' (2006: 189). For Schmitt, such a move is an impossibility given the nature of the political itself. The rationalization or juridification of politics—and war—does nothing to resolve the 'irreducible antagonism' between political entities in a world that recognizes no one sovereign. Such conflict can never be escaped. Arendt too argued that conflict of a certain kind can never or should never be avoided. But this was not a struggle to death between enemies. Unlike Schmitt, Arendt believed that the solidarity of mankind was indeed possible.[18] Yet, unlike Habermas, she rejected the notion of world citizenship and the extension of models of citizenship to a global scale.

Habermas has envisaged any 'cosmopolitan law as a law of *individuals*' rather than political communities (2006: 124).[19] Arendt's cosmopolitanism is more modest. 'Nobody can be a citizen of the world as he is a citizen of his country'. All things political are so by virtue of their dependence 'on plurality, diversity, and mutual limitations' (MDT, 81). Being an inhabitant of the earth is not the same as being a citizen of the world. One does not follow from the other, nor should it. The 'rights and duties' of citizenship, she believed, 'must be defined and limited, not only by those of his fellow citizens, but also by the boundaries of a territory' (MDT, 81). Arendt's was a politics of limits. A federated political structure more akin to Kant's 'republic of republics' is certainly compatible with her views. Indeed, such a 'framework of universal mutual agreements', she believed, was sketched in the writing of her mentor and friend, Karl Jaspers (MDT, 93). A voluntary association between republics is not the same as a global republic. It is a republic of republics, a world of *inter*national or rather inter-republic law that is the only justifiable limitation on the political world. Anything else might indeed mean the literal end of world politics.[20]

CONCLUSION

Arendt died in 1975. She did not see the end of the Cold War or witness the excitement of many about the potential for UN- and/or US-led (selective) action to prevent or end acts of ethnic cleansing. She was not a pacifist and considered genocide the worst political crime, an attack on the very basis of politics which is human diversity. Genocide destroys the very possibility of a political world. There is no doubt that she would have supported the principle of military action for the immediate and short-term goal of stopping it, as she supported an international criminal court to try and punish those responsible.[21] This was the *only* criteria for a 'necessary war' (OT, 442). All other war should be ruled out if in practice it resulted in a challenge to any 'actually existing solidarity of mankind' (MDT, 93). Conduct *in war* should also never be such that it would rule out future 'peace and reconciliation'.[22] It is for this reason, and not for any moral purpose per se, that war must be excluded from 'the arsenal of political means... because each war, no matter how limited in the use of means and in territory, immediately and directly affects all mankind' (MDT, 93).

Arendt was no less a critic of the imperial pretensions of the United States in her day than Habermas is in ours. But her response was emphatically not to replace one grand scheme of global political and military transformation with another. She was suspicious of all such radical and ideologically mandated efforts to transform political community. Arendt never outlined any sort of institutional design or framework for a worldwide federated structure, nor did she believe that any such world would lead to 'perpetual peace'.[23] She did offer multiple examples of both violent and non-violent political foundings that are very different from the bourgeois 'public sphere' that Habermas described. Her interest in evoking the memory of the formation of these councils and small-scale republics suggests her very different and more satisfying political sensibility.[24] The spontaneously formed popular bodies she described represented public spaces for discussion and action about common affairs that need not be limited by national boundaries. The only limits were to be found in the nature of the political realm itself, boundaries, laws, and other people.

Habermas hopes that 'humanitarian' war might produce (or bring forth) the very people (a global public) on whose behest he imagines them to be fought. Arendt reminds us that public, political action is world making. But this does not mean that we can or should seek to make a public that covers the entire world. The humanitarian condition of global political action does not exist. Habermas and his followers in international theory too readily turn to the idea of politics as a form of making in their effort to found a global public realm. The turn to humanitarian war as part of this effort would probably not have surprised Arendt. We do know that she viewed violence as rational only if it could be justified to others in terms of immediate and short-term ends. There is no justification of violence as such, only a sad acceptance of the demand for and attraction of violence to achieve *concrete* goals. A global public sphere is certainly 'an achievable, producible end within the world'. Yet the practical achievement of such an end as part of the justification for military action would have struck Arendt as an inhuman abstraction. The very founding of publics, including those at the global level, can be productive of the violence the creation of a public ostensibly sought to banish.

The idea that the use of force in response to genocide or ethnic cleansing must in some way, or should in some way, contribute to any grander project is an anathema to how Arendt understood the relationship between politics and war. Rather than conceive new discourses of a global public as a necessarily progressive response to US hegemony, Arendt helps us to address the potentially violent politics in the making of public realms. There is indeed much at stake in the debate between Habermas's critical theory and followers of neoconservatism over the proper legitimation of humanitarian war, including the very foundations of politics. There are various kinds of cosmopolitanism, some more genuine than others. The neoconservative agenda has already been discredited, but not by any competing theory. It has been damaged only by its confrontation with facts and events in Iraq. This is surely too costly a way to test our political theories. Arendt was significantly more cognisant of the difficult relationship between organized violence and the political than neoconservatism *and* Habermas's version of critical theory. If we listen to Arendt we will not even try the greater and potentially even more dangerous political experiment of 'making' one global public realm.

Conclusion

The lifespan of man running towards death would inevitably carry everything human to ruin and destruction if it were not for the faculty of
interrupting it and beginning something new, a faculty which is inherent
in action like an ever-present reminder that men, though they may die,
are not born in order to die but in order to begin.

—Arendt, *The Human Condition*, p. 246

Hannah Arendt's political theory makes more sense when it is understood in
the context of her thinking about war and we can think about the history
and theory of warfare in new ways by thinking with Arendt. She enables
us to come to the study of war from the perspective of its political origins
and consequences for how we think and act in the world. She helps political
and international theorists to approach the question of war with the simple
assumption that political thought 'arises out of... living experience and must
remain bound to them as the only guideposts by which to take its bearings'
(BPF, 14). This is why Arendt scholars and political theorists must be more
mindful of war. War fascinates because its myths and lies are so powerful;
because as Heraclitus saw it, war may indeed be 'the father of all things';
because it is life and death in the extreme; because it both produces and
destroys the political world; because the 'greatest fascination' with war, as
Arendt believed, was that it 'compresses the greatest opposites into the smallest
place and the shortest time' (1970*a*: xi).

War is of interest for the instrumental reason that it stops political and international theorists from lapsing into abstract thinking. It helps us to 'unlearn'
'simplification' and 'to become fluent in the art and the language of "concrete"
thoughts and feelings'. It encourages engaged social criticism of what is. Of
course, Arendt also understood that war itself is prone to some of the sins of
abstract thinking and romanticization—'the love and hatred of collectives—
my own people, the enemy' (1970*a*: viii). For that reason she offers us a model
for thinking theoretically, but also concretely about war. Abstract notions,
but especially abstract emotions, were heavily criticized throughout Arendt's
work. From accounts of the experiences of men in battle she learned that 'the

closer you were to the enemy, the less did you hate him...unless, of course, the soldier happens to be a killer, and only pacifists who hold abstract notions and emotions about war will mistake the one for the other' (1970*a*: ix).

Comment on war can easily be reduced to simplification, the kind of easy moral judgements for which Arendt had little time. Abstractions such as the love of one's own people or hatred of an enemy people indicated nothing but departure from reality and are 'false to what actually happens' (1970*a*: viii). But the solution to this problem, Arendt believed, was not to move to the highest level of abstraction, to the love of mankind in general. Allegiances of this kind are also a product of alienation from worldly reality; indeed, 'mankind collectively...is doubtless as predisposed to injustice as nations are' (Gray in Arendt 1970*a*: ix). Disillusionment with nationalism, or worse, the state of human suffering—about which we appear incapable of meaningful action— may make allegiance to humankind and an associated ethic of humanitarianism seem like the only appropriate response. And yet the abstract thinking necessary to conjure this humanitarianism may be used to justify wars that are as unjust, possibly even more brutal, than wars of liberation or national self-defence.

Arendt's thought, as well as the manner of her thinking, continues to inspire and enable others to make concrete interventions into debates about the changing character of war. This book has suggested how she helps us explore the importance of distinguishing politics from war; why we should reject the common conflation of power with violence; and how violence can mutate from an instrument for achieving policy to an even more destructive end in itself. She drew on Thucydides' telling of the Peloponnesian War and Homer's account of the Trojan War to recover a form of historiography with surprising ethical implications. Arendt wrote with great conviction and perceptiveness on the Vietnam War, including the dangers of the 'boomerang' effects from aggressive foreign policy. She drew powerful—and rather contemporary feeling—connections between nineteenth-century imperialism and twentieth-century total war in Europe and between the Greek and the Roman understandings of politics, law, and war. Arendt's writing speaks directly to contemporary public policy on insurgency; suicide bombing; wars of annihilation and genocide; the laws of war and civilian casualties; the dangers of lies and hypocrisy in wartime; and the perils as well as the progressive possibilities of forms of war that might unite instead of destroy humankind.

It may be necessary now, more than ever, to learn how to think with Arendt, a time that has delivered us moral and political catastrophes, which while not exceeding her day, strongly resemble and are directly linked to those she directly confronted. Post-colonial conflicts, revolutions, and occupations, wars of annihilation and crimes against humanity, anti-Semitism,

Islamophobia, and accusations of Islamo-fascism—these are among the social forces relating and separating peoples and states through organized violence. War is interesting, as Arendt might suggest, 'in the word's most literal significance, something which *inter-est*, which lies between people and therefore can relate and bind them together' (HC, 182; Elshtain 1987: 166). Arendt's mode of thinking, the way she would 'look upon contemporary events with the backward-directed glance of the historian and the analytical zeal of the political scientist' (OT, xxiii), remains as necessary as ever.

'There are many routes to accommodation with the powers that be', Arendt wrote in 1945. 'The only people who will count are those who refuse to identify themselves with either an ideology or a power' (AJ, 23). Freedom itself has become a central trope in the ideology of the greatest power on earth. But freedom is not just ideology. Arendt wrote *On Revolution* instead of a book on war because inherent to revolutionary action was the thirst for public freedom. Unlike revolution, war requires justification in terms of the ends it must pursue. Freedom is an absolute. It needs no other justification. For some time now, the most popular Western justification for war has been freedom. Arendt too believed that freedom was war's 'only possible justification'. But we are describing two very different conceptions. It was truly 'astounding', Arendt wrote in 1963, 'to watch how ... the idea of freedom has intruded itself into ... the discussion of war' when the very existence of all human life was at stake from a nuclear detonation (OR, 2). The language of freedom was an excuse, Arendt insisted, 'to justify what on rational grounds has become unjustifiable' (OR, 4).

In the mouth of government strategists, freedom is at best an empty cliché. At worst it is considered an achievable end-product that can be delivered through force. This march towards (or forward strategy of) freedom appears like some 'essentially assured progress ... which is only temporarily interrupted by some dark forces of the past' (BPF, 97). Both politics and war are reduced to the mere means through which 'freedom' is attained. The defeat of 'dark forces' is the goal. If freedom possesses some content, then it is the negative liberty of security necessary for elections and the principal agenda is 'freedom from' certain forms of threat. This is a powerful language but it is nonsense, a familiar intrusion into the debate about war; a language that ultimately glorifies the violence of the powers that be. In Arendt's terms, freedom is none of those things. It cannot be an end of politics or war. Politics and freedom, public freedom, are fundamentally ends themselves. Freedom is action with others 'to call something into being which did not exist before' (BPF, 151). It is the very meaning of politics, not its end.

Arendt admired J. Glenn Gray, the author of *The Warriors*, for the same reason we must admire Arendt: she 'makes opposition to war forceful and convincing by not denying the realities and by not warning us but making us understand why "there is in many today as great a fear of a sterile and unexciting peace as of a great war" ' (1970*a*: xii). We must admire Arendt because she wrote about the wrongs of war while never denying its attractiveness and what it sometimes could achieve. She sought to understand this appeal. She learned from it. And yet Arendt's ultimate heroes, those who cared for the public world the most, were the men and women who took to the streets to demand an end not to all wars but to one or more concrete acts of unjustifiable violence. When she first arrived in the United States she found that 'The republic is not a vapid illusion' (AJ, 30). Within a few years of the Cold War, when the republic was suffering deep crises, she believed that it was dissent against war that offered the best hope. It was the civil disobedients against war that would ensure the republic was not destroyed in an aggressive imperial war. It was the civil disobedients, those who acted for a cause outside themselves, who were truly great. It was they who understood the meaning of freedom. And it was they who were clearest about what they are fighting for, the *res publica* itself. If war brings 'ruin and destruction' to the human condition, then civil action and disobedience interrupt this like a new insertion into the world. It is they who end the 'ominous silence that answers us whenever we dare to ask, not "What are we fighting *against*" but "What are we fighting *for*?" ' (BPF, 27).

Notes

NOTES TO CHAPTER 1

1. The essay originally appeared in small book form and was reprinted in *Crises of the Republic*, which contains other essays written by Arendt including a response to the publication of the Pentagon Papers in 1971, the US government account of the decision-making during the Vietnam War. All references to 'On Violence' are to the version in *Crises of the Republic*.
2. In a 1954 essay 'Europe and the Atom Bomb', Arendt wrote, 'With the appearance of nuclear weapons, both the Hebrew–Christian limitation on violence and the ancient appeal to courage have for all practical purposes become meaningless, and, with them, the whole political and moral vocabulary in which we are accustomed to discuss these matters' (EU, 421).
3. Perhaps Arendt's two biggest flaws as a thinker are her utter neglect of the importance of sexism and patriarchy in shaping politics and society and her misunderstanding of black radicals in 1960s America. Arendt praised the student movements of the 1960s, describing their action as a 'real danger to the status quo precisely because it strikes at the heart of genuine political life. I can only say with Jefferson: *Centerum censeo*—the ward or council system of small republics where everyone has a voice in public affairs' (AJ, 583). In contrast, some of her comments in the same essay about black students are simply racist. Also, in a somewhat contradictory fashion to her identification as a Jew, Arendt believed that being a woman was politically irrelevant. But in the words of Bonnie Honig, 'Once we stop focusing exclusively on whether Arendt was properly attentive to women and their "experience", we can ask what resources, if any, Arendt has to offer a feminist theory and politics whose constituency is diverse and often fractious' (1995: 3; also see Dietz 2002).
4. Edward Shils and Morris Janowitz (1948) argued that low levels of breakup and collapse among the German army on the Eastern Front is explained by high levels of group cohesion, loyalty to the primary group. This is disputed by Omer Bartov (2001), who suggests that there could be no unit cohesion. Death rates were too high. It was ideological indoctrination that explains why German soldiers continued to fight under such dreadful conditions against Russian troops. Social science also calls into question the methodology behind the claim that because soldiers describe comradeship as their main motivation for fighting and fighting well this makes it so. Task cohesion, the belief in the validity of the common goal, and a desire to coordinate to achieve that goal are the best indicators of combat effectiveness (MacCoun, Kier, and Belkin 2006). This argument supports the claim that the open integration of homosexuals into the US military would not hurt combat effectiveness (Kier 1998).

5. Arendt also made some odd assertions, for example, that in the Western hemisphere 'generals are among the most peace-loving and least dangerous creatures' (1958*b*: 18).

6. Arendt also found that such functionaries, just like most regular soldiers, 'were not sadists or killers by nature' (EJ, 105). The 'great criminal of the twentieth century', those who planned, organized, and carried out the Final Solution, was not a fanatic of any sort. 'It became clear that for the sake of his pension, his life insurance, the security of his wife and children, such a man was ready to sacrifice his beliefs, his honor, and his human dignity' (EU, 128). The motives that led people to participate in mass murder were clear to her as early as 1945. There was no need, she wrote, to indulge in 'speculations about German history and the so-called German national character...There is more to be learned from the characteristic personality of the man who can boast that he was the organizing spirit of the murder. Heinrich Himmler...is a "bourgeois" with all the outer aspect of respectability, all the habits of the good *paterfamilias* who does not betray his wife and anxiously seeks to secure a decent future for his children, and he has consciously built up his newest terror organization...on the assumption that most people are...first and foremost jobholders, and good family men...It needed only the Satanic genius of Himmler to discover that after such degradation he was entirely prepared to do literally anything when the ante was raised and the bare existence of his family was threatened' (EU, 128).

NOTES TO CHAPTER 2

1. All quotes in this paragraph are taken from a speech Arendt delivered in Copenhagen, Denmark in 1975. It is digitally available from the Hannah Arendt Papers at the Library of Congress, United States, http://memory.loc.gov/ammem/arendthtml/arendthome.html

2. Arendt explained that 'when the Nazis demanded first only stateless persons for deportation, i.e. German refugees who they had deprived of their nationality, the Danes explained that because the refugees were no longer German citizens, the Nazis could not claim them without Danish ascent'. Arendt neglected to mention their collaboration with the Nazis in relation to Communists who *were* transported to internment camps.

3. Arendt challenged Franz Borkenau's argument that reactionary powers would inevitably defeat all popular revolutions in the post–Second World War period with 'the most modern, most efficient, most ruthless machinery yet in existence. It means that the age of revolutions free to evolve according to their own laws is over' (Borkenau quoted in CR, 146*f*). Arendt was less impressed by the power of technology. 'The fact is', she wrote, 'that the gap between state-owned means of violence and what people can muster by themselves—from beer bottles to Molotov cocktails and guns—has *always* been so enormous that technical improvements make hardly any difference' (CR, 147, emphasis added).

4. The anarchistic elements in Arendt's thought are discussed by Isaac (1992: 11). Arendt's description of the role of the workers' councils during the Hungarian Revolution is troubling for Joel Olson's conclusion that 'Arendt's critique of the revolutionary tradition cannot account for the fact that the Spanish Revolution's spontaneity sprang from the long-standing activities of the working class' (1997: 486; also see OT, 189).

5. Arendt did not understand revolution to be solely a two-way struggle between the revolutionists and the old regime (cf. Olson 1997: 463). Neither did she ignore 'the fact that certain groups oppose—and oppose violently—the coming together of another group to form the space of the political' (cf. McGowan 1998: 288). Writing of the Spanish Civil War (1936–9), Arendt criticized communist Russia for undermining the Spanish Republic and 'using the misfortunes of the Spanish to get even with anti-Stalinists inside and outside of the Party' (MDT, 215). She neglected to mention the abandonment of the republicans by both Britain and France. But, as a result of the rise of nationalism in the interwar period, she wrote that

> more and more persons of all countries, including the Western democracies, volunteered to fight in civil wars abroad (something which up to then only a few idealists or adventurers had done) even when this meant cutting themselves off from their national communities. This was the lesson of the Spanish Civil War and one of the reasons why the governments were so frightened of the International Brigade . . . [The] Brigade was organized into national battalions in which the Germans felt they fought against Hitler and the Italians against Mussolini, just as a few years later, in the Resistance, the Spanish refugees felt they fought against Franco when they helped the French against Vichy. What the European governments were so afraid of in this process was that the new stateless people could no longer be said to be of dubious or doubtful nationality (OT, 282–3).

6. Arendt was not popular in Zionist circles for she implied that 'as a movement of settlers originating in Europe, even if Jewish, [Zionism] was imperialist through and through' (Bar On, 2002: 140; JW 396–7). She paid a price for her outspokenness. Arendt travelled to Jerusalem to cover for *The New Yorker* magazine the trial of Adolf Eichmann, the Nazi bureaucrat charged with directing the transportation of Jews to the death camps. The essays were expanded and published in 1963 as *Eichmann in Jerusalem: A Report on the Banality of Evil.* This would undoubtedly become Arendt's most controversial book. She believed it was 'the object of an organized campaign' involving the circulation of 'lies about what [she] had written . . . and about the facts [she] had reported' (BPF, 227*f*; EJ, 282). For example, she was condemned for pointing to the fact that the Jewish Councils—the leaders not the people themselves—often cooperated with the Nazis by providing lists of names. As a result of the storm she lost many friends and her ties with the organized Jewish community in the United States were effectively severed (see Barnouw 1990; Bernstein 1996; Aschheim 2001; Zertal 2005: ch. 4).

7. Rather than support the idea of an exclusively Jewish homeland, Arendt argued for a political structure of joint Arab–Jewish local councils in a bi-national state. Jewish statelessness, she argued, 'was, indeed solved—namely, by means of a colonized and then conquered territory'. But this 'solved neither the problem of minorities nor the stateless. On the contrary, like virtually all other events of our century, the solution of the Jewish question merely produced a new category of refugees' (OT, 290). In 1948 she wrote of the dangers of chauvinism, which tended 'to divide the world into two halves, one of which is one's own nation, which fate, or ill-will, or history has pitted against a whole world of enemies...The struggle in Palestine takes place within a broad international framework, and the right distinction between friend and foe will be a life or death matter for the State of Israel' (JP, 239).

8. For Schmitt, the political was the struggle to establish the distinction between friend and enemy and always involves the potential of physical destruction. The political retains existential primacy over the moral, aesthetic, and economic spheres. It 'is the strongest and most intense of the distinctions and categorizations' (1996: 27). These potential and real physical battles, however, are not merely the continuation of politics by other means, a mere instrument to achieve a preconceived end. War is also an existential mode of being, the ultimate expression and foundation of the political.

9. In Arendt's words,

   Who has ever doubted that the violated dream of violence..., the persecuted of exchanging 'the role of the quarry for that of the hunter'...? The point, as Marx saw it, is that dreams never come true. The rarity of slave rebellions and of uprisings among the disinherited and downtrodden is notorious; on the few occasions when they occurred it was precisely 'mad fury' that turned dreams into nightmares for everybody...To identify the national liberation movements with such outbursts is to prophesy their doom—quite apart from the fact that the unlikely victory would not result in changing the world (or the system), but only its personnel (CR, 123; see Fanon 1963: 52–3).

10. Arendt's point was that, 'violence itself is incapable of speech, and not merely that speech is helpless when confronted with violence' (OR, 9). Hence, there is little contradiction between the idea of the silence of violence and the fact that Arendt wrote about the Second World War during it. Bat-Ami Bar On has sought to 'save' Arendt from this (non-)inconsistency by 'psychologizing' her. She may have been so 'emotionally overwhelmed' that she 'perceived herself as silenced by the violence of Nazism and World War II' (2002: 18, 21). Her powerful call for a Jewish army seems to undermine this idea.

11. There was a small controversy over whether Arendt helped to fund a Jewish terrorist group after the founding of Israel. The original edition of Elizabeth Young-Bruehl's 1982 biography mistakenly claimed that Arendt made financial contributions to the Jewish Defence League (JDL), a terrorist group, in 1967 and 1973, years in which Israel went to war with its neighbours. In fact, Arendt

contributed to the United Jewish Appeal, a philanthropic organization, not the JDL, which she considered to be 'fascistic'. 'She would never have contributed to it', Young-Bruehl has since written in the new edition of the definitive biography (2004: xxxv). Nonetheless, this inadvertent mistake provided grist for the mill for Edward Said's critique of how 'left liberals have altered their old views rightward as a way of not allowing these views and theories to furnish even implicit criticism of what Israel does'. Arendt's support for the JDL 'is remarkable', Said continued, 'for someone otherwise so compassionate and reflective on the subject of what Zionism did to Palestinians' (1995: 85).

12. In a letter to Mary McCarthy written in 1965, Arendt captured the point with a thought experiment. 'Suppose China declared war upon the United States tomorrow and declared unconditional surrender within the next hour or so, whereupon 5 or 6 million Chinese come marching across the border [with Vietnam] unarmed, with their hands over their heads to surrender. I suppose we would get out in a hurry' (BF, 182).

13. There is some overlap between Arendt's account of power and that of Michel Foucault. For Foucault, 'Power must be analyzed as something which circulates, or rather as something which only functions in the form of a chain. It is never localized here or there, never in anybody's hands' (1984: 212).

14. The philosophical roots of this view are in Plato's interpretation of political action 'in terms of *archein* and *prattein*—of ordering the start of an action and of executing this order' (OT, 325*f*). Thomas Hobbes then became the principal modern theorist of politics as the accumulation of power *over* others, of rulership. The social contract in the imaginary state of nature justified a relationship of rulership that was already being exercised by the King in the interests of protecting life. Arendt's criticisms of this are discussed in Chapters 7 and 8.

15. Violence is dominated by instruments to such an extent that nuclear weapons made it possible, Arendt believed, to envision 'the disappearance of war from the scene of [great power] politics even without a radical transformation of international relations and without an inner change of men's hearts and minds' (OR, 4).

16. Wisely Arendt does not offer a definition of peace. In an essay called 'Peace or Armistice in the Middle East?' Arendt presciently argued that 'Peace, as distinguished from armistice, cannot be imposed from the outside, it can only be the result of negotiations, of mutual compromise and eventual agreement between Arabs and Jews' (1950: 56).

17. This is not how Habermas understands the 'public sphere'. Arendt's emphasis on contestation and disagreement, her acceptance of the contingency of all politically relevant truth claims, is at odds with Habermas's focus on deliberative rationality and consensus-building (see Chapter 8).

18. '*Force*, which we often use in daily speech as a synonym for violence', Arendt clarified, 'especially if violence serves as a means of coercion, should be reserved, in terminological language, for...the energy released by physical or social movements' (CR, 143–4).

19. 'How could it be otherwise?', Clausewitz continued. 'Do political relations between peoples and between their governments stop when diplomatic notes are no longer exchanged? Is war not just another expression of their thoughts, another form of speech or writing? Its grammar, indeed, may be its own, but not its logic. If that is so, then war cannot be divorced from political life' (1976: 605).

20. It is certainly possible to imagine the 'internal' relations of a society to be political and the external to be war-like. Arendt was aware of this position, which is key to the Western tradition. On this view, as Arendt described it, 'Violence is traditionally the *ultima ratio* in relationships between nations and the most disgraceful of domestic actions' (BPF, 22). As we discuss throughout this book, this image imposes severe limitations on how we understand the transnational generation of military power and forms of warfare and social processes that do not neatly fit into such state-centric categories (see especially Chapters 4 and 8).

21. In 1963, Arendt wrote that 'the pretense that the aim of an armament race is to guard the peace is even older, namely as old as the discovery of propaganda lies. But the point of the matter is that today the avoidance of war is not only the true or pretended goal of an over-all policy but has become the guiding principle of the military preparations themselves' (OR, 6). She criticized the American 'arms trade and arms production' in an era when the dangers of nuclear confrontation meant that 'war as a rational means of politics has become a kind of luxury justifiable only for small powers' (RJ, 273). Here, Arendt underestimated the importance of proxy wars for the very 'rational' conduct of superpower rivalry.

22. 'Law is not pacification', in the words of Foucault, 'for beneath the law, war continues to rage in all its mechanisms of power ... War is the motor behind institutions and order. In the smallest of its cogs, peace is waging a secret war. To put it another way, we have to interpret the war that is going on beneath peace; peace itself is a coded war. We are therefore at war with one another; a battlefront runs through the whole of society, continuously and permanently ... There is no such thing as a neutral subject. We are all inevitably someone's adversary' (2003: 50–1; for an excellent discussion, see Hanssen 2000: ch. 3).

23. The meaning of politics, for Schmitt, is expressed in the distinction between friend and enemy and war is the most extreme means of expression (1996: 35). This was meant literally. Political concepts such as friend and enemy only have meaning to the extent that real physical destruction is an ever-present possibility. Without it there would be no politics or 'specifically political behavior' (1996: 34).

24. There are differences among these thinkers. For example, Virilio explicitly distinguishes himself from Baudrillard, who appears to celebrate the disappearance of politics, and seeks to 're-establish politics' (1997: 34).

25. Arendt cited Richard J. Barnet's *Roots of War* (1971), which 'tries to prove that war has become a permanent institution, that is, the kind of war we are waging in Vietnam' (BF, 316). Barnet also cites Arendt as an influence on this very argument.

26. Rather than the 'white man's burden', Arendt argued, statesmen now talked of 'commitments' and 'responsibilities' to clients. The American domino theory, in which war must be waged to halt the spread of communism to distant countries, was the new 'Great Game', in which 'whole nations' were considered 'as stepping-stones or as pawns' (OT, xviii). As it fell further and further into the quagmire in Vietnam, the actions and verbal justifications of the US government, Arendt observed, 'bear a much more portentous resemblance to the deeds and verbal justifications that preceded the outbreak of World War I, when a spark in a peripheral region of minor interest...could start a world-wide conflagration' (OT, xxi).

27. In the post-war effort to impose a Pax Americana, the temptation to imperialism was never remote. The best hope for a retreat from such urges and its 'even more ominous mentality' (OT, xxi) were only two restraining facts. These were the constitutional balance of power and the caution imposed by the nuclear balance of terror. Arendt did not live to see the removal of the Soviet restraint, but she feared that constitutional check on executive war-making power was already in grave peril. In criticizing a police gas attack against anti-Vietnam War protestors on the Berkeley campus, Arendt noted that the toxins were 'not just tear gas but also another gas, "outlawed by the Geneva Convention and used by the Army to flush out guerrillas in Vietnam"...an excellent example of this "backlash" phenomenon' (CR, 153).

28. Arendt referred to the establishment of a 'military–industrial–*labor* complex' in the post–Second World War period (CR, 111, emphasis added). The inclusion of 'labor' into President Eisenhower's original phrase is significant and is connected to her belief that in modern society there had emerged an 'unnatural growth of the natural' (HC, 47). Arendt defined labour as 'the biological process of the human body, whose spontaneous growth, metabolism, and eventual decay are bound to the vital necessities produced and fed into the life process by labor. The human condition of labor is life itself' (HC, 7). Arendt was among the first to warn of the dangers of placing the protection and the servicing of the life process at the centre of politics. Coinciding with the liberal idea that 'life is the highest good', the principle function of modern politics has become the cultivation and sustenance of 'life itself'. The results, Arendt believed, were disastrous; 'the linkage of politics and life results in an inner contradiction that cancels and destroys what is specifically political about politics' (PP, 145). This process was in no small measure due to the rise of peoples' armies and the need to secure the consent of the people for evermore costly wars. The modern nation-state was not only the possessor of force but also paradoxically the protector of 'life' within it. 'Security remained the decisive criterion', Arendt wrote, 'but not the individual's security against violent "death", as in Hobbes...but a security which should permit an undisturbed development of the life process of society as a whole' (BPF, 150). It took the introduction of nuclear weapons to bring to the international sphere what had long been established in the 'domestic' realm of the state, a concern with 'the naked existence

of us all' (PP, 145). The paradox is that at a time when the central function of the state was to protect the life of its citizens it acquired the means of destruction to destroy all human life. The related idea of 'biopolitics' has recently become popular largely through the appropriation of the writing of Arendt and Foucault by Italian philosopher Giorgio Agamben (1995; Dillon and Reid 2007; Reid 2007).

29. 'The abolition of war', Arendt wrote, 'like the abolishment of a plurality of sovereign states, would harbor its own peculiar dangers' (MDT, 93–4). This is discussed in Chapter 8.

30. Jean Bethke Elshtain has argued that Arendt's account of natality may point us in the direction of a more pacific form of politics, a 'pacific image that evokes love, not war' (1986: 110). This is a stretch, not least given Arendt's view of love as 'the most powerful of all antipolitical forces' (HC, 242; JW 466–7).

NOTES TO CHAPTER 3

1. This is not to deny that there are especially strong common feelings among soldiers and, indeed, across the 'no man's land' of the trenches in the First World War. Tony Ashworth (1980) describes the emergence of 'live and let live' systems, the growth of elements of goodwill from soldiers on both sides who saw themselves trapped in a common situation. Arendt believed that such comradeship was amoral, not immoral and observed '"inhuman cruelty" and "superhuman kindness", not as stereotype opposites but as simultaneously present in the same person' (1970a: xi).

2. If Faulkner captured the inner meaning of the First World War, then Arendt pointed to Rudyard Kipling as the author who offered nothing less than 'the foundation legend' of imperialism for those who would practise it (OT, 209).

3. There is a suggestive comment in Arendt's account of Waldemar Gurian's view that 'in the *battle* of ideas, in the nakedness of confrontation, men soar freely above their conditions and protections in the ecstasy of sovereignty, not defending but confirming with absolutely no defences *who* they are' (MDT, 260, first emphasis added).

4. As Seyla Benhabib writes, in this essay Shklar is 'quite acrimonious and at times ungenerous in spirit. Shklar reads Arendt against the grain on so many issues' (1996b: 63).

5. Benhabib (1992b) wants to abandon Arendt's potentially irresponsible and 'masculinist' Greek agonism. At best, Benhabib argues, if peers are ever to compete for excellence on the public stage (Benhabib's not Arendt's reading of agonism), this would imply a kind of moral and political homogeneity which simply does not exist in modern society. Moreover, when the 'theatre' of politics is restricted to the public stage, this rigidifies the problematic distinction between public and private that feminists have been at pains to lay to rest for decades. Arendt certainly neglected gender. But it is not the case that she wanted to simply re-institute some Greek-inspired model of the polis. Habermas has

mistakenly claimed that 'Arendt remains bound to the historical and conceptual constellation of classical Greek philosophy' (1983: 174). This is a false statement on a number of levels. For a further discussion, see Chapters 5 and 7.

6. Arendt was not inattentive to Greek imperialism, as we discuss in Chapter 5 (cf. Beiner 1997: 132; Pangle 1989: xxiv; Euben 2000: 151).

7. If the Greek experience with politics is at the bottom of the sea of our own political experience, then Arendt, borrowing her own words, is like the 'pearl diver who descends to the bottom of the sea, not to excavate the bottom and bring it to light but to pry loose the rich and the strange, the pearls and the coral in the depths and to carry them to the surface, this thinking delves into the depths of the past—but not in order to resuscitate it the way it was and to contribute to the renewal of extinct ages' (MDT, 205).

8. Schmitt is making this point to substantiate his own claim that the essence of the political is the friend–enemy distinction whose ultimate expression is war. The enemy must truly be 'the other, the stranger; and it is sufficient for his nature that he is, in a specially intense way, existentially something different and alien, so that in the extreme case conflicts with him are possible' (1996: 27).

9. 'Since Homer', Arendt noted, 'the metaphor has borne that element of the poetic which conveys cognition; its use establishes the *correspondences* between physically most remote things—as when in the *Iliad* . . . the approaching of the army moving to battle in line after line corresponds to the sea's long billows which, driven by the wind, gather head far out on the sea, roll to shore line after line, and then burst on the land in thunder' (MDT, 166).

10. 'Hobbes', Arendt wrote, 'is the only political philosopher in whose work death, in the form of fear of violent death, plays a crucial role. But it is not equality before death that is decisive for Hobbes; it is the equality of fear resulting from the equal ability to kill possessed by everyone that persuades men in the state of nature to bind themselves into a commonwealth' (CR, 165).

11. Arendt goes on to note that during war 'men are literally standing, or rather thrown, outside their selves, whether their ' "I" passes insensibly into a "we"' or they feel so much "part of this circling world", so much alive that, in seeming paradox, death no longer matters to them' (1970a: xi).

12. In essays posthumously collected in *The Jew as Pariah*, Arendt linked the possibility of suicide as an act of resistance to human spontaneity. She suggested that this was the last and possibly the only indestructible guarantee of human freedom. Suicide could be a rebellion against oblivion even when protest no longer had even 'historic importance' (Rousset quoted in OT, 451). But in *Origins*, Arendt also appeared to question whether this last guarantee was really so indestructible. She noted the apparent rarity of suicides in the camps and attributed it to 'the destruction of individuality'. Whether there is evidence to make such a claim—a low rate of suicide compared to what? (Stark 2001)—Arendt's writing on suicide is still relevant. The ability to martyr oneself was the last vestige of the moral person; to destroy this element of personhood 'is done in the main by making martyrdom, for the first time in history, impossible'

(OT, 451). As if aware of the final bond between freedom and suicide, the Nazis deliberately sought to make such 'decisions of conscience absolutely questionable and equivocal'. In Arendt's words, 'when even suicide would mean the immediate murder of his own family—how is he to decide? The alternative is no longer between good and evil but between murder and murder' (OT, 452).

13. Christopher Coker, '21st Century Warriors?', Talk at University of Oxford, 31 January 2006.

14. In fact, for Arendt, it was only the possibility of robot soldiers that might reverse the relation between power and violence discussed in Chapter 2. 'No government exclusively based on the means of violence has ever existed. Even the totalitarian ruler...needs a power basis—the secret police and its net of informers. Only the development of robot soldiers, which...would eliminate the human factor completely and, conceivably, permit one man with a push button to destroy whomever he pleased, could change this fundamental ascendancy of power over violence' (CR, 149).

15. We must at all times make a clear distinction between suicide bombing as a tactic in a struggle for national liberation and similar practices in the name of some form of Islamic imperialism espoused by Osama bin Laden (2005). There is no equivalence. The former can clearly be seen as rational and motivated (as opposed to legitimized) by a concrete political cause. The latter is an expansive, ideologically driven celebration of pure violence for religious purposes. It is anti-political in the most dangerous of senses. It is unworldly, in Arendt's terms, because bin Laden's ideas are based on a totalizing rejection of difference and plurality. They are based on a hatred of the world and those who are attracted to his ideas about violence have a hatred of life. If taken to its logical extreme, Bin Ladenism would indeed amount to totalitarianism. The yawning gap between national liberation struggles and the celebration of death found in the utterances of bin Laden may be clear from a letter Arendt wrote in 1946. The important thing about the French Resistance, she wrote, 'is that they're still ready to fight and risk their lives. We are, unfortunately, only used to our enemies being ready to risk their lives. And they do so not out of heroism but because a certain modern type will gladly run the risk of being murdered as long as he gets a chance to be a murderer himself. It isn't any great feat to be a "hero" if you hate life' (AJ, 64).

16. This insight was lost in the criticism of Susan Sontag (2001) who described as 'brave' the hijackers of 9/11. In noting this fact, Sontag was not endorsing their acts or their ends. Rather, she was pointing to the 'morally neutral virtue' of courage, or more accurately that it could not easily be said that the 9/11 hijackers were 'cowards' (also see Kateb 2004). And yet Sontag was not totally correct when she called for American citizens to examine how their own foreign policies may have led to the attacks. In response to events that seem quite literally unbelievable—a widespread feeling in the days and weeks following 9/11—there is a tendency or even a need to speculate 'about deeper causes'. Arendt suggested that this 'returns [us] from the shock of reality to what seems

plausible and can be explained in terms of what reasonable men think possible' (RJ, 261). To many after the 9/11 attacks, it seemed only plausible to point to what came before, linking the histories of the United States and the Middle East. Bin Laden has also shamelessly pointed to US support for Israel in its occupation of Palestine as some sort of motivation for his organization and its violence. The hypocrisy is startling given that there would be no place for a Palestinian nation-state in his Islamist Empire. Bin Laden's violent fanaticism is not based on rage at injustice. As Arendt pointed out, it is not the case that 'oppression [and] exploitation as such is ever the main cause for resentment' (OT, 4). This is not to dismiss the view that US foreign policy and power shaped the global context in which the 9/11 attacks happened and within which they can partly be understood (Barkawi 2004). Rather, it is to question the common sense view that violent hatred, in Arendt's words, must 'spring necessarily from great power and great abuses, and that consequently organized hatred . . . cannot but be a reaction to their importance and power' (OT, 5).

17. It has been claimed that Arendt's concept of the 'banality of evil' teaches us something about suicide bombing (Atran 2004). The analysis here suggests that this association is superficial. That ordinary people can become monstrous killers is the usual way in which her idea is rendered. The phrase comes from Arendt's account of Adolf Eichmann, the Nazi bureaucrat charged with directing the transportation of Jews to the death camps and arranging the execution of enemy populations in newly conquered territories. She observed that he was actually an 'ordinary', unremarkable functionary, not the sadistic monster many seemed to want him to be. He was not radical, but banal. 'He *merely,* to put the matter colloquially, *never realized what he was doing.* . . . That such remoteness from reality and such thoughtlessness can wreak more havoc than all the evil instincts taken together which, perhaps, are inherent to man—that was, in fact, the lesson one could learn in Jerusalem' (EJ, 287–8).

18. Evil, Arendt wrote, 'can overgrow and lay waste the whole world precisely because it spreads like a fungus on the surface. It is "thought-defying" . . . because thought tries to reach some depth, to go to the roots, and the moment it concerns itself with evil, it is frustrated because there is nothing. That is its "banality". Only the good has depth and can be radical' (JP, 251).

19. After reading Mary McCarthy's analysis of war (1967) in her book *Vietnam*, Arendt wrote, 'This still and beautiful pastoral of yours has the effect of showing the whole monstrosity of our enterprises in a harsher light than any denunciation or description of horror could' (BF, 218).

20. 'In ancient warfare', as Winston Churchill put it, 'the episodes were more important than the tendencies; in modern warfare, the tendencies are more important than the episodes' (quoted in Virilio and Lotringer 1997: 19).

21. Hans J. Morgenthau considered Arendt to be 'a historian very close up like Thucydides' (quoted in Young-Bruehl 2006: 34).

22. Arendt is quoting from Shakespeare's *The Tempest* (Act I, Scene 2; also see LM, 212). 'Full fathom five thy father lies,/ Of his bones are coral made,/ Those are

pearls that were his eyes./ Nothing of him that doth fade/ But doth suffer a sea-change/ Into something rich and strange'.

NOTES TO CHAPTER 4

1. In support of 'humanitarian intervention', Michael Walzer has argued that 'the price of silence and callousness...' about atrocities and human rights abuses abroad is that 'you will soon have to pay the political price of turmoil and lawlessness nearer home...We see the sequence most clearly', he continues, 'with Hannah Arendt's description of how European brutality in the colonies was eventually carried back to Europe itself' (2004: 74). This is a strange use of Arendt's work to support military intervention given that she was observing *European* atrocities in the colonies and how they paved the way, in part, to horrors in *Europe*.

2. Arendt's work has been used as a resource for postcolonial studies (see Williams and Chrisman 1994; Chrisman 2000: 3; Stone-Mediatore 2003). She was a critic of Marx, but she saw the appeal of his ideas that would become the basis of post-colonial history and theory. 'Those who were rejected by their own time were usually forgotten by history', she argued, 'and insult added to injury had troubled all sensitive consciences ever since faith in a hereafter where the last would be first had disappeared. Injustices in the past as well as the present became intolerable when there was no longer any hope that the scales of justice eventually would be set right. Marx's great attempt to rewrite world history in terms of class struggles fascinated even those who did not believe in the correctness of his thesis, because of his original intention to find a device by which to force the destinies of those excluded from official history into the memory of posterity' (OT, 333).

3. The suggestion that Arendt 'overemphasizes the importance of colonialism to German life', which she did not, is therefore beside the point (Gann 1977: 228).

4. For Hans J. Morgenthau (1977), Arendt's delineation of totalitarianism as a new form of government was her most important contribution to political thought.

5. I owe this point to Tarak Barkawi.

6. Many Europeans imagined themselves to be part of a civilizing mission and wars of colonial conquest were part of national identity. (Totalitarian propaganda techniques 'were prepared for them by fifty years of the rise of imperialism' (OT, 351).) Much of the conquering was done with armies drawn from the colonies. But these were not mere mercenary armies in the eyes of many Europeans. They were still 'our' men fighting for our cause. Indeed, many of those fighting also believed this to the case (Killingray and Omissi 1999). In Arendt's words, for the French, 'the colonies were considered lands of soldiers which could produce a *force noire* to protect the inhabitants of France against their national enemies...Clemenceau insisted at the peace table in 1918 that he cared about nothing but "an unlimited right of levying black troops to assist in the defence

of French territory in Europe if France were attacked in the future by Germany"'
(OT, 129).

7. In 1914, Rosa Luxemburg was indicted by a Criminal Court, in Arendt's words, 'for "inciting" the masses to civil disobedience in case of war'. This was pretty good, Arendt sarcastically wrote, 'for the woman who "was always wrong" to stand trial on this charge five months before the outbreak of the First World War, which few "serious" people had thought possible' (MDT, 37).

8. It is in this context that we must understand Arendt's (controversial) problem with the appearance of the 'body' in the political realm. The position is controversial, it has been described as 'the Arendtian taboo on the body' (Zerilli 1995: 171), because it places her at odds with feminists who have rightly stressed the centrality of the body and bodily difference to the functioning of political power. William E. Connolly has also criticized Arendt's 'tendency to reduce so much of the body to a set of automatisms and then to valorize "carefree" thinking, opinion, and engagement' (1999: 14). Arendt's apparent problem with the 'body' makes more sense in light of her fear of the *dangers* of biological categories. As we discussed in Chapter 2, Arendt rejected Fanon's idea that anti-colonial violence was a physical as well as a political revulsion against colonial domination. Arendt argued that this violence (and rage) is part of the political, the *artificial* human-made realm (also see Cocks 2002: 66).

9. The Nazi stormtroopers 'were organized after the model of criminal gangs and used for organized murder' (OT, 372). However, this is not an accurate description of colonial troops who were more disciplined than their colonial masters often expected. The Nazi belief that its system of law potentially applied to the whole world shaped the conduct of its army during occupation. In Arendt's words, the 'army was no longer an instrument of conquest that carried within it the new law of the conqueror, but an executive organ which enforced a law which already supposedly existed for everyone' (OT, 416).

10. Arendt described the 'wild murdering' in Southeast Africa, the 'extermination of the Hottentot tribes', the 'decimation of the peaceful Congo population' (OT, 185). She singled out the actions of Belgium's King Leopold II, his decimation of the Congo, as 'responsible for the blackest pages in the history of Africa' (OT, 185*f*).

11. Arendt mistakenly claimed that the first use of concentration camps was by the British in the Boer War. In fact, it was Spanish colonists who first used them in Cuba in 1895 resulting in approximately 200,000 deaths.

12. Indeed, if we broaden out the analysis to include deaths caused by famine that was a direct result of policy, the British look much worse (Davis 2002). Another important part of the early history of British air power, which was an important element of the 'total' character of the Second World War, is found in the colonies. In the interwar period, air power was seen by the British as an efficient means to police the increasingly unruly empire. Indeed, the RAF has been described as the 'midwife of modern Iraq' (Omissi 1990: 37). Without it, the British presence after the First World War, would not have been sustainable, the

pliant Arab kingdom would have collapsed and Turkey's (Ottoman) influence would have increased. Palestinians also suffered heavy casualties at the hands of the British who were mandated the territories after the collapse of the Ottoman Empire. Palestinians were resisting Jewish settlement, and the British bombed from the air to suppress them.

13. The Turkish government also continues to deny that the Ottoman Empire perpetrated genocide against the Armenians. Arendt understood early how such denials were possible. In her words, 'the very immensity of the crimes guarantees that the murderers who proclaim their innocence with all manner of lies will be more readily believed than the victims who tell the truth' (OT, 439).

14. The brutality of the fighting on the Eastern Front was not only a result of the clashing total ideologies of Nazism and Communism. As Hew Strachan has pointed out, we must clearly distinguish the concept of modern war from total war. The 'barbarization' of the Eastern Front was partly a result of the *de*modernization of the war. 'Ninety per cent of the divisions earmarked for the invasion of the Soviet Union were dependent on horse-drawn transport ... The *Wehrmacht* ... became less well-equipped, less modern, as the war progressed' (Strachan 2001*b*: 264).

15. There are some useful comparisons that can be drawn between totalitarian movements in Europe during the twentieth-century and the al-Qaeda terrorist network. Both are supranational to the extent they are not limited by territorial boundaries. Both are totally governed by an ideology that removes their followers from the common public world which is the only basis for reality. As discussed in the notes to the previous chapter, though Osama bin Laden has sought to coopt the Palestinian and the Chechen struggles for national liberation, his version of an imperialist Islam, the establishment or re-establishment of a new caliphate, is a travesty of politics more than a perversion of religion.

16. Paul Gilroy has suggested that 'the doctrine of pre-emption might, for example, be traced to these earlier colonial adventures and the forms of warfare they engendered' (2005: 15).

17. Arendt wrote that the Nazis' crimes against the Jews exploded all legal and moral frameworks. There were no laws able to properly account for the crimes that had been committed (see Chapter 5). In a letter to Karl Jaspers, she actually suggested that the breach preceded the Holocaust. 'We are simply not equipped to deal, on a human, political level, with a guilt that is beyond crime and innocence that is beyond goodness or virtue. This is the abyss that opened up before us as early as 1933 (much earlier, actually, with the onset of imperialistic politics) and to which we have finally stumbled' (AJ, 54).

18. 'English imperialism: The best thing about it', Arendt wrote, 'was how it was liquidated and also how in spite of everything the still-intact national institutions of the homeland always thwarted the real intentions of England's imperialistic party' (AJ, 167).

NOTES TO CHAPTER 5

1. For example, it has been suggested by legal scholar, Michael Byers, that 'the international rules and institutions rejected [by the Bush administration] ... are more consistent with the founding principles of the US than the imperialist principles to which they subscribe' (2002: 127).

2. Article 57 (2) of the Additional Protocol I to the Geneva Convention states that 'an attack should be cancelled or suspended if it becomes apparent that ... the attack may be expected to cause incidental loss of civilian life, injury to civilians, damage to civilian objects, or a combination thereof, which would be excessive in relation to the concrete and direct military advantage anticipated'. The United States is not a signatory to this Additional Protocol, but it did agree to many of its provisions.

3. Arendt's broader point was that, 'Terms like nationalism, imperialism, totalitarianism, etc., are used indiscriminately for all kinds of political phenomena (usually just as highbrow words for "aggression"), and none of them is any longer understood with its particular historical background. The result is generalization in which words themselves lose all meaning' (EU, 407). Elsewhere, she also noted the difficulty in comparing the British and the Roman empires 'because, though Roman rule was presumably much crueler and intemperate, it was still a genuine empire and not merely imperialism, because the Roman conquerors forced Roman law on foreign peoples and by doing so avoided the disastrous bastardized governments of modern times' (AJ, 167).

4. The power that emerged out of people acting together in the political realm, Arendt wrote, could not 'be checked, at least not reliably, by laws ... [They] are always in danger of being abolished by the power of the many, and in a conflict between law and power it is seldom the law which will emerge as victor' (OR, 150).

5. In this sense, territory does not first and foremost refer to territorial space on the earth, Arendt observed, 'as to the space between individuals in a group whose members are bound to, and at the same time separated and protected from, each other' by their traditions and laws (EJ, 262–3). The organization of politics, the human-made laws and conventions, is historically contingent as well as spatially (territorially) bound. 'Treaties and international guarantees provide an extension of this territorially bound freedom for citizens outside of their own country, but ... the elementary coincidence of freedom and a limited space remains manifest' (OR, 279; HC, 191).

6. Arendt argued that Hobbes's model of the Leviathan depended on an 'everpresent possibility of war' to survive. 'Since [for Hobbes] power is only a means to an end a community based solely on power must decay in the calm of order and stability; its complete security means that it is built on sand. Only by acquiring more power can it guarantee the status quo; only by constantly extending its authority and only through the process of power accumulation can it remain stable. Hobbes's Commonwealth is a vacillating structure and must

always provide itself with new props from outside; otherwise, it would collapse overnight into the aimless, senseless chaos of the private interests from which it sprang ... [The] ever-present possibility of war guarantees the Commonwealth a prospect of permanence because it makes it possible for the state to increase its power at the expense of other states' (OT, 142).

7. The society of European states or the comity of nations was destroyed by the events of the First World War (OT, 267); it 'went to pieces when, and because, it allowed its weakest member to be excluded and persecuted' (JP, 66).

8. 'As European states were struggling in Africa', Koskenniemi writes, '...the new generation of lawyers...used the distinction between civilized and non-civilized communities to deal with the process of European expansion. Although they discussed colonialism from a variety of perspectives...their discourse provides a uniform logic of exclusion–inclusion in which cultural arguments intersect with humanitarian ones so as to allow a variety of positions while at every point guaranteeing the controlling superiority of "Europe"' (2001: 127).

9. ' "Wherever you go, you will be a *polis*": these famous words became not merely the watchword of Greek colonization', wrote Arendt, 'they expressed the conviction that action and speech create a space between the participants which can find its proper location almost anytime and anywhere' (HC, 198). They expressed the creative and boundary-transgressing ethos of the political action of free and equal citizens.

10. Another indication that laws and legislating were considered by the Greeks as pre-political, Arendt suggests, is that the 'lawgiver did not even have to be a citizen of the city but could be engaged from outside to perform his task' (PP, 179; also see Honig 2001).

11. The significance of the fact that law is 'made' is discussed in Chapter 8.

12. In the words of one legal scholar, 'ideas from Roman law...continue to exert an influence on contemporary [legal and international legal] theory' (Mills 2006: 4).

13. Arendt argued that this sense of Western foreign policy derived from Rome was in danger of being wiped out in an era of possible nuclear wars. In such circumstances, and if we take our standard of evaluation to be human life itself, she argued the annihilation of politics was obviously preferable to the destruction of humanity in a nuclear war. 'Out of this fear arises the hope that men will come to their senses and rid the world of politics instead of humankind' (PP, 153). Of course, this was not Arendt's solution. But she believed that if wars of nuclear annihilation were to occur 'then the specifically political nature of foreign policy as practiced since the Romans will disappear, and the relations between nations fall back into an expanse that knows neither law nor politics, that destroys a world and leaves a desert' (PP, 190).

14. As we discussed in Chapter 3, Arendt faulted the Greeks for not taking further the political spirit of Homer's military history.

15. In *On Revolution*, Arendt suggested that the republican form of government is a mutual contract between equals based on respect and reciprocity; 'its actual content', she wrote, 'is a promise, and its result is indeed a "society" or "consociation" in the old Roman sense of *societas*, which means alliance. Such an alliance gathers together the isolated strength of the allied partners and binds them into a new power structure by virtue of "free and sincere promises" ' (OR, 169).

16. For an introductory discussion of different forms of international society, including their relation to imperialism and empire, see Jackson and Owens (2005).

17. Interestingly, Arendt rejected the idea that violence and war could ever be *legitimate*. The distinction between justification and legitimacy is important less for pedantic reasons than for what it reveals, again, about politics and war in Arendt's thought. Justification is the political act of claiming that something is reasonable or just. It is to offer reasons for something such as a war. Legitimacy is more precise and only forms a small part of the justification for any war. To be legitimate is to conform to existing laws or rules of the game. For Arendt, power does not need to be *justified* with reference to any other end. It is an end in itself. But it does require legitimacy. When people act in concert they construct the laws and rules of the political 'game' they make and remake their own legitimacy. In contrast, while violence may be justified, properly speaking it can never be legitimate. In Arendt's words, 'Power springs up whenever people get together and act in concert, but it derives its legitimacy from the initial getting together rather than from any action that then may follow. Legitimacy, when challenged, bases itself on an appeal to the past, while justification relates to an end that lies in the future. Violence can be justifiable, but it will never be legitimate' (CR, 151). For an application of this distinction to the 1999 Kosovo war, see the essays by Iris Marion Young (2002) and Owens (2005*a*).

18. In such questions, Arendt was far more likely to emphasize developments in technology rather than 'moral progress'. Similarly, she believed it was technical developments, the introduction of nuclear weapons, rather than any moral progress that made it possible to envision 'the disappearance of war from the scene of politics'. This point distances Arendt again from liberal or 'normative' explanations of what became known as the 'long peace', the absence of direct war between the great powers in the international system since 1945. She also argued that aggressive war was only defined as a crime and the right to self-defence was established, when the First World War 'demonstrated the horribly destructive potential of warfare under conditions of modern technology' (OR, 3).

19. The apparent dichotomy between forgiveness and punishment does not exclude the possibility of reconciliation (Schaap 2005; Young-Bruehl 2006). However, in the case of the post-war proposal by some Nazis for a 'conciliation committee' between former Nazis and Jews, Arendt nonetheless derided this as an 'outrageous cliché'.

20. Arendt distinguished between ethnic cleansing and genocide. While in practice this distinction can be enormously difficult to make and acts of ethnic cleansing can be genocidal in intent (Shaw 2003), Arendt argued that the core crime of each was different. Ethnic cleansing, the forced removal of a people from a given territory, Arendt believed to be a crime not only against those people but against other states. Genocide, the effort to blot out an entire people not only from a given territory but from the face of the earth, was not only a crime against the people but also the order of mankind (EJ, 257). Genocide is not an ordinary war crime that can be dealt with in a traditional military tribunal. 'Expulsion and genocide', she wrote, 'though both are international offences, must remain distinct; the former is an offence against fellow-nations, whereas the latter is an attack upon human diversity as such, that is, upon a characteristic of the "human status" ' (EJ, 268–9).

21. In a letter to Jaspers, Arendt intriguingly wrote, that her support for the right of Israel to try Eichmann might appear like she was 'attempting to circumscribe the political with legal concepts. And I even admit that as far as the role of the law is concerned, I have been infected by the Anglo-Saxon influence. But quite apart from that, it seems to me to be in the nature of this case that we have no tools to hand except legal ones with which we have to judge and pass sentence on something that cannot even be adequately represented either in legal terms or political terms' (AJ, 417).

22. Tarak Barkawi and Mark Laffey (2002) describe the spread of state sovereignty after de-colonization as *only juridical*, and suggest that this does not reflect social relations of sovereignty, which remain imperial. They are mostly right. But this implied dichotomy between the social and the juridical occludes the importance of the subtler role of law in constituting 'imperial social formations'.

23. Arendt believed that the international affairs of her day were 'still based upon national sovereignty' and did not make sense or 'function without force or the threat of force as the *ultima ratio* of all foreign policy'. War remained the 'last resort' and she was not confident of any progress in this area (1962: 11).

24. More generally, the United States has been reluctant to resort to legal justifications for decisions to go to war. Britain presented the principal legal defence in the case of both Kosovo and Iraq.

25. In Habermas's words, 'the neoconservatives have actually offered up as their alternative to the domestication of state power through international law … a revolutionary claim: if the regime of international law fails, then the hegemonic imposition of a global liberal order is justified, even by means that are hostile to international law' (2003: 365). Neoconservatism is discussed at length in Chapter 7.

26. The desire for domestic public legitimacy seems crucial to accounting for the ambiguous but sustained effort by US governments to demonstrate in equal measure both the atrocities of America's enemies—and the legitimacy of their own—while avoiding the explicit appearance of relying on law to justify the use of force. The mythology of the outlaw or vigilante, the notion that justice can

be done by breaking the law, not only provides a staple theme in US popular drama (Norton 1993: 142). It has also been used to defend of the principle of 'humanitarian' war in the absence of Security Council approval; the United States and its allies may act as global 'human rights' vigilantes (Wheeler 2000*b*: 146).

27. Others in favour of so-called 'humanitarian intervention' point to the failure of the draft resolution (12-3) condemning NATO's actions as a breach of Article 2 (4), 24 and 53 of the UN Charter. This is presumed to demonstrate a level of tacit acceptance of 'humanitarian' military intervention in the 'society of states' (Wheeler 2000*a*; 2000*b*).

28. In a letter to Jaspers, Arendt expressed sympathy for Israel's abduction of Eichmann in contrast to Jaspers' belief there was no justification and that he ought to be tried in an international court. Arendt argued that it was possible for Israel to claim that they captured a man who had already been indicted in Nuremberg for crimes against humanity but due to his escape he was now 'a *hostis humani generis*, the way pirates used to be'. They could also argue that he was kidnapped from Argentina because that country had 'the worst possible record for the extradition of war criminals' (AJ, 414). Later she realized that the pirate theory was inadequate because pirates act for private (financial) and not public political motives (AJ, 423).

29. Even if morality can be used to justify the right to fight a war, it might also refuse the right to do what is needed to win; 'the rules of war may at some point become a hindrance to ... victory' (Walzer 1992: 195). There is clearly a constant tension between means and ends in war. If the goal of war is peace, even if the end is victory, conquest or freedom, then it is 'in conflict with the ends for which the means of force have been mobilized' (PP, 197). For Arendt, the end of war falls easily into conflict with the goal because, as Clausewitz also argued, the most *efficient* way to achieve it is to give the means 'free rein' (PP, 199).

30. For a fuller discussion of the relationship between 'accidental' civilian deaths and technology see Owens (2003), in which the social and legal history of accidents and responsibility as it emerged in the United States in the mid-nineteenth century is compared with 'accidental' civilian deaths during the recent US-led wars. The US refusal to accept responsibility for civilian deaths parallels in interesting ways the development of the modern legal doctrine of 'negligence'. This represented a move away from strict liability for accidents, which emerged through a series of judicial rulings during the heyday of American industrialization. The doctrine helped bring into being new understandings of blame and responsibility deemed more appropriate for the industrial age, that is, in favour of risk-taking capitalists.

31. This is in spite of the historical evidence. A quantitative analysis of all interstate wars between 1815 and 1999 suggests that democracies have been *more* likely to target civilians than non-democracies (Downes 2002).

32. Donald Rumsfeld, NewsHour, PBS, 3 January 2002. Available at http://www.pbs.org/newshour/bb/terrorism/jan-june02/search_1-3.html

33. Arendt drew a link between the rise of bureaucracy and terrorism. The transformation from the age of absolutism to the era of modern bureaucratic government profoundly altered the face of terrorism. It was now obsolete to believe that an entire political system could be changed by assassinating one ruler. In modern bureaucracies, power is wielded by the elite among faceless officials. In such a system, political terrorism rather than simple assassination makes much more sense. Arendt also highlighted the stifling effects of bureaucratization on domestic politics, the expansion of the party machines in political institutions; the 'transformation of government into administration, or of republics into bureaucracies, and the disastrous shrinkage of the public realm that went with it' (CR, 178). There was an inverse relationship, she believed, between the effectiveness of channels for authentic political action and the attractiveness of violence.

34. This is nicely described by Moruzzi. 'Service in the bureaucracy allowed for a commitment to ideals of devotion and honor in a cause larger than any individual or separate purpose. These civil and military servants of empire found themselves placed upon the stage (of orientalism) in order to play out the part of dramas implicitly more significant than any they could hope to see at home' (2000: 107).

35. Donald Rumsfeld, Pentagon Briefing, 22 January 2002. Available at http://transcripts.cnn.com/TRANSCRIPTS/0201/22/se.01.html

NOTES TO CHAPTER 6

1. Also see Robert Fisk, 'Bush's and Rumsfeld's War Dossier: Blindness, Hypocrisy, Lies', *The Independent*, 16 September 2002.

2. Samantha Power reads Arendt as a supporter of the contemporary international human rights movement. Yet she acknowledges the ambivalence in Arendt's position. 'Arendt's suspicions about the false promise of liberal internationalism were well-founded, but what she underestimated was the intrinsic resonance of human rights principles around the world—a resonance that has resulted more in the bottom-up promotion of human rights than in the top-down protection envisaged in 1948' (2004: xxi).

3. Human rights have been heralded as the new standard for human dignity in the twenty-first-century. Most Arendt scholarship argues that she believed any such new principle must be political in nature. There are no grounds for human rights beyond human conventions. However, in a recent book Peg Birmingham argues that 'Arendt's entire work can be read as an attempt to work out theoretically this fundamental right to have rights' (2006: 1) and that she provides philosophical grounds for them in the concept of natality. We are *born* to have rights. Arendt certainly argued that we were born to *begin*. Natality, as we discussed elsewhere, is the ontological root of the faculty of action. It is only through action and speech that the human conventions and institutions that make up the political world come into existence. It is possible that one may

argue *from* Arendt that there are philosophical grounds for human rights. But it is difficult to argue that this was Arendt's own central preoccupation. She rarely used the term human rights. She did believe that 'human dignity needs a new guarantee' (OT, ix). But human rights themselves could scarcely be the basis of this new political principle in Arendt's thought, 'the new fundament for civilized societies' (OT, 293). As she wrote in the English edition of *Origins*, 'The concept of human rights can again be meaningful only if they are redefined as a right to the human condition itself, which depends upon belonging to some human community, the right never to be dependent upon some inborn human dignity which de facto, aside from its guarantee by fellow-men ... does not exist' (1951: 439). The only thing that could guarantee human rights and a 'home in the world', Arendt was suggesting, were contingent political circumstances.

4. 'All the so-called liberal concepts of politics', Arendt wrote, '(that is, all the pre-imperialist political notions of the bourgeoisie) ... have this in common: they simply add up private lives and personal behavior patterns and present the sum as laws of history, or economics, or politics' (OT, 145–6). But as Arendt also put it, 'whether one agrees with liberalism or not (and I may say here that I am rather certain that I am neither a liberal nor a positivist nor a pragmatist), the point is that liberals are clearly no totalitarians. This, of course, does not exclude the fact that liberal or positivistic elements also lend themselves to totalitarian thinking; but such affinities would only mean that one has to draw even sharper distinctions because of the *fact* that liberals are not totalitarians' (1953: 80).

5. Arendt did however point to concentration camps, torture and famines as conditions that dehumanize 'and under such conditions, not rage and violence, but their conspicuous absence is the clearest sign of dehumanization. Rage is by no means an automatic reaction to misery and suffering as such' (CR, 160).

6. The essence of guerrilla activity is summarized by Lawrence: 'suppose we were (as we might be) an influence, an idea, a thing intangible, invulnerable, without front or back, drifting about like a gas? Armies were like plants, immobile, firm-rooted ... We might be a vapour, blowing where we listed. Our kingdom lay in each man's mind; and as we wanted nothing material to live on, so we might offer nothing material to the killing' (1991: 192).

7. Arendt wrote movingly of the struggles of Lawrence who wanted to escape from the confinement of British social convention; he succeeded so well in assimilating himself to the cause of Arab nationalism 'that he came to believe in it himself. But then again', as Arendt continued, 'he did not belong, he was ultimately unable "to think their thought" and to "assume their character". Pretending to be an Arab, he could only lose his "English self", which is exactly what he wanted to do' (OT, 219). Lawrence's effort to transform himself into a different 'Arab' self was pure Orientalism (Said, 1978: Ch.3). As Arendt wrote, 'the so-called Eastern soul appeared to be incomparably richer, its psychology more profound, its literature more meaningful than that of the "shallow" Western democracies' (OT, 245). Returning to Britain, Lawrence needed another function or achievement to prevent 'the world from identifying him with his

deeds in Arabia, from replacing his old self with a new personality. He did not want to become "Lawrence of Arabia" ' (OT, 220). But after having lost his old self in the war he did not want to acquire a new one. For Arendt, this made some sense of his otherwise 'incomprehensible enlistment as a private in the British army, which obviously was the only institution in which a man's honor could be identified with the loss of his individual personality' (OT, 218).

8. 'The fact that the "white man's burden" is either hypocrisy or racism', Arendt wrote, 'has not prevented a few of the best Englishmen from shouldering the burden in earnest and making themselves the tragic and quixotic fools of imperialism' (OT, 209).

9. In Arendt's words,

There have always been wars of aggression; the massacre of hostile populations after a victory went unchecked until the Romans mitigated it by introducing the *parcere subjectis*; through centuries the extermination of native peoples went hand in hand with the colonization of the Americas, Australia and Africa; slavery is one of the oldest institutions of mankind and all empires of antiquity were based on the labor of state-owned slaves who erected their public buildings. Not even concentration camps are the invention of the totalitarian movements. They emerge for the first time during the Boer War ... and continued to be used in South Africa as well as India for 'undesirable elements' (OT, 440; EU, 233).

As noted in Chapter 4, the Spanish in Cuba and not the British in South Africa were the first imperialists to systematically use concentration camps.

10. Arendt described the poet Bertolt Brecht, born in 1898, as a member of 'the first of the three lost generations' that had come into being as a result of the world wars. Her words are worth quoting at length:

Men of this generation whose initiation into the world had been the trenches and the battlefields of the First World War invented or adopted the term because they felt that they had become unfit to live normal lives; normality was a betrayal of all the experience of horror, that had made them into men.... This attitude, common to the war veterans of all countries, became a sort of climate of opinion when it turned out that they were succeeded by two more such 'lost generations': the first born about ten years later, in the first decade of the century, was taught, through the rather impressive lessons of inflation, mass unemployment, and revolutionary unrest, the instability of whatever had been left in tact in Europe after more than four years of slaughter; the next, again born about ten years later, in the second decade of the century, had the choice of being initiated into the world by Nazi concentration camps, the Spanish Civil War, or the Moscow Trials. These three groups, born, roughly, between 1890 and 1920, were close enough together in age to form a single group during the Second World War, whether as soldiers or as refugees and exiles, as members of the resistance movements or as inmates of concentration and extermination camps, or as civilians under a rain of bombs (MDT, 218–9).

11. Arendt suggested that beliefs in a 'community of fate' were strong among veteran groups across Europe between the wars. (The humiliation of the Front was shared equally no matter on which side the veteran had fought.) For a while at least, until nationalism came back into the fore in preparation for war, some fascist ideologists suggested it was 'far more important to have belonged to the generation of the trenches, no matter on which side, than to be a German or a Frenchman' (OT, 329).

12. Fascism provided a satisfying answer to an 'old troublesome question' that emerged in the interwar crisis. If the question, as Arendt framed it, was 'Who am I?', then conventional bourgeois 'society insisted, "You are what you appear to be." ' But the new fascist activism replied, 'You are what you have done'. There were no moral constraints to what you may do. 'The point was to do something, heroic or criminal, which was unpredictable and undetermined by anybody else' (OT, 331).

13. 'It was characteristic of the war generation and the philosophy of the twenties in Germany', Arendt noted, 'that the experience of death attained to a hitherto unknown philosophical dignity, a dignity it had only once before, in Hobbes's political philosophy, and then only seemingly. For although the fear of death plays a central part in Hobbes, it is not fear of inevitable mortality, but of "violent death". Undoubtedly the war experience was bound up with fear of violent death; but it was precisely characteristic of the war generation that this fear was transposed into the general anxiety about death' (MDT, 126).

14. The exception here may be Lawrence who did not direct his disgust at hypocrisy into a deliberate political project to unmask it. In fact, Lawrence appeared to undertake something of a desperate effort to try on as many different masks as he could. Lawrence, of course, was not the only one of his generation to attempt such a feat. In an essay on Isak Dinesen, Arendt described a 'generation of young men whom the First World War had made forever unfit to bear the conventions and fulfill the duties of everyday life...Some of them became revolutionists and lived in the dreamland of the future; others, on the contrary, chose the dreamland of the past...They belonged together in the fundamental conviction that "they did not belong to this century". (In political parlance, one would say that they were antiliberal insofar as liberalism meant acceptance of the world as it was together with the hope for its "progress"; historians know to what extent conservative criticism and revolutionary criticism of the world of the bourgeoisie coincide)' (MDT, 101).

15. When political statements are reduced to a 'declaration of purpose' leaders are afforded an element of 'freedom from the content of their own ideologies' (OT, 387). This means that inconsistencies, glaring contradictions, and double standards can be explained away.

16. As Arendt noted, such ideas were also proffered by the Pan-Slavs in the interwar period, who produced 'an unending stream of literary variations [that] opposed the profundity and violence of Russia to the superficial banality of

the West, which did not know suffering or the meaning of sacrifice, and behind whose sterile civilized surface were hidden frivolity and triteness' (OT, 246).

17. 'Bin Laden's Warning: Full Text', BBC News, 7 October 2001. Available at http://news.bbc.co.uk/1/hi/world/south_asia/1585636.stm

18. 'Remarks by the President on Winston Churchill and the War on Terror', 4 February 2004. Available at http://www.whitehouse.gov/news/releases/2004/02/20040204-4.html

19. 'Report of the Defence Science Board Task Force on Strategic Communication', Department of Defence, September 2004. Available at http://www.acq.osd.mil/dsb/reports/2004-09-Strategic_Communication.pdf

20. Arendt was much more critical of what she described as 'the Viet Cong terror' than Chomsky, just as she opposed 'the terror of the National Liberation Army in Algeria. People who did agree with this terror and were only against the French counter-terror, of course, were applying a double standard' (1971: 114). She was therefore rightly critical of 'a number of people in the so-called New Left—who are against our country's intervention in Vietnam (as I am, too) would like us to interfere, only in favor of the other side' (1971: 115). Though it would less 'horrible' to support the other side it would still be wrong and would do nothing to overcome the perception around the world of US foreign policy as 'moralistic'.

21. Arendt was forced into making such public comments about love or her lack of love for any 'people' as a result of the controversy around her *Eichmann* book. One critic, Gershom Scholem, accused the book of heartlessness and demonstrating a lack of *Ahabath Israel*, or love of the Jewish people (quoted in JP, 241; Ring 1997).

22. At the beginning of 1933 she presciently wrote, 'Germany means my mother tongue, philosophy, and literature. I can and must stand by all that. But I am obliged to keep my distance, I can be neither for nor against when I read Max Weber's wonderful sentence where he says that to put Germany back on her feet he would form an alliance with the devil himself' (AJ, 16).

23. *For the Love of the World* is the subtitle of Arendt's biography by Elisabeth Young-Bruehl (1982).

24. As we discussed in Chapter 3, Arendt understood political action to be inspired by the achievement of 'worldly immortality', not the Christian effort 'to remedy the consequences of human sinfulness' or the modern state's interest in 'cater[ing] to the legitimate wants and interests of earthly life' (HC, 314).

25. If the public realm is constituted by what appears, then it has great difficulty confronting that which cannot be displayed. Arendt viewed Christian thought as especially unpolitical because it drew attention away from public spiritedness and the necessary sense of a public world, 'which can form only in the interspaces between men in all their variety' (MDT, 31). The difference is

evident when we compare conscientious objection to war and civil disobedience against war. Arendt claimed that statements that evoke conscience cannot be generalized. 'What I cannot live with may not bother another man's conscience'; conscience is largely 'unpersuasive of others' (CR, 64, 67). It is true that a growth in the number of conscientious objectors to a particular war might galvanize others to oppose the war and participate in acts of civil disobedience. But these acts of civil disobedience are not justified in terms of conscience. They are public acts based on the concern for the republic. Of course, the conscientious objectors who have resisted participating in the 2003 invasion and occupation of Iraq did so for a wide range of reasons. But the political significance of such objections emerges precisely 'when a number of consciences happen to coincide, and the conscientious objectors decide to ... make their voices heard in public' (CR, 67–8). It is at this stage, Arendt pointed out, that they 'actually no longer rely on themselves alone' (CR, 68). They now make arguments that are capable of persuading others of an action or inaction 'for the future course of the world', not for the sake of the self or their own soul or conscience. There is an important distinction between claims on behalf of 'the individual self' (such as conscience) and claims made as a citizen, as 'the member of the community' (CR, 62, 60).

26. 'The Christian can love all people', she wrote, 'because each one is only an occasion, and that occasion can be everyone. It is not really the neighbor who is loved ... it is love itself' (LSA, 97). Waldemar Gurian, the Jewish convert to Catholicism, thus viewed politics, in Arendt's words, as 'a battlefield not of bodies, but of souls and ideas ... In this sense, politics was ... a kind of realization of philosophy' (MDT, 259). For a discussion of Arendt's criticisms of the anti-political character of philosophy, see Chapter 7.

27. Friendship, not intimacy, solidarity not pity and compassion were Arendt's remedies for the reality of human suffering. Arendt was also against all forms of 'sentimental utopianism' and the 'reducing of horror to sentimentality'. She pointed to the success of *The Diary of Anne Frank* as evidence of this trend (MDT, 5, 19).

28. Arendt did not believe that we must always tolerate that of which we morally disapprove (cf. Williams 2002). John Williams suggests that an 'Arendtian' reading of 'toleration' accounts for the importance of territorial borders in protecting the intrinsic good of the diversity of state forms in the international system and provides the basis for 'a pluralistic ethical agenda rooted in the virtue of toleration' (2002: 751). But Arendt is not really a theorist of 'toleration'. For example, she believed that Adolf Eichmann had committed acts that were *intolerable* and ought to hang for it. In her word, his 'open purpose was to eliminate forever certain "races" from the surface of the earth'; hence he too 'had to be eliminated' (EJ, 277). Arendt wished the judges had said the following when announcing his fate: 'And just as you supported and carried out a policy of not wanting to share the earth with the Jewish people and the people of a number of other nations ... we find that no one, that is, no member of the

human race, can be expected to want to share the earth with you. This is the reason, and the only reason, you must hang' (EJ, 279). Arendt's lack of tolerance on this issue is queried by Tzvetan Todorov (1999: 218). 'If that is the only reason, then in my opinion Eichmann should have been allowed to live. I do not understand the argument that, because he excluded certain human beings from the ranks of the human race, we in turn should exclude him. Why repeat his actions? In what way is that an improvement on the law of an "eye for an eye"?'

29. Arendt feared the 'sinister potentiality' of genocide to recur in the future with even greater frequency and linked both the general and the particular reasons to her wider political theory. The general reason is that she believed it was in 'the very nature of things human that every act that has once made its appearance and has been recorded in the history of mankind stays with mankind as a potentiality long after it actually has become a thing of the past' (EJ, 273). The more particular reason genocide might recur with even greater frequency in the post-war period was the global problem of 'superfluous-ness'. 'The frightening coincidence of the modern population explosion with the discovery of technical devices that, through automation, will make large sections of the population "superfluous" even in terms of labor, and that, through nuclear energy, make it possible to deal with this twofold threat by the use of instruments beside which Hitler's gassing installations look like an evil child's fumbling toys, should be enough to make us tremble' (EJ, 273).

30. As we discussed in Chapter 3, the world comes into its full reality, Arendt argued, when the 'thing or event' in 'all its aspects' has 'been discovered, all its sides revealed, and it has been acknowledged and articulated from every possible stand-point within the human world' (PP, 174).

NOTES TO CHAPTER 7

1. There are differences in emphasis among neoconservative foreign policy thinkers. For example, Charles Krauthammer (2004), a self-described 'democratic realist', differs from William Kristol and Robert Kagan (2003) who are more interventionist, more moralist, less classically 'realist'.

2. President Bush's own religiosity should not be taken to assume that most neoconservative intellectuals are also Christian, or even especially religious. And it must not be confused with any idea that foreign policy neoconservatives are pursuing a specific religious agenda such as Zionism. There is more continuity than change in Bush's religious rhetoric. Every presidential inaugural address has evoked the guiding hand of a Christian God. I thank Dan Twining for this point.

3. 'Liberal idealism', in the words of Jeanne Kirkpatrick, 'need not be identical with masochism, and need not be incompatible with the defence of freedom and the national interest' (1979: 45).

4. 'Bush's advocacy of "regime change"—which avoids the pitfalls of a wishful global universalism on the one hand, and a fatalistic cultural determinism on

the other—is a not altogether unworthy product of Strauss's rehabilitation of the notion of regime' (Lenzner and Kristol 2003: 38).

5. US Representative Henry A. Waxman collected 237 specific misleading statements from high-ranking Bush administration officials about the threat from Iraq. Available at http://www.ratical.org/ratville/CAH/IraqORreport.pdf (also see Corn 2003; Dean 2004).

6. It is possible to argue that Strauss believed that those who possessed wisdom about the natural (hierarchical) order of social and political life must be cautious about the diffusion of this knowledge; for the sake of the people and for the sake of the philosopher's safety. He thus appeared to suggest that philosophers ought to conceal their doubts about religion and truth to sustain a number of functional myths. Through the concealment of dangerous truths both the philosopher and the political order are protected. To lie, therefore, may be moral; it protects the wise and maintains social order. The morally and intellectually inferior must believe in 'noble lies', 'statements which, while being useful for the political community, are nevertheless lies' (Strauss 1989: 69, 66).

7. We are focused less on individuals and more on ideas and ideology. There is already a large literature on the role of influential individuals in shaping the justification and conduct of the invasion of Iraq (Steinfels 1980; Ehrman 1995; Mann 2004). Leading architects of Bush's foreign policy and influential advisers most often labelled as 'neoconservative' are Paul Wolfowitz, Richard Perle, Robert Kagan, Elliot Abrams, William Kristol, and Max Boot. This chapter does not rely on any claims about the direct influence of Strauss on these men or their acceptance of the neoconservative label (see Kagan 2006).

8. For an excellent account of the similarities and divergences between Arendt and classical realists such as Morgenthau and Kennan, see Klusmeyer (2005). Arendt and Morgenthau were friends. According to a student of both, she considered 'heroic' his 'resignation from the National Security Council—. . . the only member of Lyndon Johnson's administration to take such a step—in protest over the Vietnam War' (Young-Bruehl 2006: 34).

9. The influence of neoconservatism in the Republican Party is obviously important. But we should not assume that neoconservative foreign policy ideas are only attractive to those on the political right (Cushman 2005; Kamm 2005).

10. Arendt understood ideologies as powerful political weapons, given their 'tremendous power of persuasion' (OT, 163). They appealed to 'immediate political needs' without which the specifics of the ideologies could not have even been imagined (OT, 159).

11. One historian of neoconservatism has noted that Jeanne Kirkpatrick's 'views were crystallized when she heard Hannah Arendt speak . . . Arendt, who taught that the left was just as capable of mounting terror as the right, was one of the shaping forces of neoconservatism' (Friedman 2005: 154). Norton (2004: 128) also argues that neoconservative ideas about the Soviet Union were partly based on readings of *The Origins of Totalitarianism*. In fact, Arendt was horrified that her book became a staple of Cold War propaganda and was infuriated

because in the United States 'every little idiot thinks he has the right and duty
to look down on Marx now' (AJ, 137). She did not view the Cold War as a
struggle between the forces of freedom and a monolithic Communism. 'If we
would only leave well enough alone', she wrote, 'we would get...a variety of
Socialist to Communist regimes with which we could live very well, some of
which would be Russian-oriented and some more inclined to China' (BF, 181).
In 1966, Arendt criticized the US Cold War stance of viewing China as part of
a global Communist conspiracy. In this she was correct, yet Arendt was clearly
unaware of the extent of the terror perpetuated by Mao, when she wrote, 'it was
obvious that Mao Tse-tung's "thought" did not run along the lines laid down by
Stalin (or Hitler, for that matter), that he was not a killer by instinct, and that
nationalist sentiment, so prominent in all revolutionary upheavals in formerly
colonial countries, was strong enough to impose limits upon total domination'
(OT, xxvi–xxvii).

12. Some of Arendt's concerns about politics in the modern age also echo those of
Irving Kristol. Arendt argued that the increasing identification of freedom with
the ability to accumulate personal wealth, and the triumph of the archetypal
liberal freedom *from* politics, deformed the political sphere. But the spirit of
the American founding praised by Strauss and Kristol is very different from
Arendt's. For example, Arendt praised, rather than criticized, the counter-
culture, civil rights movements, and anti-Vietnam War activists that so bothered
the American right (e.g. see Kirkpatrick 2004: 235–40).

13. Arendt rarely referred to neoconservatism and died before the full political
force of neoconservative ideas were felt in the United States. In a 1956 essay
she wrote, 'Neo-conservativism, which has won a surprisingly large following
in recent years, is primarily cultural and educational, and not political or social
in outlook; it appeals to a mood and concern which are direct results of the
elimination of authority from the relationship between young and old, teacher
and pupil, parents and children' (1956: 404).

14. This has led to false accusations of nostalgia and Hellenism (even by Straussians!) in Arendt's work (see Pangle 1999: xxiv).

15. Of course, Arendt believed that thinking and acting were connected. However,
she rejected the effort to ensure that the mentality of one enjoyed hegemony
over the other.

16. This particular critique of neoconservatism also applies to some critical international theory (see Chapter 8). According to Andrew Linklater, the 'fundamental
conflict in the world system' is not between states, but competing *ideologies*—
emancipatory versus all others (1990: 21).

17. Arendt was unimpressed by the efforts of military technicians to overcome the
unexpected in war; 'nowhere does Fortuna, good or ill luck play a more fateful
role in human affairs than on the battlefield'. This element of the unexpected
could not 'be eliminated by simulations, scenarios, game theories, and the like'
(CR, 106). And yet Arendt also wrote that it was possible for 'non-technical
factors in warfare, such as troop morale, strategy, general competence and even

sheer chance, [to be] completely eliminated so that results can be calculated with perfect precision in advance' (OR, 7; 1962, 15). This is certainly an exaggeration in all contexts except perhaps for nuclear war. It does not apply, as Arendt well knew, to guerrilla warfare and counter-insurgency.

18. NATO's Kosovo intervention was billed as a 'social democratic' war because it was fought under the Democratic Presidency of Bill Clinton and the New Labour government of Tony Blair. However, the intervention also played an important role in the transformation of foreign policy views in the Republican Party in the United States, turning many into neoconservatives broadly defined. Many Republicans opposed the Kosovo intervention on the grounds that it was counter to traditional (realist) national interests. But Republicans such as Senator John McCain, though ambivalent until NATO started dropping bombs, became much more interventionist. At the same time, influential neoconservative writers, such as William Kristol, were arguing for the moral imperative to intervene and supported McCain over George W. Bush in the Republican primaries of 2000 because he was potentially more 'neocon'.

19. According to Kaplan and Kristol, when Europeans complain about 'unilateral' US actions in favour of some 'consensus of the "world community"' they are actually 'practicing a form of power politics dressed up as international morality' (2003: 92). And, anyway, 'what is wrong with dominance, in the service of sound principles and high ideals?' (2003: 112) Moreover, the UN, a collection of nation-states, most of them corrupt, should not be considered a higher moral authority than the United States. For neoconservatives, this is to falsely assume that US interests and those of 'humanity are inherently incompatible' (2003: 93).

20. This practice is not unique to neoconservatives. President Clinton pointed to the historical struggles over the place of multicultural diversity in the United States as part of the 'liberal' narrative of 'humanitarian war' over Kosovo in 1999.

21. Anti-war dissenters are prototypical actors in Arendt's political theory. The civil disobedient 'shares with the revolutionary the wish to "change the world", and the changes he wishes to accomplish can be drastic indeed' (CR, 77). For example, on 7 April 2003, several hundred Americans picketed outside the offices of Stevedoring Services, which handles military cargo, in the Port of Oakland, California. Thirty seconds after ordering the group to disperse and without violent provocation according to a UN report on the incident, the police opened fire using wooden pellets, sting ball grenades, shot-filled bean bags, and tear gas. Twenty protesters were injured and thirty arrested. Twenty-five of the arrested, the 'Oakland 25', were put on trial but the cases were dismissed. Days before the protest, a spokesperson for the California Anti-Terrorism Information Center said, 'You can make an easy kind of a link that, if you have a protest group protesting a war where the cause that's being fought against is international terrorism, you might have terrorism at that [protest] ... You can almost argue that a protest against that is a terrorist act'. However, as Arendt might put

it, the 'distinction between an open violation of the law' in a public act of civil disobedience and a 'clandestine' act of crime or terrorism 'is so glaringly obvious that it can be neglected only by prejudice or ill will' (CR, 75). On 24 March 2004, the UN released a report on the Protection and Promotion of Human Rights and Human Rights Defenders by the Special Representative of the Secretary General on the situation of human rights defenders. Available at http://www.unhchr.ch/pdf/chr60/94add3AV.pdf

22. For a discussion of Arendt's criticisms of compassion in the context of war refugees, see Owens (2004). The argument is that goodness and an associated 'ethic of care' potentially collapses the 'worldly' differences between the people supposed to be helped. This is a potentially serious flaw in efforts to establish political justice and ethical political action.

23. 'President Addresses the Nation in Prime Time Press Conference', 13 April 2004. Available at http://www.whitehouse.gov/news/releases/2004/04/20040413-20.html

24. Total ideological explanations for world history are so destructive of political freedom. In Arendt's words, 'For respect for human dignity implies the recognition of my fellow-men or our fellow-nations as subjects, as builders of worlds or cobuilders of a common world. No ideology which aims at the explanation of all historical events of the past and at mapping out the course of events of the future can bear the unpredictability which springs from the fact that men are creative, that they can bring forward something so new that nobody ever foresaw it' (OT, 458).

25. Arendt observed during the Vietnam War that 'people who had lived for so long in the euphoric mood of "Nothing succeeds like success", the logical consequence that "nothing fails like failure" was not easy to accept' (RJ, 268). She was not impressed with the effort to explain away the defeat critiquing 'the stab-in-the-back legend, generally invented by generals who have lost a war' (RJ, 269); 'such general notions as "Greek tragedy" [are] ... always dear to warmongers in defeat' (CR, 33). Arendt had opposed the undeclared war in Vietnam and was not persuaded by the Munich analogies to justify it. However, it must be noted that Arendt's views of the Korean War are more amenable to such analogies. In a letter to Karl Jaspers she wrote, 'Whenever somebody tells me again that Stalin certainly can't make war right now or doesn't have any interest in it, I always have to think of a Jewish joke: A Jew is afraid of a dog that is barking loudly. Someone says to placate him: You surely know that dogs that bark a lot don't bite. To which he replies: Yes, I know, but do I know that he knows that? And so I continue to be afraid' (AJ, 150–1). She nonetheless also viewed the 'war mood' in the United States at the time to be 'crazy and dangerous' (AJ, 160). This was confirmed by the end of the military campaign and the return home of the US prisoners of war. She noted that 'the army issued a statement in all the papers saying that the first thing that would be done with any of the prisoners who had been "infected" with Communism would be to put them in psychiatric clinics! I don't believe that was actually done. But the thinking is typically American' (AJ, 214).

26. In a footnote Arendt wrote,

> I hope no one will tell me any more that Plato was the inventor of the 'noble lie'. This belief rested on a misreading of a crucial passage (414C) in *The Republic*, where Plato speaks of one his myths...as a ψεῦδος. Since the same Greek word signifies 'fiction', 'error', and 'lie' according to context—when Plato wants to distinguish between error and lie, the Greek language forces him to speak of 'involuntary' and 'voluntary' ψεῦδος ...; under no circumstances can it be understood as a recommendation of lying as we understand it. Plato, of course, was permissive about occasional lies to deceive the enemy or insane people...But contrary to the cave allegory, no principle is involved in these passages (BPF 298 *f*).

NOTES TO CHAPTER 8

1. There are other grounds on which thinkers have justified 'humanitarian war' by drawing on Habermas. Nicholas J. Wheeler (2000) argues that NATO's Kosovo intervention was legitimate because it reflected a growing consensus in the society of states about the contingent nature of sovereignty when human rights are being systematically abused. Wheeler also argues that communicative discourse matters. If states cannot come up with plausible legitimating reasons for 'humanitarian intervention' (e.g. 'saving the Kosovars') their actions will necessarily be constrained (2000: 2; Crawford, 2002; cf. Owens, 2004). This chapter is about a different justification for 'humanitarian war'—one based on appeals to an emerging global (rather than international) public sphere of world citizens (rather than states).

2. The language of humanitarianism is not limited to interventions justified principally in these terms. 'As we pursue the terrorists in Afghanistan', promised the 2002 US National Security Strategy, 'we will continue to work with international organizations...to provide the humanitarian, political, economic, and security assistance necessary to rebuild Afghanistan so that it will never again abuse its people'. See http://www.whitehouse.gov/nsc/nss.html

3. Much of the new critical and normative literature on the 'mutually constitutive' relationship between publics and war is useful because the relation between them in traditional accounts is not very satisfactory. The literature on war propaganda, public opinion research, and the 'CNN-effect' normally considers the relation between war and publics as dependent on political calculation (Holsti 1996; Minear et al. 1996; McInnes 2002; Robinson 2002). State officials deploy military power (or not) in response to diverse but pre-given 'public opinion'. The (usually singular) public is presented as an empirically extant object to be analysed via the accumulated polling data. These methods lead social scientists to consider the existence of 'publics' as separate from analysis of the mode and effect of particular kinds of public circulation or address. Indeed, 'counting

noses in opinion-polls' (CR, 141), as Arendt would say, is partly constitutive of the idea of 'the public' such surveys seek to describe (also see Warner 2002).

4. 'Absolutely central to the notion of the public sphere in all its versions is the opposition between reason and force' (Hill and Montag 2000: 6), between peaceful dialogue and violence.

5. Habermas's conceptions of legitimacy, 'communicative', and 'strategic' action have been applied to the international realm both with and without explicit reference to 'publics'. Even where democratic forums are absent, it has been suggested that politics at the international level might be legitimated, or at least better understood, via an account of communicative action theory, good justifications, or arguments (Onuf 1989; Kratochwil 1991; Reus-Smit 1997; Crawford 2002; Steffek 2003).

6. The international public sphere was central to the effort of the European great powers to manage the balance of power in nineteenth-century Europe. Jennifer Mitzen suggests that 'in the Concert period a critical public was aware of and commenting on foreign affairs, which influenced the changes in diplomatic practice in a process that might be seen as an international corollary to the processes Habermas chronicles' (2005: 414).

7. Not only did Arendt directly influence Habermas, Seyla Benhabib has performed a 'Habermasian' rendering of Arendt (1992*a*, 1996*a*). Others have explicitly resisted this effort (Honig 1993*a*, 1993*b*; Villa 1999: 143). As Margaret Canovan notes, Arendt did not believe in 'anything remotely resembling universal concurrence in objective truth' or that political disputes could be resolved 'by purely rational means' (1983: 109).

8. Habermas has argued that Arendt's thought is incapable of dealing with 'structural violence' (1983: 179) by which he means 'unconscionable social inequality, degrading discrimination, pauperization, and marginalization' (Habermas and Borradori 2003: 35). He argues that Arendt subsumes the strategic action of war, which she distinguishes from politics, with instrumental action. In his words, 'since the purposive deployment of military means seems to have the same structure as the use of instruments for producing objects or transforming the goods of nature, Arendt, in a kind of shorthand, equates strategic action with instrumental action. She demonstrates that in the waging of war strategic action is as violent as it is instrumental; an action of this type stands outside the realm of the political' (1983: 180). Habermas then points out that forms of strategic action also took place inside the Greek polis and that strategic action has been institutionalized in the forms of legal political parties and labour conflicts in modern mass societies. The point is to suggest that we must include forms of legitimate strategic action in our understanding of 'the political'. 'The concept of the political', he concludes, 'has to be extended to include the strategic competition for political power and the use of power within the political system' (1983: 183). In turn, this facilitates an understanding of the way in which structural violence serves to 'keep other individuals or groups from perceiving their interests. In this sense, violence has always belonged to the means for acquiring and holding onto power' (1983: 181). But Arendt simply has a different name

for what Habermas calls 'structural violence'. It is old-fashioned domination and she showed how it worked in her analysis of ideologies and her criticism of Greek slavery. She was clearly aware that 'strategic action' took place in the polis (see CR, 149; 2002: 285) and in modern mass societies.

9. Arendt elaborated a tripartite distinction between labour, work and action, and she understood the activities as conditioning, but not wholly determining, the human world. The human condition is not human nature; it 'never conditions us absolutely'. When we act in the public world we 'constantly create' our own 'self-made conditions' (HC, 11, 9). Here we need only distinguish between work and action. Labour, humans as *animal laborans*, is the activity most closely corresponding to the needs of biological necessity. Labour is necessary for humans to sustain life and regenerate their existence on earth. In Marxist terminology, it is ' "man's metabolism with nature" ' (HC, 98). Historically, it has also been associated with violence. As Arendt wrote, 'It was the arts of violence, the arts of war, piracy, and ultimately absolute rule which brought the defeated into the services of the victors and thereby held necessity in abeyance for the longer period of recorded history' (HC, 129).

10. In contrast to Hobbes's account of the absorption of public power into the hands of the amoral Leviathan, free debate in public, Kant argued, could be the bridge between politics and morality. When people joined together to debate their common affairs they bequeath the critical use of reason onto the political realm.

11. In an interview with Günter Gaus in 1964 for German television Arendt protested the label of 'philosopher'. 'I do not belong to the circle of philosophers. My profession...is political theory...In my opinion, I have said good-bye to philosophy once and for all...The expression "political philosophy", which I avoid, is extremely burdened by tradition...There is a kind of enmity against all politics in most philosophers, with very few exceptions' (EU, 1–2).

12. As Michael Walzer put it, the tension between *jus ad bellum* (the right to war) and *jus in bello* (what is right to do *in* war) is summed up as the 'dilemma of winning and fighting well: the military form of the means/end problem, the central issue in political ethics' (1992: xxx–xxxi). The *end* of a war is only manifest after hostilities cease and can be described in terms of self-defence, conquest, domination, even freedom. This end, in the sense of what is supposed to be achieved, tends to be more or less firmly fixed (or it should be) and is future-oriented. The end product is tangible, and it is directly related to the means meant to achieve it.

13. As Peter Baehr has written, 'few authors of the twentieth-century offered a more comprehensive alternative to Weber's political and sociological thought than Arendt did' (2001: 307). And yet she seldom addressed the writings of Weber directly. There is strong evidence that she believed to do so would compromise her close friendship with Karl Jaspers, her doctoral supervisor and former student of Weber. As a result, in Baehr's words, 'Weber appears not in his own right, worthy of detailed rebuttal [like Marx], but as part of a broader tradition, and it is this that constitutes the target of Arendt's strictures' (2001: 323).

14. 'Textbook instructions on "how to make a revolution" in a step-by-step progression from dissent to conspiracy, from resistance to armed uprising, are based on the mistaken notion that revolutions are "made"' (CR, 147).
15. Indeed, this was not only the case for major campaigns against great power enemies in Europe. With the slow extension of the franchise, working-class publics in the metropolis grew keenly interested in the military adventures of 'their' armies during the so-called 'small wars' of colonial conquest (MacKenzie 1986). We also know that in the contemporary post-colonial period, democracies find it difficult to fight and win 'small wars', even against technologically inferior enemies, if there is little will to fight (Merom 2003).
16. The 'shrinkage of the earth' and reality of 'humanity' is by no means necessarily a good thing; the price could well be the alienation of humanity from its 'immediate earthly surroundings' (HC, 251).
17. Arendt was a critic of the liberal idealists after the First World War who argued for a world government. 'The presently popular liberal notion of World Government is based', she wrote, 'like all liberal notions of political power, on the same concept of individuals submitting to a central authority which "overawes them all", except that nations are now taking the place of individuals. The World Government is to overcome and eliminate authentic politics, that is, different peoples getting along with each other in the full force of their power' (OT, 142 *f*).
18. Arendt wrote that it was in the 'genuine equal plurality of peoples in whose complete multitude alone mankind can be realized' (OT, 167). She believed that Hobbes's political theory excluded 'in principle the idea of humanity which constitutes the sole regulating idea of international law. With the assumption that foreign politics is necessarily outside of the human contract...Hobbes affords the best possible theoretical foundation for those naturalistic ideologies which hold nations to be tribes...without any connection whatever, unconscious of the solidarity of mankind and having in common only the instinct for self-preservation which man shares with the animal world' (OT, 157). In this scenario, the clash of civilizations—or tribes—is inevitable (for a discussion of Schmitt on this point, see Mouffe 2005*b*).
19. This should not be taken to mean that Arendt was some kind of communitarian. She was too suspicious of group identity to be readily associated with such a theory (see Beiner 2000: 44).
20. Arendt perhaps also feared that a world republic might eventually lead to a global civil war. In *On Revolution*, she evoked the spectre of such a war 'in which it is as though even the fury of war was merely the prelude, a preparatory stage to the violence unleashed by revolution...of where, on the contrary, a world war appears like the consequences of revolution, a kind of civil war raging all over the earth as even the Second World War was considered by a sizeable portion of public opinion and with considerable justification' (OR, 8).
21. As noted in Chapter 5, Arendt distinguished the (international) crimes of expulsion and ethnic cleansing from the crime (against humanity) that was genocide (EJ, 268–9). We do not know whether she would have supported

action to halt ethnic cleansing, as distinct from genocide, or how in concrete situations she would have distinguished between them.

22. For Kant, the goal of war was peace, even if the end was self-defence or conquest. To say that 'peace' is the goal of war, Arendt suggests, implies that the standard by which we judge each action in war is the following: 'nothing should be allowed to happen in war that would make a subsequent peace impossible' (PP, 198). It is here that we may also find a possible way to alleviate the 'murderous' clash between ends and means in war. This is possible if actors do not lose sight of the *goal* of war, which is peace. The goal refers to the 'guidelines and directives by which we orient ourselves' (PP, 193). It is far more fluid than the end; it is 'never cast in stone' but is what political actors keep in mind as they act and it sets 'the standards by which everything that is done must be judged' (PP, 194). Unlike the *meaning* of politics or war which ceases to exist the moment the action is complete the goal can continue to exert an influence. But 'it must remain constantly present, and precisely during times when it is not yet achieved' (PP, 198). Conquest, self-defence and freedom, the ends of various wars, are themselves in tension with peace. But if peace is the goal of war, then its obvious purpose is to constrain brute force.

23. 'What interests Kant in the abolition of war', Arendt wrote, '…is…not even the elimination of cruelty, the bloodshed, the atrocities of warfare. It is, as he sometimes even grudgingly concludes (grudgingly, because…there is something sublime in the sacrifice of life; etc.), the necessary condition for the greatest possible enlargement of the enlarged mentality' (LK, 73). By enlarged mentality Kant meant the republic of world citizens that would follow from perpetual peace. In Kant's own words, 'War itself, provided it is conducted with order and a sacred respect for the rights of civilians, has something sublime about it…On the other hand, a prolonged peace favours the predominance of a mere commercial spirit, and with it a debasing self-interest, cowardice, and effeminacy, and tends to degrade the character of the nation' (1952: 112–13).

24. Indeed, Habermas very nicely describes 'the motif that inspired' Arendt. In his words, 'she is interested in the power of common conviction: the withdrawal of obedience in relation to institutions that have lost their legitimacy, the confrontation of power generated by free coalition with the physically coercive means of a violent yet impotent state apparatus, the originative act of a new political power and the attempt—the pathos of a new beginning—to hold onto the revolutionary point of departure, to prolong institutionally the communicative engendering of power…When revolutionaries seize power that lies in the streets, when a populace resolved upon passive resistance confront alien tanks with their bare hands, when convinced minorities dispute the legitimacy of current laws and organize civil disobedience, when in the course of the protest movement there is manifest a "pure pleasure in action" on the part of the students—in all this there seems to be confirmed again and again that no one really possesses power; it "springs up between them when they act"' (1983: 177).

Bibliography

Agamben, Giorgio (1995). *Homo Sacer: Sovereign Power and Bare Life* (trans. Daniel Heller-Roazen). Stanford, CA: Stanford University Press.

——— (2005). *State of Exception* (trans. Kevin Attell). Chicago, IL: University of Chicago Press.

Anderson, Benedict (1992). *Imagined Communities: Reflections on the Origin and Spread of Nationalism*. London: Verso.

Angell, Norman (1913). *The Great Illusion: a Study of the Relation of Military Power to National Advantage*. London: Heinemann.

Anghie, Anthony (2004). *Imperialism, Sovereignty and the Making of International Law*. Cambridge: Cambridge University Press.

Appadurai, Arjun (1996). *Modernity at Large: Cultural Dimensions of Globalization*. Minneapolis, MN: University of Minnesota Press.

——— (1998). 'Full Attachment', *Public Culture*, 10(2): 443–49.

Aquinas, Saint Thomas (1988). *On Law, Morality, and Politics* (edited by William P. Baumgarth and Richard J. Regan). Indianapolis, IN: Hackett.

Arendt, Hannah (1943). 'Why the Crémieux Decree was Abrogated', *Contemporary Jewish Record*, 6(2): 115–23.

——— (1946). 'Imperialism: Road to Suicide', *Commentary*, 1: 27–35.

——— (1950). 'Peace or Armistice in the Near East', *Review of Politics*, 12: 56–82.

——— (1951). *The Burden of Our Time*. London: Secker and Warburg.

——— (1953). 'A Reply', *Review of Politics*, 15(1): 76–85.

——— (1956). 'Authority in the Twentieth Century', *Review of Politics*, 18(4): 403–17.

——— (1958*a*). *The Human Condition*. Chicago, IL: University of Chicago Press.

——— (1958*b*). 'Totalitarian Imperialism: Reflections on the Hungarian Revolution', *Journal of Politics*, 20(1): 5–43.

——— (1961). 'Freedom and Politics' in Albert Hunold (ed.), *Freedom and Serfdom: An Anthology of Western Thought*. Dordrecht: D. Reidel, pp. 191–217.

——— (1962). 'The Cold War and the West', *Partisan Review*, 29(1): 10–19.

——— (1966 [1951]). *The Origins of Totalitarianism* (new edition with added prefaces). New York: Harcourt Brace Jovanovich.

——— (1968*a*). *Between Past and Future: Eight Exercises in Political Thought*. New York: Viking.

——— (1968*b*). *Men in Dark Times*. New York: Harcourt, Brace, and World.

——— (1968*c* [1963]). *Eichmann in Jerusalem: A Report on the Banality of Evil*. New York: Viking.

——— (1969). 'Reflections on Violence', *Journal of International Affairs*, 23(1): 1–35.

——— (1970*a*). 'Introduction', in J. Glenn Gray (ed.), *The Warriors: Reflections on Men in Battle*. London: University of Nebraska Press, pp. vii–xiv.

—— (1970*b* [1963]). *On Revolution*. New York: Viking.

—— (1970*c*). 'Introduction: Walter Benjamin: 1892–1940', in Walter Benjamin (ed.), *Illuminations* (edited and with an Introduction by Hannah Arendt) (trans. Harry Kohn). London: Jonathan Cape, pp. 1–55.

—— (1971). 'The Legitimacy of Violence as a Political Act? Panel discussion between Hannah Arendt, Noam Chomsky, Robert Lowell and Conor Cruise O'Brien', in Alexander Klein (ed.), *Dissent, Power, and Confrontation: Theatre for Ideas/Discussions No. 1*. New York: McGraw-Hill, pp. 95–133.

—— (1972). *Crises of the Republic*. New York: Harcourt Brace Jovanovich.

—— (1974 [1958]). *Rahel Varnhagen: The Life of a Jewish Woman* (trans. Richard and Clara Winston) (rev. edn). New York: Harcourt Brace Jovanovich.

—— (1978*a*). *The Jew as Pariah: Jewish Identity and Politics in the Modern Age* (edited and introduction by Ron H. Feldman). New York: Grove Press.

—— (1978*b*). *Life of the Mind*. New York: Harcourt Brace Jovanovich.

—— (1979). 'On Hannah Arendt', in Melvyn Hill (ed.), *Hannah Arendt: The Recovery of the Public World*. New York: St. Martin's Press, pp. 301–39.

—— (1982). *Lectures on Kant's Political Philosophy* (edited and with an interpretive essay by Ronald Beiner). Chicago, IL: University of Chicago Press.

—— (1994). *Essays in Understanding, 1930–1954* (edited by Jerome Kohn). New York: Harcourt Brace.

—— (1996). *Love and Saint Augustine* (edited and with an interpretive essay by Joanna Vecchiarelli Scott and Judith Chelius Stark). Chicago, IL: University of Chicago Press.

—— (2000). 'The Jewish Army—the Beginning of a Jewish Politics?', in *The Portable Hannah Arendt* (edited by Peter Baehr). London: Penguin, pp. 46–8.

—— (2002). 'Karl Marx and the Tradition of Western Political Thought', *Social Research*, 69(1): 273–319.

—— (2003). *Responsibility and Judgement* (edited and with an introduction by Jerome Kohn). New York: Schocken.

—— (2004). 'Philosophy and Politics', *Social Research*, 71(3): 427–54.

—— (2005). *The Promise of Politics* (edited and with an introduction by Jerome Kohn). New York: Schocken.

—— (2007). *The Jewish Writings* (edited by Jerome Kohn and Ron H. Feldman). New York: Schocken.

—— and Heinrich Blücher (2000). *Within Four Walls: The Correspondence Between Hannah Arendt and Heinrich Blücher, 1936–1968*. New York: Harcourt Brace Jovanovich.

—— and Karl Jaspers (1992). *Correspondence, 1926–1969* (edited by Lotte Kohler and Hans Saner) (trans. by Robert and Rita Kimber). New York: Harcourt Brace Jovanovich.

—— and Mary McCarthy (1995). *Between Friends: The Correspondence of Hannah Arendt and Mary McCarthy, 1949–1975* (edited and with an introduction by Carol Brightman). London: Secker and Warburg.

Aron, Raymond (1993). 'The Essence of Totalitarianism According to Hannah Arendt', *Partisan Review*, 60(3): 366–76.

Aschheim, Steven E. (ed.) (2001). *Hannah Arendt in Jerusalem*. Berkeley, CA: University of California Press.

Ashworth, Tony (1980). *Trench Warfare, 1914–1918: The Live and Let Live System*. London: Macmillan.

Atran, Scott (2004). 'Mishandling Suicide Terrorism', *Washington Quarterly*, 27(3): 67–90.

Axtmann, Roland (2006). 'Globality, Plurality and Freedom: The Arendtian Perspective', *Review of International Studies*, 32(1): 93–117.

Bacevich, Andrew J. and Eliot A. Cohen (eds.) (2001). *War Over Kosovo: Politics and Strategy in a Global Age*. New York: Columbia University Press.

Baehr, Peter (2001). 'The Grammar of Prudence: Arendt, Jaspers, and the Appraisal of Max Weber', in Steven E. Ashheim (ed.), *Hannah Arendt in Jerusalem*. Berkeley, CA: University of California Press, 306–24.

——— (2002). 'Identifying the Unprecedented: Hannah Arendt, Totalitarianism, and the Critique of Sociology', *American Sociological Review*, 67(6): 804–31.

——— (2005). 'Personal Dilemma or Intellectual Influence? The Relationship Between Hannah Arendt and Max Weber', *Max Weber Studies*, 5(1): 125–30.

Bar On, Bat-Ami (2002). *The Subject of Violence: Arendtean Exercises in Understanding*. Oxford: Rowman and Littlefield.

Barkawi, Tarak (2004). 'On the Pedagogy of "Small Wars"', *International Affairs*, 80(1): 19–38.

——— (2006). *Globalization and Warfare*. London: Rowman and Littlefield.

——— and Mark Laffey (1999). 'The Imperial Peace: Democracy, Force and Globalization', *European Journal of International Relations*, 5(4): 403–34.

——— (2002). 'Retrieving the Imperial: *Empire* and International Relations', *Millennium: Journal of International Studies*, 31(1): 109–27.

——— (2006). 'The Postcolonial Moment in Security Studies', *Review of International Studies*, 32(2): 329–52.

Barnet, Richard J. (1971). *Roots of War: The Men and Institutions Behind U.S. Foreign Policy*. London: Penguin.

Barnett, Michael and Raymond Duvall (2005). 'Power in Global Governance', in Barnett and Duvall (eds.), *Power in Global Governance*. Cambridge: Cambridge University Press, pp. 1–32.

Barnouw, Dagmar (1990). *Visible Spaces: Hannah Arendt and the German-Jewish Question*. Baltimore, MD: Johns Hopkins University Press.

Bartov, Omer (2001). *The Eastern Front 1941–45: German Troops and the Barbarisation of Warfare*. London: Palgrave.

——— (2003). 'Seeking the Roots of Modern Genocide: On the Macro- and Microhistory of Mass Murder', in Robert Gellately and Ben Kiernan (eds.), *The Specter of Genocide: Mass Murder in Historical Perspective*. Cambridge: Cambridge University Press, pp. 75–96.

Baudrillard, Jean (1991). *The Gulf War Did Not Take Place* (trans. and with introduction by Paul Patton). Bloomington, IN: Indiana University Press.

Beck, Ulrich (2002). 'The Cosmopolitan Perspective: Sociology in the Second Age of Modernity', in Steven Vertovec and Robin Cohen (eds.), *Conceiving Cosmopolitanism: Theory, Context, and Practice*. Oxford: Oxford University Press, pp. 61–85.

—— (2005). *Power in the Global Age*. Cambridge: Polity.

—— (2006). *The Cosmopolitan Vision*. Cambridge: Polity.

Beiner, Ronald (1982). 'Interpretative Essay: Hannah Arendt on Judging', in Hannah Arendt (ed.), *Lectures on Kant's Political Philosophy*. Chicago, IL: University of Chicago Press, pp. 89–156.

—— (1990). 'Hannah Arendt and Leo Strauss: The Uncommenced Dialogue', *Political Theory*, 18(2): 238–54.

—— (1996). 'Love and Worldliness: Hannah Arendt's Reading of Saint Augustine', in Larry May and Jerome Kohn (eds.), *Hannah Arendt: Twenty Years Later*. Cambridge, MA: MIT Press, pp. 269–84.

—— (1997). *Philosophy in a Time of Lost Spirit: Essays on Contemporary Theory*. Toronto: University of Toronto Press.

—— (2000). 'Arendt and Nationalism', in Dana Villa (ed.), *The Cambridge Companion to Hannah Arendt*. Cambridge: Cambridge University Press, pp. 44–62.

Bell, Vikki (2005). 'The Scenography of Suicide: Terror, Politics and the Humiliated Witness', *Economy and Society*, 34(2): 241–60.

Benhabib, Seyla (1992a). 'Models of Public Space: Hannah Arendt, the Liberal Tradition, and Jürgen Habermas', in Craig Calhoun (ed.), *Habermas and the Public Sphere*. Cambridge, MA: MIT Press, pp. 73–98.

—— (1992b). *Situating the Self: Gender, Community and Postmodernism in Contemporary Ethics*. New York: Routledge.

—— (1995). 'The Pariah and Her Shadow: On the Invisibility of Women in Hannah Arendt's Political Philosophy', *Political Theory*, 23(1): 5–24.

—— (1996a). *The Reluctant Modernism of Hannah Arendt*. Thousand Oaks, CA: Sage Publications.

—— (1996b). 'Judith Shklar's Dystopic Liberalism', in Bernard Yack (ed.), *Liberalism Without Illusions: Essays on Liberal Theory and the Political Vision of Judith N. Shklar*. Chicago, IL: University of Chicago Press, pp. 55–63.

—— (2002). *The Claims of Culture: Equality and Diversity in the Global Era*. Princeton, NJ: Princeton University Press.

—— (2004). *The Rights of Others*. Cambridge: Cambridge University Press.

Benjamin, Walter (1970). *Illuminations* (edited and with an introduction by Hannah Arendt) (trans. Harry Kohn). London: Jonathan Cape.

Bennett, William (2003). *Why We Fight: Moral Clarity and the War on Terrorism*. Washington DC: Regnery.

Berlant, Lauren (1997). *The Queen of America Goes to Washington City: Essays on Sex and Citizenship*. Durham, NC: Duke University Press.

—— (ed.) (2004). *Compassion: The Culture and Politics of an Emotion*. London: Routledge.

Bernstein, Richard J. (1996). *Hannah Arendt and the Jewish Question*. Cambridge: Polity Press.

―― (2005). *The Abuse of Evil: The Corruption of Politics and Religion since 9.11*. Cambridge: Polity Press.

Bessel, Richard (2004). *Nazism and War*. London: Phoenix.

Bhabha, Homi K. (1994). *The Location of Culture*. London: Routledge.

―― (2004). 'Foreword', in Franz Fanon, *The Wretched of the Earth* (trans. by Richard Philcox, foreword by Homi K. Bhabha and preface by Jean-Paul Sartre). New York: Grove Press, pp. vii–xlii.

Bin Laden, Osama (2005). *Messages to the World: The Statements of Osama Bin Laden* (edited and introduced by Bruce Lawrence) (trans. James Howarth). London: Verso.

Birmingham, Peg (1994). 'Arendt/Foucault: Power and the Law', in Arleen B. Dallery and Stephen H. Warson with E. Marya Bower (eds.), *Transitions in Continental Philosophy*. New York: State University of New York Press, pp. 21–32.

―― (2006). *Hannah Arendt and Human Rights: The Predicament of Common Responsibility*. Bloomington, IN: Indiana University Press.

Bley, Helmut (1996). *Namibia under German Rule* (trans. Hugh Ridley). Hamburg: Lit Verlag.

Bohman, James (1997). 'The Public Spheres of the World Citizen', in James Bohman and Matthias Lutz-Bachmann (eds.), *Perpetual Peace: Essays on Kant's Cosmopolitan Ideal*. Cambridge, MA: MIT Press, pp. 179–200.

―― (1999). 'Citizenship and Norms of Publicity: Wide Public Reason in Cosmopolitan Societies', *Political Theory*, 27(2): 176–202.

―― and Matthias Lutz-Bachmann (eds.) (1997). *Perpetual Peace: Essays on Kant's Cosmopolitan Ideal*. Cambridge, MA: MIT Press.

Bond, Brian (1998). *War and Society in Europe: 1870–1970*. Gloucestershire: Sutton.

Boot, Max (2003). *Savage Wars of Peace: Small Wars and the Rise of American Power*. New York: Basic Books.

―― (2004). 'Myths about Neoconservativism', in Irwin Stelzer (ed.), *The Neocon Reader*. New York: Grove Press, pp. 43–52.

Booth, Ken (ed.) (2000). *The Kosovo Tragedy: The Human Rights Dimensions*. London: Frank Cass.

Brown, Chris (2003). 'Selective Humanitarianism: In Defence of Inconsistency', in Deen K. Chatterjee and Don E. Scheid (eds.), *Ethics and Foreign Intervention*. Cambridge: Cambridge University Press, pp. 31–50.

Buchanan, Patrick (2004). *Where the Right Went Wrong: How Neoconservatives Subverted the Reagan Revolution and Hijacked the Bush Presidency*. New York: St. Martin's Press.

Buckley, William Joseph (ed.) (2000). *Kosovo: Contending Voices on Balkan Interventions*. Michigan, MI: Eerdmans Publishing.

Bull, Hedley (1966). 'The Grotian Conception of International Society', in Martin Wight and Herbert Butterfield (eds.), *Diplomatic Investigations: Essays in the Theory of International Politics*. London: Allen and Unwin, pp. 51–73.

——(1977). *The Anarchical Society: A Study of Order in World Politics*. London: Macmillan.

——(ed.) (1984). *Intervention in World Politics*. Oxford: Clarendon Press.

Butler, Judith (2000). *Antigone's Claim: Kinship between Life and Death*. New York: Columbia University Press.

——(2004). *Precarious Life: The Powers of Mourning and Violence*. London: Verso.

Buzan, Barry (2004). *From International to World Society? English School Theory and the Social Structure of Globalization*. Cambridge: Cambridge University Press.

Byers, Michael (1999). *Custom, Power and the Power of Rules: International Relations and Customary International Law*. Cambridge: Cambridge University Press.

——(2002). 'Terror and the Future of International Law', in Ken Booth and Tim Dunne (eds.), *Worlds in Collision: Terror and the Future of Global Order*. London: Palgrave, pp. 118–27.

——(2003). 'Preemptive Self-Defense: Hegemony, Equality and Strategies of Legal Change', *Journal of Political Philosophy*, 11(2): 171–90.

—— and Georg Nolte (eds.) (2003). *United States Hegemony and the Foundations of International Law*. (Cambridge: Cambridge University Press.

——and Simon Chesterman (2003). 'Changing the Rules about Rules? Unilateral Humanitarian Intervention and the Future of International Law', in J. L. Holzgrefe and Robert O. Keohane (eds.), *Humanitarian Intervention: Ethical, Legal, and Political Dilemmas*. Cambridge: Cambridge University Press, pp. 177–203.

Calhoun, Craig (ed.) (1992). *Habermas and the Public Sphere*. Cambridge, MA: MIT Press.

Callwell, C. E. (1896). *Small Wars: A Tactical Textbook for Imperial Soldiers*. New York: Presidio.

Caney, Simon (2005). *Justice Beyond Borders: A Global Political Theory*. Oxford: Oxford University Press.

Canovan, Margaret (1983). 'A Case of Distorted Communication: A Note on Habermas and Arendt', *Political Theory*, 11(1): 105–16.

——(1992). *Hannah Arendt: A Reinterpretation of Her Political Thought*. Cambridge: Cambridge University Press.

——(1996). 'Hannah Arendt as a Conservative Thinker', in Larry May and Jerome Kohn (eds.), *Hannah Arendt: Twenty Years Later*. Cambridge, MA: MIT Press, pp. 11–32.

Carr, E. H. (1939). *The Twenty Years' Crisis, 1919–1939: An Introduction to the Study of International Relations*. London: Macmillan.

Carter, April (2001). *The Political Theory of Global Citizenship*. London: Routledge.

Cassese, Antonio (1988). *Violence and Law in the Modern Age*. Princeton, NJ: Princeton University Press.

Char, René (1956). *Hypnos Waking: Poetry and Prose by René Char* (selected and trans. by Jackson Mathews). New York: Random House.

Charlesworth, Hilary (1995). 'Worlds Apart: Public/Private Distinctions in International Law', in Margaret Thornton (ed.), *Public and Private: Feminist Legal Debates*. Oxford: Oxford University Press, pp. 243–60.

Chomsky, Noam (1971). 'The Legitimacy of Violence as a Political Act? Panel discussion between Hannah Arendt, Noam Chomsky, Robert Lowell and Conor Cruise O'Brien', in Alexander Klein (ed.), *Dissent, Power, and Confrontation: Theatre for Ideas/Discussions No. 1.* New York: McGraw-Hill, pp. 95–133.

_____(1999). *The New Military Humanism: Lessons From Kosovo.* Monroe, ME: Common Courage Press.

_____(2000). 'The Kosovo Peace Accord', in Tariq Ali (ed.), *Masters of the Universe? NATO's Balkan Crusade.* London: Verso, pp. 387–96.

Chrisman, Laura (2000). *Rereading the Imperial Romance: British Imperialism and South African Resistance in Haggard, Schreiner, and Plaatje.* Oxford: Oxford University Press.

Clark, General Wesley K. (2001). *Waging Modern War: Bosnia, Kosovo, and the Future of Combat.* New York: Public Affairs.

Clark, Ian (2005). *Legitimacy in International Society.* Oxford: Oxford University Press.

Clausewitz, Carl von (1976). *On War* (edited by Michael Howard and Peter Paret). Princeton, NJ: Princeton University Press.

Cochran, Molly (2002). 'A Democratic Critique of Cosmopolitan Democracy: Pragmatism from the Bottom-Up', *European Journal of International Relations*, 8(4): 517–48.

Cocks, Joan (2002). *Passion and Paradox: Intellectuals Confront the National Question.* Princeton, NJ: Princeton University Press.

Cohen, Richard (1999). 'A Look Into The Void: Kosovo as Holocaust Analogy', *The Washington Post*, April 16.

Coker, Christopher (1994). *War in the Twentieth Century.* London: Brassey's.

_____(2001). *Humane Warfare.* London: Routledge.

_____(2004). *The Future of War: The Re-Enchantment of War in the Twenty-First Century.* Oxford: Blackwell.

Connolly, William E. (1999). *Why I Am Not a Secularist.* Minneapolis, MN: University of Minnesota Press.

Coole, Diana (2000). 'Cartographic Convulsions: Public and Private Reconsidered', *Political Theory*, 28(3): 337–54.

Cooter, Roger and Bill Luckin (1997). 'Accidents in History: An Introduction', in Roger Cooter and Bill Luckin (eds.), *Accidents in History: Injuries, Fatalities and Social Relations.* Atlanta, GA: Editions Rodopi, pp. 1–16.

Corn, David (2003). *The Lies of George W. Bush: Mastering the Politics of Deception.* New York: Crown Publishers, 2003.

Cotter, Bridget (2005). 'Hannah Arendt and "the Right to Have Rights" ', in Anthony F. Lang Jr. and John Williams (eds.), *Hannah Arendt and International Relations: Readings Across the Lines.* London: Palgrave Press, pp. 95–112.

Crawford, Neta C. (2002). *Argument and Change in World Politics: Ethics, Decolonization, and Humanitarian Intervention.* Cambridge: Cambridge University Press.

Curtis, Kimberley (1999). *Our Sense of the Real: Aesthetic Experience and Arendtian Politics.* Ithaca, NY: Cornell University Press.

Cushman, Thomas (ed.) (2005). *A Matter of Principle: Humanitarian Arguments for War in Iraq*. Berkeley, CA: University of California Press.

d'Entrèves, Maurizio Passerin (1994). *The Political Philosophy of Hannah Arendt*. London: Routledge.

Davis, Mike (2002). *Late Victorian Holocausts: El Niño Famines and the Making of the Third World*. London: Verso.

Dawson, Doyne (1996). *The Origins of Western War: Militarism and Morality in Ancient Greece*. Boulder, CO: Westview.

De Greiff, Pablo and Ciaran Cronin (eds.) (2002). *Global Justice and Transnational Politics*. Cambridge: MIT Press.

Dean, John W. (2004). *Worse than Watergate: The Secret Presidency of George W. Bush*. New York: Little, Brown and Co.

Deleuze, Gilles and Felix Guattari (1987). *A Thousand Plateaus: Capitalism and Schizophrenia* (trans. and forward by Brian Massumi). Minneapolis, MN: University of Minnesota Press.

DeMuth, Christopher and William Kristol (eds.) (1995). *The Neoconservative Imagination: Essays in Honor of Irving Kristol*. Washington DC: AEI Press.

Der Derian, James (2001a). *Virtuous War: Mapping the Military-Industrial-Media-Entertainment Network*. Boulder, CO: Westview.

—— (2001b). 'Global Events, National Security, and Virtual Theory', *Millennium: Journal of International Studies*, 30(3): 669–90.

Derrida, Jacques (1992). 'Force of Law: The "Mystical Foundations of Authority" ', in Drucilla Cornell, Michael Rosenfeld, and David Gray Carlson (eds.), *Deconstruction and the Possibility of Justice*. London: Routledge, pp. 3–68.

Desch, Michael C. (2005). 'What Would Strauss Do?', *The American Conservative*, 17 January.

Detter, Ingrid (2000). *The Law of War* (2nd edn). Oxford: Oxford University Press.

Deutsch, Kenneth L. and John A. Murley (eds.) (1999). *Leo Strauss, the Straussians, and the American Regime*. London: Rowman & Littlefield.

Dietz, Mary G. (2002). *Turning Operations: Feminism, Arendt, and Politics*. London: Routledge.

Dillon, Michael (1996). *Politics of Security: Toward a Political Philosophy of Continental Thought*. London: Routledge.

—— and Julian Reid (2007). *The Liberal Way of War: The Martial Face of Global Biopolitics*. London: Routledge.

Disch, Lisa (1993). 'More Truth than Fact: Storytelling as Critical Understanding in the Writings of Hannah Arendt', *Political Theory*, 21(4): 665–94.

—— (1994). *Hannah Arendt and the Limits of Philosophy*. Ithaca, NY: Cornell University Press.

Dolan, Frederick M. (2000). 'Arendt on Philosophy and Politics', in Dana Villa (ed.), *The Cambridge Companion to Hannah Arendt*. Cambridge: Cambridge University Press, pp. 261–76.

—— (2005). 'The Paradoxical Liberty of Bio-power: Hannah Arendt and Michel Foucault on Modern Politics', *Philosophy & Social Criticism*, 31(3): 369–80.

Dorrien, Gary (2004). *Imperial Designs: Neoconservatism and the New Pax Americana.* London: Routledge.

Downes, Alexander (2002). 'Targeting Civilians in War: Does Regime Type Matter?', Paper presented at the American Political Science Association, Boston.

Doyle, Michael (1983). 'Kant, Liberal Legacies and Foreign Affairs', Parts 1 and 2, *Philosophy and Public Affairs*, Part 1, 12(3): 205–35, Part 2, 12(4): 323–53.

——— (1997). *Ways of War and Peace: Realism, Liberalism, and Socialism.* New York: W. W. Norton.

Drake, Michael (2002). *Problematics of Military Power: Government, Discipline and the Subject of Violence.* London: Frank Cass.

Drury, Shadia B. (1997). *Leo Strauss and the American Right.* New York: St. Martin's Press.

——— (2005). *The Political Ideas of Leo Strauss* (updated edition, new introduction). New York: Palgrave.

Dryzek, John S. (2000). *Deliberative Democracy and Beyond: Liberals, Critics, Contestations.* Oxford: Oxford University Press.

Duarte, André (2005). 'Biopolitics and the Dissemination of Violence: the Arendtian Critique of the Present', HannahArendt.net, available at http://hannaharendt.net/research/biopolitics.html.

Duffield, Mark (2001). *Global Governance and the New Wars: The Merging of Development and Security.* London: Zed Books.

Dumm, Thomas L. (1987). *Democracy and Punishment: Disciplinary Origins of the United States.* Wisconsin, WI: University of Wisconsin Press.

Edkins, Jenny (2003). *Trauma and the Memory of Politics.* Cambridge: Cambridge University Press.

Ehrman, John (1995). *The Rise of Neoconservatism: Intellectuals and Foreign Affairs 1945–1994.* New Haven, CT: Yale University Press.

Elliott, Lorraine and Graeme Cheeseman (eds.) (2004). *Forces for Good: Cosmopolitan Militaries in the Twenty-First Century.* Manchester: Manchester University Press.

Elshtain, Jean Bethke (1986). *Meditations on Modern Political Thought: Masculine/Feminine Themes from Luther to Arendt.* New York: Praeger.

——— (1987). *Women and War.* New York: Basic Books.

——— (1993). *Public Man, Private Woman: Women in Social and Political Thought.* (2nd edn). Princeton, NJ: Princeton University Press.

——— (2003). *Just War against Terror: The Burden of American Power in a Violent World.* New York: Basic Books.

Euben, J. Peter (2000). 'Arendt's Hellenism', in Dana Villa (ed.), *The Cambridge Companion to Hannah Arendt.* Cambridge: Cambridge University Press, pp. 151–64.

Euben, Roxanne L. (2002). 'Killing (for) Politics: *Jihad*, Martyrdom, and Political Action', *Political Theory*, 30(1): 4–35.

Fanon, Franz (1963). *The Wretched of the Earth.* New York: Grove Press.

——— (1967). *Black Skin, White Masks.* New York: Grove Press.

Faulkner, William (1978). *A Fable.* New York: Vintage.

Ferguson, Niall (2003). *Empire: How Britain Made the Modern World*. London: Penguin.

Ferguson, Robert (1984). *Law and Letters in American Culture*. Cambridge, MA: Harvard University Press.

Fine, Robert (2000). 'Crimes against Humanity: Hannah Arendt and the Nuremburg Debates', *European Journal of Social Theory*, 3(3): 293–311.

—— (2001). *Political Investigations: Hegel, Marx and Arendt*. London: Routledge.

Finnemore, Martha (1996). 'Constructing Norms of Humanitarian Intervention', in Peter J. Katzenstein (ed.), *The Culture of National Security: Norms and Identity in World Politics*. New York: Columbia University Press, pp. 153–85.

—— (2003). *The Purpose of Intervention: Changing Beliefs about the Use of Force*. Ithaca NY: Cornell University Press.

Foucault, Michel (1978). *The History of Sexuality*. London: Penguin.

—— (1984). 'The Juridical Apparatus', in William Connolly (ed.), *Legitimacy and the State*. Oxford: Basil Blackwell, pp. 201–22.

—— (1995). *Discipline and Punish: The Birth of the Prison*. New York: Vintage.

—— (2003). *Society Must be Defended*. New York: Picador.

Frampton, Kenneth (1979). 'The Status of Man and the Status of His Objects: A Reading of *The Human Condition*', in Melvyn Hill (ed.), *Hannah Arendt: The Recovery of the Public World*. New York: St. Martin's Press, pp. 101–30.

Fraser, Nancy (1997). *Justice Interruptus: Critical Reflections on the 'Postsocialist' Condition*. London: Routledge.

Freedman, Lawrence (1981). *The Evolution of Nuclear Strategy*. New York: St. Martin's Press.

Friedman, Murray (2005). *The Neoconservative Revolution: Jewish Intellectuals and the Shaping of Public Policy*. Cambridge: Cambridge University Press.

Friedrichsmeyer, Sara, Susanne Zantop, and Sara Lennox (eds.) (1998). *The Imperialist Imagination: German Colonialism and Its Legacy*. Lansing, MI: University of Michigan Press.

Fukuyama, Francis (2006). *America at the Crossroads: Democracy, Power, and the Neoconservative Legacy*. New Haven, CT: Yale University Press.

Gambetta, Diego (ed.) (2005). *Making Sense of Suicide Missions*. Oxford: Oxford University Press.

Gann, L. H. (1977). *The Rulers of German Africa, 1884–1914*. Stanford, CA: Stanford University Press.

George, Jim (2005). 'Leo Strauss, Neoconservativism and US Foreign Policy: Esoteric Nihilism and the Bush Doctrine', *International Politics*, 42(2): 174–202.

Gerson, Mark (1995). 'Reflections of a Neoconservative Disciple', in Christopher DeMuth and William Kristol (eds.), *The Neoconservative Imagination: Essays in Honor of Irving Kristol*. Washington DC: AEI Press, pp. 165–72.

—— (1996). *The Neoconservative Vision: From the Cold War to the Culture War*. London: Madison Books.

Giddens, Anthony (1995). *The Nation State and Violence*. Cambridge: Polity.

Gilpin, Robert G. (1986). 'The Richness of the Tradition of Political Realism', in Robert O. Keohane (ed.), *Neorealism and its Critics*. New York: Columbia University Press, pp. 301–45.

——— (2005). 'War is Too Important to be Left to Ideological Amateurs', *International Relations*, 19(1): 5–18.

Gilroy, Paul (2001). *Against Race: Imagining Political Culture Beyond the Color Line*. Cambridge, MA: Harvard University Press.

——— (2005). *Postcolonial Melancholia*. New York: Columbia University Press.

Glaser, Daryl (2006). 'Does Hypocrisy Matter? The Case of US Foreign Policy', *Review of International Studies*, 32(2): 251–68.

Glazer, Nathan (1975). 'Hannah Arendt's America', *Commentary*, 60(1): 61–7.

Glennon, Michael J. (2001). *Limits of Law, Prerogatives of Power: Interventionism after Kosovo*. New York: Palgrave.

Gold, Philip (2004). *Take Back the Right: How the Neocons and the Religious Right Have Hijacked the Conservative Movement*. New York: Carroll and Graf.

Goldstein, Judith, Miles Kahler, Robert O. Keohane, and Anne-Marie Slaughter (2001). 'Introduction: Legalization and World Politics', in Judith Goldstein, Miles Kahler, Robert O. Keohane, and Anne-Marie Slaughter (eds.), *Legalization and World Politics*. Cambridge, MA: MIT Press, pp. 1–15.

Goodman, Nan (1998). *Shifting the Blame: Literature, Law, and the Theory of Accidents in Nineteenth Century America*. Princeton, NJ: Princeton University Press.

Gottlieb, Susannah Young-ah (2003). *Regions of Sorrow: Anxiety and Messianism in Hannah Arendt and W. H. Auden*. Stanford, CA: Stanford University Press.

Gottsegen, Michael G. (1994). *The Political Thought of Hannah Arendt*. New York: State University of New York Press.

Grant, Ruth W. (1997). *Hypocrisy and Integrity: Machiavelli, Rousseau, and the Ethics of Politics*. Chicago, IL: University of Chicago Press.

Gray, Christine (2000). *International Law and the Use of Force*. Oxford: Oxford University Press.

Gray, Colin S. (1999). *Modern Strategy*. Oxford: Oxford University Press.

Gray, J. Glenn (1970). *The Warrior: Reflections on Men in Battle* (introduction by Hannah Arendt). London: University of Nebraska Press.

Grovogui, Siba N'Zatioula (1996). *Sovereigns and Quasi Sovereigns, and Africans: Race and Self-Determination in International Law*. Minneapolis, MN: University of Minnesota Press.

Habermas, Jürgen (1969). *Toward a Rational Society: Student Protest, Science and Politics*. London: Heinemann.

——— (1983). 'Hannah Arendt: On the Concept of Power', *Philosophical-Political Profiles*. London: Heinemann, pp. 171–87.

——— (1984a). 'What does a Legitimation crisis mean today? Legitimation Problems in Late Capitalism', in William Connolly (ed.), *Legitimacy and the State*. Oxford: Basil Blackwell, pp. 134–55.

——— (1984b). *Theory of Communicative Action* (trans. Thomas McCarthy). Boston, MA: Beacon Press.

—— (1987). *The Philosophical Discourse of Modernity: Twelve Lectures* (trans. Frederick G. Lawrence). Cambridge, MA: MIT Press.

—— (1991). *The Structural Transformation of the Public Sphere: An Inquiry into a Category of Bourgeois Society*. Cambridge, MA: MIT Press.

—— (1992). 'Further Reflections on the Public Sphere', in Craig Calhoun (ed.), *Habermas and the Public Sphere*. Cambridge, MA: MIT Press, pp. 421–61.

—— (1996). *Between Facts and Norms: Contributions to a Discourse Theory of Law and Democracy* (trans. William Rehg). Cambridge: Polity Press.

—— (1998a). 'The European Nation-State: On the Past and Future of Sovereignty and Citizenship', *Public Culture*, 10(2): 397–414.

—— (1998b). 'Paradigms of Law', in Michael Rosenfeld and Andrew Arato (eds.) *Habermas on Law and Democracy: Critical Exchanges*. Berkeley, CA: University of California Press, pp. 13–25.

—— (1998c). *The Inclusion of the Other: Studies in Political Theory*. Cambridge, MA. MIT Press.

—— (2000). 'Bestiality and Humanity: A War on the Border between Law and Morality', in William Joseph Buckley (ed.), *Kosovo: Contending Voices on Balkan Interventions*. Michigan, MI: Eerdmans Publishing, pp. 306–316.

—— (2001a). *On the Pragmatics of Social Interaction: Preliminary Studies in the Theory of Communicative Action* (trans. Barbara Fultner). Cambridge, MA: MIT Press.

—— (2001b). *The Post-National Constellation: Political Essays*. Cambridge: Polity Press.

—— (2002). 'Letter to America', *The Nation*, 15, 16 December.

—— (2003). 'Interpreting the Fall of a Monument', *Constellations*, 10(3): 364–70.

—— (2006). *The Divided West* (edited and trans. by Ciaran Cronin). Cambridge: Polity.

—— and Eduardo Mendieta (2004). 'America and the World: A Conversation with Jürgen Habermas', *Logos*, 3(3): 1–22. Available at http://www.logosjournal.com/habermas_america.pdf.

—— and Giovanna Borradori (2003). 'Fundamentalism and Terror: A Dialogue with Jürgen Habermas', in Giovanna Borradori (ed.), *Philosophy in a Time of Terror: Dialogues with Jürgen Habermas and Jacques Derrida*. Chicago, IL: University of Chicago Press, pp. 25–43.

Halper, Stefan and Jonathan Clarke (2004). *America Alone: The Neo-conservatives and the Global Order*. Cambridge: Cambridge University Press.

Hammer, Dean (2002). 'Hannah Arendt and Roman Political Thought: The Practice of Theory', *Political Theory*, 30(1): 124–49.

Hammes, Thomas X. (2004). *The Sling and the Stone: On War in the 21st Century*. Osceola, WI: Zenith Press.

Hansen, Lene (2006). *Security as Practice: Discourse Analysis and the Bosnian War*. London: Routledge.

Hanson, Victor Davis (1989). *The Western Way of War: Infantry Battle in Classical Greece* (with an introduction by John Keegan) (2nd edn). Berkeley: University of California Press.

Hanson, Victor Davis (2005). 'Genesis of the Infantry', 'From Phalanx to Legion' and 'The Roman Way of War', in Geoffrey Parker (ed.), *The Cambridge History of Warfare*. Cambridge: Cambridge University Press, pp. 15–58.

Hanssen, Beatrice (2000). *Critique of Violence: Between Poststructuralism and Political Theory*. London: Routledge.

Hardt, Michael and Antonio Negri (2001). *Empire*. Cambridge, MA: Harvard University Press.

Hartz, Louis (1955). *The Liberal Tradition in America*. New York: Harcourt Brace.

Harvey, David (2003). *The New Imperialism*. Oxford: Oxford University Press.

Herman, Edward S. and Noam Chomsky (2002). *Manufacturing Consent: The Political Economy of the Mass Media* (with a new introduction by the authors). New York: Pantheon Books.

Herzog, Annabel (2004). 'Political Itineraries and Anarchic Cosmopolitanism in the Thought of Hannah Arendt', *Inquiry*, 47(1): 20–41.

Hill, Melvyn (ed.) (1979). *Hannah Arendt: The Recovery of the Public World*. New York: St. Martin's Press.

Hill, Mike and Warren Montag (2000). 'What Was, What Is, the Public Sphere?', in Hill and Montag (eds.), *Masses, Classes, and the Public Sphere*. London: Verso, pp. 1–10.

Hitchens, Christopher (2003). *A Long Short War: The Postponed Liberation of Iraq*. New York: Plume.

Hobbes, Thomas (1968). *Leviathan* (edited and with an introduction by C. B. Macpherson). London: Penguin.

Holquist, Peter (2001). 'To Count, to Extract, and to Exterminate: Population Statistics and Population Politics in Late Imperial and Soviet Russia', in Ronald Grigor Suny and Terry Martin (eds.), *A State of Nations: Empire and Nation-Making in the Age of Lenin and Stalin*. Oxford: Oxford University Press, pp. 111–44.

Holsti, Ole R. (1996). *Public Opinion and American Foreign Policy*. Ann Arbor, MI: University of Michigan Press.

Honig, Bonnie (1991). 'Declarations of Independence: Arendt and Derrida on the Problem of Founding a Republic', *American Political Science Review*, 85(1): 97–114.

_____ (1993*a*). *Political Theory and the Displacement of Politics*. Ithaca, NY: Cornell University Press.

_____ (1993*b*). 'The Politics of Agonism: A Critical Response to "Beyond Good and Evil: Arendt, Nietzsche, and the Aestheticization of Political Action" by Dana R. Villa', *Political Theory*, 21(3): 528–33.

_____ (1995). 'Introduction', in Bonnie Honig (ed.), *Feminist Interpretations of Hannah Arendt*. Pennsylvania: Pennsylvania State University Press, pp. 1–16.

_____ (2001). *Democracy and the Foreigner*. Princeton, NJ: Princeton University Press.

Howard, Michael (1978). *War and the Liberal Conscience*. New Brunswick, NJ: Rutgers University Press.

_____ (1983). *Clausewitz*. Oxford: Oxford University Press.

Hull, Isabel V. (2003). 'Military Culture and the Production of "Final Solutions" in the Colonies: The Example of Wilhelminian Germany', in Robert Gellately and

Ben Kiernan (eds.), *The Specter of Genocide: Mass Murder in Historical Perspective.* Cambridge: Cambridge University Press, pp. 141–62.

—— (2005). *Absolute Destruction: Military Culture and the Practices of War in Imperial Germany.* Ithaca, NY: Cornell University Press.

Ignatieff, Michael (2003). *Empire Lite: Nation-Building in Bosnia, Kosovo and Afghanistan.* London: Vintage.

—— (2004). *The Lesser Evil: Political Ethics in an Age of Terror.* Princeton, NJ: Princeton University Press.

Isaac, Jeffrey C. (1992). *Arendt, Camus, and Modern Rebellion.* New Haven: Yale University Press.

—— (1996). 'A New Guarantee on Earth: Hannah Arendt on Human Dignity and the Politics of Human Rights', *American Political Science Review*, 90(1): 61–73.

—— (1998). *Democracy in Dark Times.* Ithaca, NY: Cornell University Press.

—— (2002). 'Hannah Arendt on Human Rights and the Limits of Exposure, or Why Noam Chomsky is Wrong about the Meaning of Kosovo', *Social Research*, 69(2): 263–95.

Jackson, Robert (2000). *The Global Covenant: Human Conduct in a World of States.* Oxford: Oxford University Press.

Jackson, Robert H. and Patricia Owens (2005). 'The Evolution of International Society', in John Baylis and Steve Smith (eds.), *The Globalization of World Politics.* Oxford: Oxford University Press, pp. 45–62.

James, Joy (2003). 'All Power to the People! Hannah Arendt's Theory of Communicative Power in a Racialized Democracy', in Robert Bernasconi (ed.), *Race and Racism in Continental Philosophy.* Bloomington, IN: Indiana University Press, pp. 249–66.

Jaspers, Karl (1957). *Man in the Modern Age* (trans. by Eden and Cedar Paul). New York: Doubleday.

—— (1961). *The Atom Bomb and the Future of Man* (trans. by E. E. Ashton). Chicago, IL: University of Chicago Press.

Jay, Martin (1993). *Force Field: Between Intellectual History and Cultural Critique.* New York: Routledge.

Joas, Hans (2003). *War and Modernity.* Cambridge: Polity Press.

Johnson, Chalmers (2004). *Blowback: The Costs and Consequences of American Empire* (2nd edn). New York: Owl Books.

—— (2004). *The Sorrows of Empire: Militarism, Secrecy, and the End of the Republic.* New York: Henry Holt.

Jonassohn, Kurt (1999). *Genocide and Gross Human Rights Violations.* New Brunswick, NJ: Transaction.

Jünger, Ernst (1929). *The Storm of Steel* (introduction by Paddy Griffith). London: Chatto and Windus.

Kagan, Robert (2003). *Of Paradise and Power: America and Europe in the New World Order.* New York: Vintage.

—— (2006). 'I Am Not a Straussian: At Least, I Don't Think I am', *Weekly Standard*, 11(20).

Kagan, Robert and William Kristol (1999*a*). 'Kosovo and the Republican Future', *The Weekly Standard*, April 5–12.

——— (1999*b*). 'Win It', *The Weekly Standard*, April 19.

——— (eds.) (2000). *Present Dangers: Crisis and Opportunity in American Foreign and Defense Policy.* San Francisco, CA: Encounter Books.

Kaldor, Mary (1998). 'Reconceptualizing Organized Violence', *Re-imagining Political Community: Studies in Cosmopolitan Democracy.* Cambridge: Polity, pp. 91–110.

——— (1999). *New and Old Wars.* Cambridge: Polity.

——— (2001). 'A Decade of Humanitarian Intervention: The Role of Global Civil Society', in Helmut Anheier, Marlies Glasius, and Mary Kaldor (eds.), *Global Civil Society 2001.* Oxford: Oxford University Press, pp. 109–43.

——— (2003). *Global Civil Society: An Answer to War.* Cambridge: Polity.

Kalyvas, Andreas (2004). 'From the Act to the Decision: Hannah Arendt and the Question of Decisionism', *Political Theory*, 32(3): 320–46.

Kant, Immanuel (1952). *Critique of Judgment* (trans. and with analytical indexes by James Creed Meridith). Oxford: Clarendon Press.

Kant, Immanuel (1970). *Kant: Political Writings* (edited by Hans Reiss, trans. H. B. Nisbet). Cambridge: Cambridge University Press.

Kaplan, Lawrence F. and William Kristol (2003). *The War over Iraq: Saddam's Tyranny and America's Mission.* San Francisco, CA: Encounter Books.

Kateb, George (1984). *Hannah Arendt: Politics, Conscience, Evil.* Totowa, NJ: Rowman and Allanheld.

——— (1987). 'Death and Politics: Hannah Arendt's Reflections on the American Constitution', *Social Research*, 54(3): 605–16.

——— (1995). 'The Questionable Influence of Arendt (and Strauss)', in Peter Graf Kielmansegg, Horst Mewes, and Elisabeth Glaser-Schmidt (eds.), *Hannah Arendt and Leo Strauss: German Emigrés and American Political Thought after World War II.* Cambridge: Cambridge University Press, pp. 29–43.

——— (2000). 'Political Action: Its Nature and Advantages', in Dana Villa (ed.), *The Cambridge Companion to Hannah Arendt.* Cambridge: Cambridge University Press, pp. 130–48.

——— (2004). 'Courage as a Virtue', *Social Research*, 71(1): 39–72.

Katzenstein, Peter J. (ed.) (1996). *The Culture of National Security: Norms and Identity in World Politics.* New York: Columbia University Press.

Katznelson, Ira (2003). *Desolation and Enlightenment: Political Knowledge after Total War, Totalitarianism, and the Holocaust.* New York: Columbia University Press.

Keal, Paul (2003). *European Conquest and the Rights of Indigenous Peoples: The Moral Backwardness of International Society.* Cambridge: Cambridge University Press.

Keane, John (1996). *Reflections on Violence.* London: Verso.

——— (2003). *Global Civil Society?.* Cambridge: Cambridge University Press.

——— (2004). *Violence and Democracy.* Cambridge: Cambridge University Press.

Keene, Edward (2002). *Beyond the Anarchical Society: Grotius, Colonialism and Order in World Politics.* Cambridge: Cambridge University Press.

Kennedy, David (2004). *The Dark Sides of Virtue: Reassessing International Humanitarianism.* Princeton, NJ: Princeton University Press.

Kielmansegg, Peter Graf (1995). 'Introduction', in Peter Graf Kielmansegg, Horst Mewes, and Elisabeth Glaser-Schmidt (eds.), *Hannah Arendt and Leo Strauss: German Emigrés and American Political Thought after World War II*. Cambridge: Cambridge University Press, pp. 1–8.

Kier, Elizabeth (1998). 'Homosexuals in the U.S. Military: Open Integration and Combat Effectiveness', *International Security*, 23(2): 5–39.

Kiernan, V. G. (1998). *Colonial Empires and Armies 1815–1960*. Stroud: Sutton.

Killingray, David and David Omissi (eds.) (1999). *Guardians of Empire: the Armed Forces of the Colonial Powers, c.1700–1964*. Manchester: Manchester University Press.

Kinsella, Helen M. (2004). 'The Image Before the Weapon: A Critical History of the Distinction of "Combatant" and "Civilian" in International Law and Politics', PhD dissertation, University of Minnesota.

—— (2005*a*). 'Discourses of Difference: Civilians, Combatants, and Compliance with the Laws of War', *Review of International Studies*, 31 (special issue): 163–85.

—— (2005*b*). 'Securing the Civilian: Sex and Gender and Laws of War', in Michael Barnett and Raymond Duvall (eds.), *Power in Global Governance*. Cambridge: Cambridge University Press, pp. 249–72.

—— (2006). 'Gendering Grotius: Sex and Sex Difference in the Laws of War', *Political Theory*, 34(2): 161–191.

Kirkpatrick, Jeanne (1979). 'Dictatorships and Double Standards', *Commentary*, 68(5): 34–45.

—— (2004). 'Neoconservatism as a Response to the Counter-Culture', in Irwin Stelzer (ed.), *The Neocon Reader*. New York: Grove Press, pp. 235–40.

Klusmeyer, Douglas (2005). 'Hannah Arendt's Critical *Realism*: Power, Justice, and Responsibility', in Anthony F. Lang Jr. and John Williams (eds.), *Hannah Arendt and International Relations: Readings Across the Lines*. London: Palgrave, pp. 113–78.

Knightley, Philip (2000). *The First Casualty: The War Correspondent as Hero and Myth-Maker from the Crimea to Kosovo* (new introduction by John Pilger) (2nd edn). London: Prion.

Köhler, Martin (1998). 'From the National to the Cosmopolitan Public Sphere', in Daniele Archibugi, David Held, and Martin Köhler (eds.), *Re-imagining Political Community: Studies in Cosmopolitan Democracy*. Cambridge: Polity, pp. 58–71.

Koskenniemi, Martti (2001). *The Gentle Civilizer of Nations: The Rise and Fall of International Law, 1870–1960*. Cambridge: Cambridge University Press.

Krasner, Stephen D. (1999). *Sovereignty: Organized Hypocrisy*. Princeton, NJ: Princeton University Press.

Kratochwil, Friedrich V. (1991). *Rules, Norms, and Decisions: On the Conditions of Practical and Legal Reasoning in International Relations and Domestic Affairs*. Cambridge: Cambridge University Press.

—— (2000). 'How Do Norms Matter?', in Michael Byers (ed.), *The Role of Law in International Politics: Essays in International Relations and International Law*. Oxford: Oxford University Press, pp. 35–68.

Krauthammer, Charles (2004). 'In Defense of Democratic Realism' *The National Interest*, Fall no. 77.

Krieger, Leonard (1976). 'The Historical Hannah Arendt', *The Journal of Modern History*, 48(4): 672–84.

Kristeva, Julia (2001). *Hannah Arendt* (trans. Ross Guberman). New York: Columbia University Press.

Kristol, Irving (1978). *Two Cheers for Capitalism*. New York: Basic Books.

―――― (1983). *Reflections of a Neoconservative: Looking Back, Looking Ahead*. New York: Basic Books.

―――― (2003). 'The Neoconservative Persuasion', *Weekly Standard*, 8(47), 25 August.

Kristol, William and Vance Serchuk (2004). 'End the Genocide Now', *Washington Post*, 22 September.

Kurth Cronin, Audrey (2003). 'Terrorists and Suicide Attacks', CRS Report for Congress #RL 32058. Washington, DC.: Congressional Research Service.

Lang Jr., Anthony F. (2001). *Agency and Ethics: The Politics of Military Intervention*. New York: State University of New York Press.

―――― (2005). 'Governance and Political Action: Hannah Arendt on Global Political Protest', in Anthony F. Lang, Jr. and John Williams (eds.), *Hannah Arendt and International Relations: Readings Across the Lines*. London: Palgrave Press, pp. 179–98.

―――― and John Williams (eds.) (2005). *Hannah Arendt and International Relations: Readings Across the Lines*. London: Palgrave.

Laqueur, Walter (1976). *Guerrilla: A Historical and Critical Study*. Boston, MA: Little, Brown and Co.

Latham, Robert (1997). *The Liberal Moment: Modernity, Security, and the Making of Postwar International Order*. New York: Columbia University Press.

Lawrence, T. E. (1991). *Seven Pillars of Wisdom: A Triumph*. New York: Anchor Books.

Lebow, Richard Ned (2003). *The Tragic Vision of Politics: Ethics, Interests and Orders*. Cambridge: Cambridge University Press.

Lee, Benjamin (1998). 'Peoples and Publics', *Public Culture*, 10(2): 371–94.

Lenzner, Steven and William Kristol (2003). 'What was Leo Strauss up to?', *The Public Interest*, 153 (Fall): 19–39.

Lindqvist, Sven (1996). *Exterminate All the Brutes*. New York: New Press.

Linklater, Andrew (1998). *The Transformation of Political Community: Ethical Foundations of the Post-Westphalian Era*. Cambridge: Polity Press.

―――― (2000). 'The Good International Citizen and the Crisis in Kosovo', in A. Schabel and R. Thakur (eds.), *Kosovo and the Challenge of Humanitarian Intervention*. Tokyo: UN Press, pp. 482–95.

―――― (2005). 'Discourse Ethics and the Civilizing Process', *Review of International Studies*, 31(1): 145–54.

Locke, John (1963). *Two Treaties of Government* (with Introduction and notes by Peter Laslett). Cambridge: Cambridge University Press.

Long, David and Brian C. Schmitt (eds.) (2005). *Imperialism and Internationalism in the Discipline of International Relations*. New York: State University of New York Press.

Luban, David (1983). 'Explaining Dark Times: Hannah Arendt's Theory of Theory', *Social Research*, 50(1): 215–48.

—— (1997). *Legal Modernism*. Michigan, MI: University of Michigan Press.

Lukes, Steven (2005). *Power: A Radical View* (2nd edn). London: Palgrave.

Lynch, Marc (1999). *State Interests and Public Spheres: The International Politics of Jordan's Identity*. New York: Columbia University Press.

—— (2002). 'Why Engage? China and the Logic of Communicative Engagement', *European Journal of International Relations*, 8(2): 187–230.

—— (2005). 'Transnational Dialogue in an Age of Terror', *Global Society*, 19(1): 5–28.

—— (2006). 'Critical Theory: Dialogue, Legitimacy, and Justifications for War', in Jennifer Sterling-Folker (ed.), *Making Sense of International Relations Theory*. Boulder, CO: Lynne Rienner, pp. 255–75.

MacCoun, Robert, Elizabeth Kier and Aaron Belkin (2006). 'Does Social Cohesion Determine Motivation in Combat?: An Old Question with an Old Answer', *Armed Forces & Society*, 32(4): 646–54.

Machiavelli, Niccolò (1961). *The Prince* (trans. and with introduction by George Bull). London: Penguin.

—— (1970). *The Discourses* (edited and with an introduction by Bernard Crick). Middlesex: Penguin.

MacKenzie, John M. (ed.) (1986). *Popular Imperialism and the Military*. Manchester: Manchester University Press.

Mahan, A. T. (1895). *The Influence of Sea Power on History*. London: Sampson Low, Marston, Searle, and Rivington.

Mann, James (2004). *Rise of the Vulcans: The History of Bush's War Cabinet*. New York: Viking Penguin.

Mann, Michael (1986). *The Sources of Social Power*. Cambridge: Cambridge University Press.

—— (1988). *States, War and Capitalism: Studies in Political Sociology*. Oxford: Blackwell.

—— (2005). *The Dark Side of Democracy*. Cambridge: Cambridge University Press.

Markell, Patchen (2003). *Bound by Recognition*. Princeton, NJ: Princeton University Press.

Marks III, Frederick W. (1987). *Independence on Trial: Foreign Affairs and the Making of the Constitution*. Wilmington, DE: Scholarly Resources Inc.

Mathewes, Charles T. (2001). *Evil and the Augustinian Tradition*. Cambridge: Cambridge University Press.

Mayer, Arno J. (2000). *Furies: Violence and Terror in the French and Russian Revolutions*. Princeton, NJ: Princeton University Press.

McCarthy, Mary (1967). *Vietnam*. New York: Harcourt, Brace and World.

McGowan, John (1998). 'Must Politics Be Violent? Arendt's Utopian Vision', in Craig Calhoun and John McGowan (eds.), *Hannah Arendt and the Meaning of Politics*. Minneapolis, MN: University of Minnesota Press, pp. 263–96.

McGuigan, Jim (1996). *Culture and the Public Sphere*. London: Routledge.

McNeill, William H. (1982). *The Pursuit of Power: Technology, Armed Forces, and Society Since A.D 1000*. Chicago, IL: University of Chicago Press.

Mearsheimer, John and Stephen Walt (2003). 'An Unnecessary War', *Foreign Policy*, 137 (Jan–Feb): 51–62.

Meier, Heinrich (ed.) (1995). *Carl Schmitt and Leo Strauss: The Hidden Dialogue* (trans. J. H. Lomax). Chicago, IL: Chicago University Press.

Merom, Gil (2003). *How Democracies Lose Small Wars: State, Society and the Failures of France in Algeria, Israel in Lebanon, and the United States in Vietnam*. Cambridge: Cambridge University Press.

Mertus, Julie A. (2004). *Bait and Switch: Human Rights and US Foreign Policy*. London: Routledge.

Mills, Alex (2006). 'The Private History of International Law', *International & Comparative Law Quarterly*, 55(1): 1–49.

Minear, Larry, Colin Scott, and Thomas G. Weiss (1996). *The News Media, Civil War, and Humanitarian Action*. Boulder, CO: Lynne Rienner.

Minow, Martha (1999). 'Institutions and Emotions: Redressing Mass Violence', in Susan A. Bandes (ed.), *The Passions of Law*. New York: New York University Press, pp. 265–81.

Mitzen, Jennifer (2005). 'Reading Habermas in Anarchy: Multilateral Diplomacy and Public Spheres', *American Political Science Review*, 99(3): 401–17.

Mommsen, Wolfgang J. (1989). *The Political and Social Theory of Max Weber*. Cambridge: Polity.

Montesquieu, Charles (1989). *The Spirit of the Laws* (edited by Anne M. Cohler, Basia C. Miller, and Harold S. Stone). Cambridge: Cambridge University Press.

Moran, Daniel (2001). *Wars of National Liberation*. London: Cassell & Co.

Morgenthau, Hans J. (1946). *Scientific Man versus Power Politics*. Chicago, IL: University of Chicago Press.

——— (1948). *Politics Among Nations: The Struggle for Power and Peace*. New York: Alfred A. Knopf.

——— (1960). *The Purpose of American Politics*. New York: Knopf.

——— (1970). *Truth and Power: Essays of a Decade*. New York: Knopf.

——— (1977). 'Hannah Arendt on Totalitarianism and Democracy', *Social Research*, 44(1): 127–31.

Moruzzi, Norma Claire (1991). 'Re-placing the Margin: (Non) Representations of Colonialism in Hannah Arendt's *The Origins of Totalitarianism*', *Tulsa Studies in Women's Literature*, 10(1): 109–20.

——— (2000). *Speaking Through the Mask: Hannah Arendt and the Politics of Social Identity*. Ithaca, NY: Cornell University Press.

——— (2004). 'The Dark Heart of the Liberal Project: *Imperialism* in Hannah Arendt's *The Origins of Totalitarianism*', Paper presented at American Political Science Association, Chicago.

Mouffe, Chantal (2005*a*). *On the Political*. London: Routledge.

——— (2005*b*). 'Schmitt's Vision of a Multipolar World Order', *The South Atlantic Quarterly*, 104(2): 245–51.

Münkler, Herfried (2005). *New Wars*. Cambridge: Polity Press.

Muravchik, Joshua (2004). 'The Neoconservative Cabal', in Irwin Stelzer (ed.), *The Neocon Reader*. New York: Grove Press, pp. 243–57.

Negt, Oskar and Alexander Kluge (1993). *Public Sphere and Experience: Toward an Analysis of the Bourgeois and Proletarian Public Sphere* (foreword by Miriam Hansen, trans. Peter Labanyi, Jamie Owen Daniel, and Assenka Oksiloff). Minneapolis, MN: University of Minnesota Press.

Nelson, Deborah (2004). 'Suffering and Thinking: The Scandal of Tone in *Eichmann in Jerusalem*', in Lauren Berlant (ed.), *Compassion: The Culture and Politics of an Emotion*. London: Routledge, pp. 219–44.

_____ (2006). 'The Virtues of Heartlessness: Mary McCarthy, Hannah Arendt, and the Anesthetics of Empathy', *American Literary History*, 18(1): 86–101.

Nelson, John S. (1978). 'Politics and Truth: Arendt's Problematic', *American Journal of Political Science*, 22(2): 270–301.

Niebuhr, Reinhold (1960). *Moral Man and Immoral Society: A Study in Ethics and Politics*. New York: Scribner.

Nietzsche, Friedrich (1956). *The Birth of Tragedy and The Genealogy of Morals* (trans. Francis Golffing). London: Anchor Books.

Norton, Anne (1993). *Republic of Signs: Liberal Theory and American Popular Culture*. Chicago, IL: University of Chicago Press.

_____ (1995). 'Heart of Darkness: Africa and African Americans in the Writings of Hannah Arendt', in Bonnie Honig (ed.), *Feminist Interpretations of Hannah Arendt*. University Park, PA: Pennsylvania State University Press, pp. 247–61.

_____ (2004). *Leo Strauss and the Politics of American Empire*. New Haven, CT: Yale University Press.

Nussbaum, Martha (1996). 'Compassion: The Basic Social Emotion', *Social Philosophy and Policy*, 13(1): 27–38.

Nye, Andrea (1994). *Philosophia: The Thought of Rosa Luxemburg, Simone Weil, and Hannah Arendt*. London: Routledge.

Olasky, Marvin (2000). *Compassionate Conservatism: What it is, What is Does, and How it can Transform America* (foreword by George W. Bush). New York: Free Press.

Olson, Joel (1997). 'The Revolutionary Spirit: Hannah Arendt and the Anarchists of the Spanish Civil War', *Polity*, 29(4): 461–88.

Omissi, David E. (1990). *Air Power and Colonial Control: The Royal Air Force, 1919–1939*. Manchester: Manchester University Press.

Onuf, Nicholas G. (1989). *World of Our Making: Rules and Rule in Social Theory and International Relations*. Columbia, SC: University of South Carolina Press.

_____ (2003). 'Normative Frameworks for Humanitarian Intervention', in Anthony F. Lang Jr. (ed.), *Just Intervention*. Washington, DC: Georgetown University Press, pp. 28–45.

Orford, Ann (2003). *Reading Humanitarian Intervention*. Cambridge: Cambridge University Press.

Osiel, Mark J. (2001). *Mass Atrocity, Ordinary Evil, and Hannah Arendt: Criminal Consciousness in Argentina's Dirty War*. New Haven, CT: Yale University Press.

Owen, John M. (1997). *Liberal Peace, Liberal War: American Politics and International Security.* Ithaca, NY: Cornell University Press.

Owen, Roger and Bob Sutcliffe (eds.) (1972). *Studies in the Theory of Imperialism.* London: Longman.

Owens, Patricia (2004*a*). 'Xenophilia, Gender and Sentimental Humanitarianism', *Alternatives*, 29(3): 285–304.

——— (2004*b*). 'Review Article: Theorising Military Intervention', *International Affairs*, 80(2): 355–65.

——— (2005*a*). 'Hannah Arendt, Violence, and the Inescapable Fact of Humanity', in Anthony F. Lang Jr. and John Williams (eds.), *Hannah Arendt and International Relations: Readings Across the Lines.* London: Palgrave Press, pp. 41–65.

——— (2005*b*). 'Hannah Arendt: A Biographical and Political Introduction', in Anthony F. Lang Jr. and John Williams (eds), *Hannah Arendt and International Relations: Readings Across the Lines.* London: Palgrave Press, pp. 27–40.

——— (forthcoming). *Security and War: An Introduction.* Cambridge: Polity Press.

Pangle, Thomas L. (1989). 'Editor's Introduction', in Leo Strauss (ed.), *The Rebirth of Classical Political Rationalism: an Introduction to the Thought of Leo Strauss.* Chicago, IL: University of Chicago Press, vii–xxxviii.

Pape, Robert (2005). *Dying to Win: The Strategic Logic of Suicide Terrorism.* New York: Random House.

Parekh, Bhikhu (1981). *Hannah Arendt and the Search for a New Political Philosophy.* London: Macmillan.

Paret, Peter (ed.) (1986). *Makers of Modern Strategy.* Oxford: Oxford University Press.

Passavant, Paul A. (2004). 'Postmodern Republicanism', in Paul A. Passavant and Jodi Dean (eds.), *Empire's New Clothes: Reading Hardt and Negri.* London: Routledge, pp. 1–20.

Payne, Rodger A. (2001). 'Persuasion, Frames and Norm Construction', *European Journal of International Relations*, 7(1): 37–61.

——— and Nayef H. Samhat (2004). *Democratizing Global Norms: Discourse Norms, International Regimes, and Political Community.* New York: State University of New York Press.

Pedahzur, Ami (ed.) (2006). *Root Causes of Suicide Terrorism: Globalization of Martyrdom.* London: Routledge.

Pick, Daniel (1993). *War Machine: The Rationalisation of Slaughter in the Modern Age.* London: Yale University Press.

Pietz, William (1988). 'The "Post-Colonialism" of Cold War Discourse', *Social Text*, 19–20: 55–75.

Pitkin, Hanna Fenichel (1998). *The Attack of the Blob: Hannah Arendt's Concept of the Social.* Chicago, IL: University of Chicago Press.

Plato (1941). *The Republic* (trans. and with introduction and notes by Francis Macdonald Cornford) Oxford: Oxford University Press.

Podhoretz, Norman (1999). *Ex-friends: Falling out with Allen Ginsberg, Lionel & Diana Trilling, Lillian Hellman, Hannah Arendt, and Norman Mailer.* New York: Free Press.

Power, Samantha (2004). 'Introduction', in Hannah Arendt, *Origins of Totalitarianism*. New York: Schoken Books, pp. ix–xxiv.

Rampton, Sheldon, and John Stauber (2003). *Weapons of Mass Deception: The Uses of Propaganda in Bush's War on Iraq*. New York: Penguin/Tarcher.

Rawls, John (1971). *A Theory of Justice*. Oxford: Oxford University Press.

—— (1999). *The Laws of People*. Cambridge, MA: Harvard University Press.

Reid, Julian (2006). 'Re-appropriating Clausewitz: The Neglected Dimensions of Counter-Strategic Thought', in Beate Jahn (ed.), *Classical Theory in International Relations*. Cambridge: Cambridge University Press, pp. 277–95.

—— (2007). *The Biopolitics of the War on Terror: Life Struggles, Liberal Modernity and the Defence of Logistical Societies*. Manchester: Manchester University Press.

Reinhardt, Mark (1997). *The Art of Being Free: Taking Liberties with Tocqueville, Marx, and Arendt*. Ithaca, NY: Cornell University Press.

—— (2003). 'What's New in Arendt?', *Political Theory*, 31(3): 443–60.

Report from Iron Mountain: On the Possibility and Desirability of Peace (with introductory material by Leonard C. Lewin). London: Macdonald.

Reus-Smit, Christian (1997). 'The Constitutional Structure of International Society and the Nature of Fundamental Institutions', *International Organization*, 51(4): 555–89.

—— (ed.) (2004). *The Politics of International Law*. Cambridge: Cambridge University Press.

Richardson, John (1994). 'The Administration of the Empire', in J. A. Crook et al. (eds.), *The Cambridge Ancient History, Volume IX: The Last Age of the Roman Republic, 146–43 B.C.* (2nd edn). Cambridge: Cambridge University Press, pp. 564–98.

Rieff, David (2002). *A Bed for the Night: Humanitarianism in Crisis*. New York: Simon and Schuster.

—— (2005). *At the Point of a Gun: Democratic Dreams and Armed Intervention*. New York: Simon and Schuster.

Ring, Jennifer (1997). *The Political Consequences of Thinking: Gender and Judaism in the Work of Hannah Arendt*. Albany, NY: State University of New York.

Robin, Corey (2004). *Fear: The History of a Political Idea*. Oxford: Oxford University Press.

Robinson, Fiona (1999). *Globalizing Care: Ethics, Feminist Theory, and International Relations*. Boulder, CO: Westview.

Rosenberg, Justin (1994). *The Empire of Civil Society: A Critique of the Realist Theory of International Relations*. London: Verso.

Rothberg, Michael (2000). *Traumatic Realism: The Demands of Holocaust Representation*. Minneapolis, MN: University of Minnesota Press.

Rousseau, Jean-Jacques (1947). *The Social Contract* (introduction by Charles Frankel). New York: Hafner Publishing.

Runciman, David (2006). *The Politics of Good Intentions: History, Fear, and Hypocrisy in the New World Order*. Princeton, NJ: Princeton University Press.

Russett, Bruce (1993). *Grasping the Democratic Peace: Principles for a Post-Cold War World*. Princeton, NJ: Princeton University Press.

Said, Edward W. (1978). *Orientalism*. London: Penguin.

———(1995). *The Politics of Dispossession: The Struggle for Palestinian Self-Determination 1969–1994*. London: Verso.

———(1997). *Covering Islam: How the Media and the Experts Determine How we see the Rest of the World* (rev. edn). New York: Vintage.

Samhat, Nayef H. and Rodger A. Payne (2003). 'Regimes, Public Spheres and Global Democracy: Towards the Transformation of Political Community', *Global Society*, 17(3): 273–95.

Santosuosso, Antonio (1997). *Soldiers, Citizens and the Symbols of War: From Classical Greece to Republican Rome, 500–167 B.C.* Boulder, CO: Westview Press.

Sartre, Jean-Paul (1963). 'Preface', in Franz Fanon, *The Wretched of the Earth*. New York: Grove Press, pp. 7–31.

———(2006). *Colonialism and Neocolonialism* (trans. Azzedine Haddour, Steve Brewer, and Terry McWilliams) (preface by Robert Young and new introduction by Azzedine Haddour). London: Routledge.

Saurette, Paul (1996). '"I Mistrust All Systematizers and Avoid Them": Nietzche, Arendt and the Crisis of the Will to Order in International Relations Theory', *Millennium: Journal of International Studies*, 25(1): 1–28.

Scarry, Elaine (1985). *The Body in Pain: The Making and the Unmaking of the World*. Oxford: Oxford University Press.

Schaap, Andrew (2005). 'Forgiveness, Reconciliation and Transitional Justice', in Anthony F. Lang, Jr. and John Williams (eds.), *Hannah Arendt and International Relations: Readings Across the Lines*. London: Palgrave Press, pp. 67–93.

Scheuerman, William E. (1998). 'Revolutions and Constitutions: Hannah Arendt's Challenge to Carl Schmitt', in David Dyzenhaus (ed.), *Law as Politics: Carl Schmitt's Critique of Liberalism* (foreword by Ronald Beiner). Durham, NC: Duke University Press, pp. 252–280.

Schmitt, Carl (1996). *The Concept of the Political*. Chicago, IL: University of Chicago Press.

———(2004). *The Theory of the Partisan: A Commentary/Remark on the Concept of the Political* (trans. A. C. Goodson). East Lansing, MI: Michigan State University Press.

Scott, Shirley (2003). 'The Impact on International Law of US Noncompliance', in Michael Byers and Georg Nolte (eds.), *United States Hegemony and the Foundations of International Law*. Cambridge: Cambridge University Press, pp. 427–55.

———(2004). 'Is There Room for International Law in *Realpolitik*?: Accounting for the US "Attitude" Towards International Law', *Review of International Studies*, 30(1): 71–88.

Scott-Smith, Giles (2002). *The Politics of Apolitical Culture: The Congress for Cultural Freedom, the CIA and Post-War American Hegemony*. London: Routledge.

Sebald, W. G. (1999). *On the Natural History of Destruction*. New York: Modern Library.

Sennett, Richard (1976). *The Fall of Public Man*. Cambridge: Cambridge University Press.

—— (2003). *Respect: The Formation of Character in an Age of Inequality*. London: Penguin.

Serequeberhan, Tsenay (1994). *The Hermeneutics of African Philosophy: Horizon and Discourse*. London: Routledge.

Shaw, Martin (1988). *Dialectics of War: An Essay in the Social Theory of Total War and Peace*. London: Pluto.

—— (1991). *Post-Military Society: Militarism, Demilitarization and War at the End of the Twentieth Century*. Cambridge: Polity Press.

—— (1996). *Civil Society and Media in Global Crisis*. London: Pinter.

—— (2000). *Theory of the Global State: Globality as an Unfinished Revolution*. Cambridge: Cambridge University Press.

—— (2002). 'Risk-Transfer Militarism, Small Massacres, and the Historic Legitimacy of War', *International Relations*, 16(3): 343–60.

—— (2003). *War and Genocide*. Cambridge: Polity.

—— (2005). *The New Western Way of War: Risk-Transfer War and the Crisis in Iraq*. Cambridge: Polity Press.

—— (ed.) (1984). *War, State and Society*. London: Macmillan.

Shils, Edward and Morris Janowitz (1948). 'Cohesion and Disintegration in the Wehrmacht in World War II', *Public Opinion Quarterly*, 12(2): 280–315.

Shklar, Judith N. (1984). *Ordinary Vices*. Cambridge: Belknap.

—— (1998). *Political Thought and Political Thinkers*. Chicago, IL: University of Chicago Press.

Shorris, Earl (2004). 'Ignoble Liars: Leo Strauss, George Bush and the Philosophy of Mass Deception', *Harpers Magazine*, June.

Shy, John and Thomas W. Collier (1986). 'Revolutionary War', in Peter Paret (ed.), *The Makers of Modern Strategy: From Machiavelli to the Nuclear Age*. Princeton, NJ: Princeton University Press, pp. 815–62.

Sidebottom, Harry (2004). *Ancient Warfare: A Very Short Introduction*. Oxford: Oxford University Press.

Sitton, John (1994). 'Hannah Arendt's Argument for Council Democracy', in Lewis P. Hinchman and Sandra K. Hinchman (eds.), *Hannah Arendt: Critical Essays*. New York: State University of New York Press, pp. 307–34.

Smith, Adam (1982). *Wealth of Nations: Books I-III*. London: Penguin.

Somers, Margaret R. (1999). 'The Privatization of Citizenship: How to Unthink a Knowledge Culture', in Victoria E. Bonnell and Lynn Hunt (eds.), *Beyond the Cultural Turn: New Directions in the Study of Society and Culture*. Berkeley, CA: University of California Press, pp. 121–61.

Sontag, Susan (2001). 'Talk of the Town', *The New Yorker*, 24 September.

—— (2003). *Regarding the Pain of Others*. London: Penguin.

Sorel, Georges (1999). *Reflections on Violence* (edited by Jeremy Jennings). Cambridge: Cambridge University Press.

Sparrow, Bartholomew (1996). *From Outside In: World War II and the American State*. Princeton, NJ: Princeton University Press.

Stark, Jared (2001). 'Suicide after Auschwitz', *Yale Journal of Criticism*, 14(1): 93–114.

Steffek, Jens (2003). 'The Legitimation of International Governance: A Discourse Approach', *European Journal of International Relations*, 9(2): 249–75.

Steiner, Hadas A. (2007). *Beyond Archigram: The Structure of Circulation*. London: Routledge.

Steinfels, Peter (1980). *The Neoconservatives: The Men Who are Changing America's Politics*. New York: Simon and Schuster.

Stone-Mediatore, Shari (2003). *Reading Across Borders: Storytelling and Postcolonial Struggles*. London, Palgrave.

Strachan, Hew (1983). *European Armies and the Conduct of War*. London: Allen & Unwin.

____ (2001a). *The First World War, I: Call to Arms*. Oxford: Oxford University Press.

____ (2001b). 'Total War in the Twentieth Century', in Arthur Marwick, Clive Emsley, and Wendy Simpson (eds.), *Total War and Historical Change: Europe 1914–1955*. Buckingham: Open University Press, pp. 255–83.

____ (2005a). 'The Lost Meaning of Strategy', *Survival*, 47(3): 33–54.

____ (2005b). 'Existential Struggle: Review of Isabel V. Hull, *Military Culture and the Practices of War in Imperial Germany*', *Times Literary Supplement*, 29 July.

Strauss Clay, Jenny (2003). 'The Real Leo Strauss', *New York Times*, 7 June 2003.

Strauss, Leo (1950). *Natural Right and History*. Chicago, IL: University of Chicago Press.

____ (1958). *Thoughts on Machiavelli*. Chicago, IL: University of Chicago Press.

____ (1964). *The City and Man*. Chicago, IL: University of Chicago Press.

____ (1968). *Liberalism Ancient and Modern*. New York: Basic Books.

____ (1988a). *Persecution and the Art of Writing*. Chicago, IL: University Of Chicago Press.

____ (1988b). *What is Political Philosophy? And Other Studies*. Chicago, IL: University of Chicago Press.

____ (1989). *The Rebirth of Classical Political Rationalism: An Introduction to the Thought of Leo Strauss* (selected and introduced by Thomas L. Pangle) Chicago, IL: University of Chicago Press.

____ (1996). 'Notes on Carl Schmitt, *The Concept of the Political*' (trans. by J. Harvey Lomax) in Carl Schmitt, *The Concept of the Political*. Chicago, IL: University of Chicago Press, pp. 83–107.

Taminiaux, Jacques (1997). *The Thracian Maid and the Professional Thinker: Arendt and Heidegger*. New York: State University of New York Press.

____ (2000). 'Athens and Rome', in Dana Villa (ed.), *The Cambridge Companion to Hannah Arendt*. Cambridge: Cambridge University Press, pp. 165–77.

Telhami, Shibley (2004). 'Reaching the Public in the Middle East', in William A. Rugh (ed.), *Engaging the Arab and Islamic Worlds Through Public Diplomacy*. Washington, DC: Public Diplomacy Council, pp. 4–10.

Thomas, Ward (2001). *The Ethics of Destruction: Norms and Force in International Relations*. Ithaca, NY: Cornell University Press.

Thoreau, Henry David (1937). *Walden and Other Writings* (edited and with an introduction by Brooks Atkinson, forward by Townsend Scudder). New York: The Modern Library.

Tilly, Charles (1990). *Coercion, Capital, and European States, AD 990–1990*. Oxford: Blackwell.

Tjalve, Vibeke Schou (2005). 'American Jeremiahs: Reinhold Niebuhr, Hans J. Morgenthau and the Realist Recovery of a Republican Peace'. Ph.D. Dissertation, University of Copenhagen.

Tocqueville, Alexis de (1969). *Democracy in America*. New York: Harper.

Todorov, Tzvetan (1999). *Facing the Extreme: Moral Life in the Concentration Camps* (trans. by Arthur Denner and Abigail Pollack). London: Phoenix.

Tsao, Roy (2002*a*). 'Arendt against Athens: Rereading *The Human Condition*', *Political Theory*, 30(1): 97–123.

——(2002*b*). 'The Three Phases of Arendt's Theory of Totalitarianism', *Social Research*, 69(2): 579–619.

——(2004). 'Arendt and the Modern State: Variations on Hegel in *The Origins of Totalitarianism*', *Review of Politics*, 66(11): 105–36.

Turner, Scott (2003). 'The Dilemma of Double Standards in US Human Rights Policy', *Peace and Change*, 28(4): 524–54.

Unger, Roberto (1976). *Law in Modern Society: Toward a Criticism of Social Theory*. New York: Free Press.

Vertovec, Steven and Robin Cohen (eds.) (2002). *Conceiving Cosmopolitanism: Theory, Context, and Practice*. Oxford: Oxford University Press.

Villa, Dana R. (1992*a*). 'Postmodernism and the Public Sphere', *American Political Science Review*, 86(3): 712–21.

——(1992*b*). 'Beyond Good and Evil: Arendt, Nietzsche, and the Aestheticization of Political Action,' *Political Theory*, 20(2): 274–308.

——(1996). *Arendt and Heidegger: The Fate of the Political*. Princeton, NJ: Princeton University Press.

——(1999). *Politics, Philosophy, Terror: Essays on the Thought of Hannah Arendt*. Princeton, NJ: Princeton University Press.

——(2000). 'Introduction: The Development of Arendt's Political Thought', in Dana Villa (ed.), *The Cambridge Companion to Hannah Arendt*. Cambridge: Cambridge University Press, pp. 1–21.

——(2001). *Socratic Citizenship*. Princeton, NJ: Princeton University Press.

Vincent, R. J. (1986). *Human Rights and International Relations*. Cambridge: Cambridge University Press.

Virilio, Paul and Sylvère Lotringer (1997). *Pure War* (rev. edn) (trans. by Mark Polizzotti, postscript trans. by Brian O'Keefe). New York: Semiotext(e).

Vitalis, Robert (2000). 'The Graceful and Generous Liberal Gesture: Making Racism Invisible in American International Relations', *Millennium: Journal of International Studies*, 29(2): 331–56.

Vollrath, Ernst (1977). 'Hannah Arendt and the Method of Political Thinking', *Social Research*, 44(1): 170–82.

Waltz, Kenneth N. (1959). *Man, the State and War: A Theoretical Analysis*. New York: Columbia University Press.

——(1979). *Theory of International Politics*. New York: Random House.

Walzer, Michael (1992). *Just and Unjust Wars: A Moral Argument with Historical Illustrations* (2nd edn), New York: Basic Books.

―― (2004). *Arguing about War*. New Haven, CT: Yale University Press.

Warner, Michael (1990). *Letters of the Republic: Publication and the Public Sphere in Eighteenth-Century America*. Cambridge, MA: Harvard University Press.

―― (2002). *Publics and Counterpublics*. New York: Zone Books.

Watts, Steven (1987). *The Republic Reborn: War and the Making of Liberal America, 1790–1820*. Baltimore, MD: Johns Hopkins University Press.

Weber, Max (1946). *From Max Weber: Essays in Sociology* (trans., edited, and intro. H. H. Gerth and C. Wright Mills). Oxford: Oxford University Press.

―― (1976). *The Protestant Ethic and the Spirit of Capitalism* (new introduction by Anthony Giddens, trans. Talcott Parsons). New York: Charles Sribner's Sons.

―― (1978). *Economy and Society: An Outline of Interpretive Sociology*. Berkeley, CA: University of California Press.

Weinstein, Kenneth R. (2004). 'Philosophic Roots, the Role of Leo Strauss, and the War in Iraq', in Irwin Stelzer (ed.), *The Neocon Reader*. New York: Grove Press, pp. 201–12.

Weintraub, Jeff and Kristin Kumar (eds.) (1997). *Public and Private in Thought and Practice: Perspectives on a Grand Dichotomy*. Chicago, IL: Chicago University Press.

Weller, Marc (2000). 'The Kosovo Indictment of the International Criminal Tribunal for Yugoslavia', in Ken Booth (ed.), *The Kosovo Tragedy: The Human Rights Dimensions*. London: Frank Cass, pp. 207–22.

Welsh, Jennifer (ed.) (2003). *Humanitarian Intervention and International Relations*. Oxford: Oxford University Press.

Wendt, Alexander (1999). *Social Theory of International Politics*. Cambridge: Cambridge University Press.

―― (2000). 'What is IR For? Notes Toward a Post-Critical View', in Richard Wyn Jones (ed.), *Critical Theory and World Politics*. Boulder, CO: Lynne Rienner, pp. 205–24.

―― (2003). 'Why a World State is Inevitable', *European Journal of International Relations*, 9(4): 491–542.

Werner, Emmy E. (2002). *A Conspiracy of Decency: The Rescue of the Danish Jews During World War II*. Cambridge, MA: Westview.

Wheeler, Nicholas J. (2000a). *Saving Strangers: Humanitarian Intervention in International Society*. Oxford: Oxford University Press.

―― (2000b). 'Reflections on the Legality and Legitimacy of NATO's Intervention in Kosovo', in Ken Booth (ed.), *The Kosovo Tragedy: The Human Rights Dimensions*. London: Frank Cass, pp. 145–63.

―― (2002). 'Dying for Enduring Freedom: Accepting Responsibility for Civilian Casualties in the War Against Terrorism', *International Relations*, 16(2): 205–25.

―― (2004). 'The Humanitarian Responsibilities of Sovereignty', in Jennifer Welsh (ed.), *Humanitarian Intervention in International Relations*. Oxford: Oxford University Press, pp. 29–51.

Williams, Garrath (1998). 'Love and Responsibility: A Political Ethic for Hannah Arendt', *Political Studies*, 46(5): 937–50.

Williams, John (2002). 'Territorial Borders, Toleration and the English School', *Review of International Studies*, 28(4): 737–58.

———— (2005). 'Hannah Arendt and the International Space In-Between?', in Anthony F. Lang Jr. and John Williams (eds.), *Hannah Arendt and International Relations: Readings Across the Lines*. London: Palgrave Press, pp. 199–220.

Williams, Michael C. (2005a). 'What is the National Interest? The Neoconservative Challenge in IR Theory', *European Journal of International Relations*, 11(3): 307–37.

———— (2005b). *The Realist Tradition and the Limits of International Relations*. Cambridge: Cambridge University Press.

———— (forthcoming). 'Morgenthau Now: Neoconservatism, National Greatness, and Realism', in Michael C. Williams (ed.), *Realism Reconsidered: The Legacy of Hans Morgenthau in International Relations*. Oxford: Oxford University Press.

Williams, Patrick and Laura Chrisman (eds.) (1994). *Colonial Discourse and Post-Colonial Theory: A Reader*. New York: Columbia.

Wilson, Richard A. (ed.) (2005). *Human Rights and the 'War on Terror.'* Cambridge: Cambridge University Press.

Wolin, Sheldon S. (1994). 'Hannah Arendt: Democracy and the Political', in Lewis P. Hinchman and Sandra K. Hinchman (eds.), *Hannah Arendt: Critical Essays*. New York: State University of New York Press, pp. 289–306.

Yablonka, Hanna (1999). *Survivors of the Holocaust: Israel after the War*. New York: Macmillan.

Young, Iris Marion (2002). 'Power, Violence, and Legitimacy: A Reading of Hannah Arendt in an Age of Police Brutality and Humanitarian Intervention', in Martha Minow (ed.), *Breaking the Cycle of Hatred: Memory, Law, and Repair*. Princeton, NJ: Princeton University Press, pp. 260–87.

Young-Bruehl, Elisabeth (1977). 'Hannah Arendt's Storytelling', *Social Research*, 44(1): 183–90.

———— (1982). *Hannah Arendt: For Love of the World*. New Haven, CT: Yale University Press.

———— (2004). 'Preface to the Second Edition', in *Hannah Arendt: For Love of the World* (2nd edn). New Haven, CT: Yale University Press, pp. ix–xxxvi.

———— (2006). *Why Arendt Matters*. New Haven, CT: Yale University Press.

Zerilli, Linda M. G. (1995). 'The Arendtian Body', in Bonnie Honig (ed.), *Feminist Interpretations of Hannah Arendt*. Pennsylvania, PA: Pennsylvania State University Press, pp. 167–93.

Zertal, Idith (2005). *Israel's Holocaust and the Politics of Nationhood* (trans. Chaya Galai). Cambridge University Press.

Zimmerer, Jürgen (2004). 'Colonialism and the Holocaust: Towards and Archaeology of Genocide', in A. Dirk Moses (ed.), *Genocide and Settler Society: Frontier Violence and Stolen Indigenous Children in Australian History*. New York: Berghahn, pp. 49–76.

Index

9 780199 299362